# The Art of Lobbying

# The Art of Lobbying

## Building Trust and Selling Policy


Bertram J. Levine

*Rutgers University*

A Division of SAGE

Washington, D.C.

CQ Press
2300 N Street, NW, Suite 800
Washington, DC 20037

Phone: 202-729-1900; toll-free, 1-866-4CQ-PRESS (1-866-427-7737)

Web: www.cqpress.com



Cover design: Silverander Communications, Santa Barbara, California
Composition: Alliance Publishing, Glen Rock, New Jersey

♾ The paper used in this publication exceeds the requirements of the American National Standard for Information Sciences—Permanence of Paper for Printed Library Materials, ANSI Z39.48-1992.

Printed and bound in the United States of America

12 11 10 09 08 1 2 3 4 5

**Library of Congress Cataloging-in-Publication Data**
Levine, Bertram J.
The art of lobbying : building trust and selling policy / Bertram J. Levine.
p. cm.
Includes bibliographical references and index.
ISBN 978-0-87289-462-4 (pbk. : alk. paper) 1. Lobbying—United States. I. Title.

JK1118.L48 2009
328.73'078—dc22

2008045115

*For Shelly.*

*This book would not have been possible without her.*

# Contents

# Preface

Lobbyists are sometimes called the "fourth branch of government" or the "third house of Congress." Many lobbyists likely would consider these designations to indicate an elevation in their status—and a well-earned one at that. They are pleased. Other people, on the contrary, may see an ill-gotten usurpation of authority. They are not so pleased; in fact, they are horrified.

Whatever one's view, this much is clear: Lobbyists are indispensable players in the business of national policymaking. Whether representing a business, an industry, a nonprofit institution, a public interest group, or a faith-based organization, lobbyists are the means by which the private sector participates in the give-and-take of lawmaking in Washington, D.C. When viewed as special interest pleaders, they are likened to interlopers, trespassers upon a public domain rightfully reserved for duly empowered public officials. When seen as citizens' representatives performing an essential function in a complex world, they not so problematically can be regarded as the fourth branch or a third house.

The distinction is important, especially in the aftermath of the lobbying scandals of the early 2000s involving Jack Abramoff and Rep. Tom DeLay, R-Texas, when indignant members of Congress tried to outbid each other in regulating lobbyist–lawmaker relationships. Their indignation is understandable, but indignation alone does not beget intelligent response—far from it. Overzealous remediation, designed more for public consumption than for optimal policy results, is the all too frequent outcome of bidding contests among tough-guy legislators. Congress has responded to the Abramoff scandal by ratcheting down on permissible social contact between lobbyists and lawmakers and by slowing the "revolving door" between government service and private-sector positions.[a] These new laws

a. Some individuals have moved from one sector to the other several times. It is alleged that these people are able to use their contacts in government to benefit their private-sector employers.

may at first seem to be reasonable responses to corrupt behavior, but are they? Or are they unnecessary barriers to open and trusting exchanges of information and ideas, the sort of exchanges that promote fully informed deliberation?

What is both troublesome and ironic is that each new limitation on lobbyist–lawmaker interaction signals diminished confidence by Congress in its own integrity. Lobbyists cannot answer "yea" or "nay" to roll call votes, offer amendments, insert language into committee reports, speak on the floor of either chamber in Congress, question witnesses at hearings, or gavel a markup session to order. At any given time only 535 people—the members of Congress—can do these things. Lobbyists may influence how and when members cast their votes, and how members participate in legislative activity. But influence is one thing; authority to do these things is another. Members have this authority; lobbyists do not. Thus lobbyists can wine and dine, contribute funds, and raise as much political money for the candidates of their choice as they are able to do, but unless members are amenable to being swayed by these or other forms of largesse, no undue influence will come of the lobbyists' efforts. The member who claims otherwise might as well claim "the devil made me do it."

Academic journals and lay publications bulge with articles on this subject. Is there really such a devil at work? Maybe so, but this book will not contribute to the bulge in any important way.[b] It is well conceded that money plays a role in gaining access to members of Congress and that it likely plays a role in how some members vote some of the time. But, according to current and former lawmakers and staff, much else, other than campaign money, goes into forging a successful lobbyist–member relationship. Among the other "elses" are a manifest concern for the common good, sensitivity, intelligence, and good old-fashioned savvy.

This book is a qualitative examination of the elses.[c] It is designed to discover what members of Congress and their staffers consider, consciously or intuitively, when deciding which lobbyists they will hear, which arguments they will take seriously, and with whom they will establish ongoing relationships.

The primary research method for this book was one-on-one interviews that I conducted with sixty-five present and former—mostly former—federal policymakers and eight practicing lobbyists. (There will be more on the interviews in chapter 1.) My objective here is to provide readers with

b. The one exception will be a few pages in chapter 4 that are directed to the subject.

c. I do not attempt to prove what makes for a successful or unsuccessful relationship. My objective is antecedent to that work; here I set out to identify the key variables that those who were lobbied self-reported as having influenced their relationships with lobbyists.

something closer to a Socratic learning experience than a how-to manual—though in chapter 7 I provide some general guidance on what lobbyists should think about as they design their legislative strategies. As much as possible, however, I let the legislators and staff provide the insights.

Notwithstanding the obvious concerns about vested interests, personal bias, and false honor, it would be absurd to dismiss the observations of veteran policymakers with a simple "They're all a bunch of crooks." They are not. Richard F. Fenno's view that "good public policy" is among the three basic "goals espoused by members" of Congress remains accepted wisdom.[1] Many hundreds of hours of conversation with the study cohort convinced me that Fenno was dead on.

The interviews were supplemented by what Fenno and Richard L. Hall call "soaking and poking, or just hanging around." Hall explains the value of this research technique: "If such an experience does not provide what normally gets labeled data, it certainly improves the ability of the researcher to do better in the (unscientific) social science enterprise of moving from results to interpretations. And, in the end, of course, the interpretations matter."[2]

One such interpretation that came out of the interviews I conducted is this: With but a few exceptions there is little that resembles an *absolute* in the lobbying profession. There is no equation that provides the practitioner with a constant, predictable outcome. The work is too complex, too varied, and too personal for that. In addition, it is too situation-driven and too issue-dependent to be quantified. Thus the title of this book: Lobbying is not a science but an art. Moreover, it is an art within an art—the art of politics. And as in both the performance arts and the fine arts, the critics matter: The extent to which lobbyists succeed or fail, perform a positive or less admirable role in congressional deliberations, and are accepted or spurned on Capitol Hill is a function of what the ultimate critics, the policymakers, demand and value—not more, not less.

This book is about those demands and those values.

In conducting the research for this book I drew upon my personal experiences as a lobbyist and congressional counsel for one, and only one, purpose: The interview process was informed by my "on the ground" experience of nearly three decades. From the first interview forward this experience proved an important asset in identifying and then probing for second and third levels of information. The ability to say to an interviewee, "I understand your point; but isn't this also true?" often led to a more precisely honed and more productive exchange.

The result, I believe, is a worthwhile look at what constitutes effective (and ineffective) lobbying from the vantage point of those who should know best—people who have been lobbied and who have seen the best and the worst of the lobbying profession.[d]

## Acknowledgments

The writing of this book became a family project in many ways. My son, Mike Levine—attorney turned football coach—was my go-to person. (The football metaphors that follow are mine, but Mike did review them for accuracy.) He read virtually every word, commented on content, and rewrote with immense energy and skill. Over and again he exhibited a remarkable ability to make my sometimes-choppy prose more readable. In addition, he provided much-needed support throughout.

My wife, Shelly, a master English teacher, did the presubmission editing for every chapter. (As a card-carrying dyslexic I can safely venture that no one, other than my fellow dyslexics, can understand how important her help has been for me.) She too gave excellent advice about organization and content. And my daughter, Robin, herself a former English teacher, offered several astute observations and provided helpful advice.

For many academics there is another sort of family, our colleagues. Among these I have been blessed by the friendship and wisdom of some invaluable mentors and role models—most of whom are many years my junior. Stan Brubaker and Mike Johnston of Colgate University are each the embodiment of the university scholar, as dedicated to their teaching as they are to their research, and superb at doing both. They have been constant sources of inspiration, willing and constructive critics, and just plain good listeners. Dan Tichenor, for many years at Rutgers and now at the University of Oregon, has given continuous encouragement and good advice. He epitomizes the selfless educator and scholar. Beth Leech of Rutgers is never too busy to act as a sounding board and always has right-on responses. In many ways, she is responsible for this book coming to life. Ross Baker, seventeen years ago, when I was a practicing lobbyist, made this suggestion: "Gee, Bert, you should think about auditing a PhD course or two." With that advice he launched me on a personal adventure that has ranged beyond anything I could ever have dreamed. Many other colleagues read parts of the manuscript, made thoughtful observations, and offered suggestions for changes; they too gave useful advice, some of it on tactical

d. Many people—primarily the people who consented to providing interviews that often lasted well over an hour—have been very generous with their time and with the information they provided. That information *is* this book. For that reason, and in order to remain faithful to their contributions, I include many (many!) quotations—some of them lengthy. This provides the reader with valuable insights into what goes through the minds of policymakers as they listen to endless hours of entreaties from the good, the bad, and everyone in between.

matters such as interviewing techniques. Lyle Dennis, a true friend, was a constant source of good advice. Megan Hoover, a Rutgers undergraduate who provided me with invaluable support on some of the technical pieces of my work, was a tremendous help.

Several academics took time to review this project at both the proposal and the manuscript stages. Thanks to John C. Berg, Joseph M. Gardner, Gregory G. Lebel, and Robert Nixon for their feedback.

Of course, there are the people without whom there never could have been a book. The seventy-three interview subjects—members of Congress, former members, staff, former staff, lobbyists, and former career service executives—were unbelievably generous with their time and willing to share opinions, observations, and, best of all, countless anecdotes. The fifty-four former legislators who responded to my survey also were generous with their time and willing to share their views on some key points. Several took time to write additional observations on the subject matter of the book.

I would also like to acknowledge the never mets (or almost never mets)—scholars of the first rank whose work has been essential to my understanding of Congress. Foremost are Richard Hall, whose *Participation in Congress* I believe to be one of the finest books ever written about the work of Congress, and Thomas Mann of the Brookings Institution, who has provided a stream of invaluable insights into the political and substantive work of legislators and lobbyists. Other scholars whose work I admire and reread, each time learning more, are R. Douglas Arnold, Frank Baumgartner, Jeffrey Berry, Diana Evans, Marie Hojnacki, Laura Langbein, Norman Ornstein, Kay Schlozman, Barbara Sinclair, and John Wright. And of course, there are the giants of our profession: Richard Fenno, John Kingdon, David Mayhew, and the late Richard Neustadt.

Finally, thanks to the CQ Press staff. Dwain Smith, the development editor for this project, is the personification of the always pleasant, on-point, laid-back but very much in charge professional. His knowledge of how to put together a book is to me nothing short of remarkable. I will truly miss working with him. He has made what could have been a nerve-racking task a pleasure—well, almost. Ann Davies, who copyedited the manuscript, is of the same ilk. Her extraordinary skill (and I mean extraordinary), unflappable demeanor, and lovely sense of humor made addressing the myriad unfinished details that I imagined would just go away with no further input from me, including running down all of my not-quite-finished citations, a near . . . . pleasant experience. (Yes, I know; ellipses were not correctly used in this sentence. Eat your heart out, Ann!) Gwenda Larsen, the production editor, managed somehow to create organization out of my disorganization and to bring the project "home." And finally, Charisse Kiino, chief acquisitions editor in the College Publishing Group, who encouraged me to take on this project in the first place, is another first-rate professional.

I am certain that I have left out many people who should have been included here, but these are the folks who immediately come to mind. To all of them, all the thanks I know how to give.

## Notes

1. Richard F. Fenno Jr., *Congressmen in Committees* (Boston: Little, Brown, 1973), 1.
2. Richard L. Hall, *Participation in Congress* (New Haven, Conn.: Yale University Press, 1996), 17.

# 1 Introduction

Dr. Cutler came to the meeting well prepared. He had asked the right people to arrange the meeting, and he had lined up a number of legislators to vouch for him. When the meeting began, he was careful not to launch straight away into a litany of requests and supporting arguments. The venerated figure who now sat before him would enjoy a healthy dose of small talk before getting down to business. He would likely value the opportunity to take the measure of the man who had come so far to make his acquaintance and to ask him for a favor. Thus Cutler opened the conversation by raising matters about which he and his host shared a common interest—science and philosophy. The strategy paid off: Cutler's host relaxed, enjoyed the conversation, and took an immediate liking to him.

In addition to learning about the elderly statesman, Cutler had been active in doing a different sort of homework: He had met with other influential officials—many of less intellectual scope than the gentleman he now engaged in conversation. He had been able to convince these people that his project had the potential to benefit them either personally or by enriching their constituents, or both. He knew he could count on them for support should they be consulted.

Little more than two centuries after the Reverend Doctor Manasseh Cutler met Benjamin Franklin under a mulberry tree in the latter's garden, a much less cordial meeting was unfolding in the office of Rep. Fortney "Pete" Stark, a California Democrat. The issue under consideration was a request from President George H. W. Bush's administration for an extension of a tax credit designed to stimulate scientific research conducted abroad. Under the provision, Section 861 of the Internal Revenue Code, companies could reduce their U.S. taxes by an amount equal to the taxes paid to foreign countries in which they were doing research and development.[a] The extension was to be included in the 1990 deficit reduction bill.

Among the independent lobbyists leading the charge for the companies was Stuart Eizenstat, a prominent Democrat and a former high-ranking official in President Jimmy Carter's administration. Eizenstat was this day leading a sizable delegation of scientists, many of them under contract to the beneficiary companies, on rounds of visits to congressional offices.

The meeting with Stark was confrontational from the beginning. The representative landed the first shot. "Stuart, I thought you were bringing two people," reports author Jeffrey Birnbaum. The frequently brusque Stark did not offer seats to his overflow guests. Instead, he instructed the distinguished researchers to "stand or sit on the floor."

Eizenstat and Stark sparred for a while; then after a few additional insults from Stark, Eizenstat landed his own jab. According to Birnbaum, "Eizenstat had had enough. . . . He decided to remind Stark that he [Stark] had helped to keep the R&D credit alive during the tax bill of 1986. 'You were really one of our chief champions in 1986.' "

Stark, long a critic of the pharmaceutical industry, noted that the big drug companies were among the major supporters of the extension and accused Eizenstat of allying himself "with some squirrelly characters. . . . You've got bad companies, that's all."

Birnbaum's report ends with this exchange:

> "We shouldn't be blinded by your problems with the pharmaceuticals," Eizenstat said, asserting a new air of authority. I have worked here [Washington, D.C.] on and off for twenty years. We have to compete on innovation. . . . Any person sitting on Mount Olympus would want this done. . . ."
>
> Stark pulled back after Eizenstat's rebuttal, and they began to talk like two old political pros. . . .
>
> "Let's talk politics," Stark continued. "The practical politics are that if you don't do all of the extenders . . . you don't do any of them. . . ."
>
> "So," Stark continued, "you guys should be praying for a big tax bill. That's when you have a chance."
>
> "That's what we are praying for," Eizenstat conceded and then added with a smile, "Let me just thank you for your previous championing of this." [1]

So what is the point here?

Separated by two centuries, lobbying in distinct political venues, for entirely different purposes, one in a comfortable setting and the other in a

a. The R&D tax credit was intended to ensure that U.S. companies doing research abroad would not be taxed twice—once in the country in which the research was being conducted and again in the United States.

much more hostile environment, Cutler and Eizenstat each understood the first rule of lobbying: Know your customer. Each had done his homework and had done it well. Each had acquired a solid fix on the person with whom he would be doing business.

In Cutler's case the result was straightforward, at least to the extent that he was able to meet with Franklin. The two gentlemen had never set eyes on each other before their mulberry tree meeting, yet, by the sparse accounts available, the meeting seems to have gone off swimmingly. This result was no accident; Cutler had taken the time to learn what Franklin liked and did not like when encountering strangers—especially strangers who would be asking a favor of him. Before entering the garden he understood that Franklin was not a get-right-to-the-point person. He knew that it would be necessary to gain Franklin's confidence, and he understood that some discussion about matters scientific would move his meeting with Franklin in the right direction. Whether or not Franklin ever did follow up is a matter lost to history; but we do know that the doctor from Connecticut was able to have his audience with the doctor from Pennsylvania—one of the most celebrated men of his age.

Preparation for the Eizenstat–Stark meeting must have been of a very different stripe. Because the two men had known each other for many years before Eizenstat escorted the delegation of scientists into the representative's office, some of the groundwork had already been done. Eizenstat was well prepared for a sharp-tongued, less than hospitable, welcome. He knew his own arguments and the congressman's history on the issue at hand, and he knew that Pete Stark would bully the daylights out of him if he were to show weakness or indicate that he was in any way not prepared. So Eizenstat stood toe to toe, gave as good as he got, and managed to get Stark to back off, just enough to create a reasonably comfortable atmosphere for the rest of the meeting.

One more thing—one might call it "a lifetime of preparation": Eizenstat was extraordinarily well respected among policy elites in Washington. He could afford to stand up to Stark; he did not have to worry about being tossed out of the office.

Back to the first rule, the fundamental understanding so well shared by Manasseh Cutler and Stuart Eizenstat: Lobbyists (or any sales people for that matter) must know their customer. During each session of Congress, 535 elected officials, supported by countless staffers, go about the business of making policy for the United States. Each of those 535 members approaches the assignment in a different way, with different experiences, different likes and dislikes, different priorities, different levels of ability, and different needs. Adding to the mix are the ever-changing political, policy, and private pressures that bear upon each legislator and each staff person.

No lobbyist can account for all of these variables; some things about policymakers they cannot know. But lack of information does not change the rules; it merely adds to the challenge of the work.

Keeping these thoughts in mind, I have predicated this book on a simple principle: No one knows the customers better than the customers. As much as I am able to do, I permit them to speak for themselves.

## The Interviews and the Survey

The material for this book is drawn from personal interviews that I conducted with forty-four veteran lawmakers, seventeen current and former congressional staff members, eight experienced lobbyists, and four members of the Executive Branch Career Service—in other words, bureaucrats. In all, eighty-one interviews were conducted. I contacted some subjects two or more times—most in person but some by telephone. As noted in the preface, this work was supplemented by extensive "soaking and poking"—informal conversations with current and past staffers and legislators.[2] Many of these conversations, a number of them lengthier than the formal interviews, occurred over a sandwich in one of the congressional cafeterias.[b]

I also mailed more than 200 surveys to former members of Congress, both senators and representatives. Because my goal was to maximize the number of responses, I assured recipients that they could complete the document within ten minutes. For this reason the survey was limited in scope; it was not designed to collect data on all issues covered in this study. Rather, questions were structured to perform two functions: first, to provide further information on responses from interviewees that I had found surprising, and, second, to expand upon my information base for subjects that several interviewees found particularly interesting. Because I used the survey solely as an information tool to help round out my interview-based research, and because it was in no way scientifically constructed, I do not include the data generated from it in this book (though in a limited number of instances I do note responses to specific questions).

Fifty-four former members were kind enough to complete and return the survey. Almost 20 percent of these accepted my invitation, enclosed with the survey, to volunteer for a follow-up telephone interview, several of which proved to be extremely productive. In all, 127 research subjects, not including the "soaking and poking" contributors, produced information used in this study.

---

b. On one occasion two of my luncheon partner's colleagues joined us, and an informal roundtable developed. As if to prove the adage "better lucky than smart," this chance meeting resulted in a marvelous series of discussions during which I was primarily an observer and scribe.

Each of the former members and staffers who were interviewed, with only a few exceptions, had worked on Capitol Hill for at least four terms (eight years)—most for a longer period. And although the full cohort includes five former legislators who left Congress as early as 1990, I place primary reliance on "recent formers"—those who retired from Congress between 2000 and 2008. There are three reasons for selecting this cohort.

First, experience in interviewing both current and former members and staff has taught me that formers, especially former members, tend to be more forthcoming than the people now sitting. One former member paraphrased an old Washington adage: "If you don't want to see it on the front page of the *Washington Post*, don't say it." Sitting members are well aware of the risks and protect themselves accordingly. Thus, the extent to which a researcher can depend on them for uncompromised observations about what works and what does not work in the lobbyist–member exchange is limited.

Two examples help to illustrate the case: the importance of socializing and the presence of the "revolving door" between Congress and the lobbyists' world. Formers were outspoken on both of these subjects in ways that could not have been expected of sitting lawmakers—especially in the current political environment that has been so deeply affected by the Abramoff–DeLay scandals.[c] They—the formers—were virtually unanimous in their belief that Congress has gone too far in curtailing and, in some cases, eliminating these activities. They see benefits to the commonweal in providing legislators and lobbyists with opportunities to socialize in a "reasonable way." A relaxed social environment allows participants to take the measure of one another and to pursue ideas at length—in contrast to the frenetic pace of the congressional office or the theatrical environment of a public hearing. The formers also see revolving-door lobbyists as being helpful on both procedural and policy matters. The time they have spent on the Hill has taught them how to be on point and efficient with members' time. (We will look more closely at these matters in later chapters.)

Second, because so many of the interviewees had served within the past few years, it is likely that their views on what constitutes effective lobbying are consistent with the thinking of current members. Indeed, I found no evidence to refute this view.

---

c. Rep. Tom DeLay, R-Texas, then House majority leader, was charged with violating campaign finance laws in 2005 and did not seek reelection; Jack Abramoff, a businessman and lobbyist, was convicted of fraud and corruption in 2006. Abramoff had hosted DeLay on a golf outing to Scotland in 2000. The trip occurred just before major house action on legislation opposed by an Abramoff client. Subsequently, DeLay helped to kill the legislation. The outing helped to spark congressional ethics and lobbying reform legislation in 2007. More will be said about this in subsequent chapters.

The third reason is time. No productive first-round interview for this book lasted less than one hour; many interviews were longer.[d] Former members had the time to give, and they gave it generously—in some cases on more than one occasion. It was more difficult to get time with sitting members. Although many sitting members professed and frequently demonstrated interest in the project, they were often pressed to move on to their next obligation. Getting a half-hour with them was a bonus.

Adequate interview time with the formers permitted impromptu digressions, second- and third-order questions, and the luxury of dwelling on a topic in which the former member or staffer had a special interest. Although I came into each interview with a predetermined opening question ("What, in your mind, makes for a good or a bad lobbyist?") and follow-up questions, I let the interviews go where the subjects took them. I was more than willing to sacrifice breadth for depth. When an interviewee became passionate about a position or began to recount on-point, often-colorful, anecdotes, I listened carefully. I was especially attentive when a former added nuance on top of nuance, or suggested that I needed to supplement my investigation with an additional line of questions. This was welcome advice that I almost always heeded—especially since many of these advisers had been highly regarded lawmakers during their tenure on the Hill. They knew what they were talking about.

## Research Regime, Significance, and Scope of the Investigation

This book is largely qualitative. There is a reason for this: Much scholarship and journalistic reporting that purports to analyze what contributes to lobbying effectiveness relies on independent variables that are easily quantifiable—for example, numbers of lobbying visits to congressional offices, amounts of money contributed, and support by coalitions. This work is valuable, providing much to think about as we evaluate the effectiveness of lobbying tools or the normative questions that are raised when clearly self-interested, often well-heeled organizations attempt to insert themselves into the policymaking process.

But in many cases the proverbial cart seems to be ahead of the horse. There are two unknowns that confound students of interest groups and lobbying. The first: What is it that is discussed behind the closed doors that shield lobbyists and members as they discuss policy, procedure, and

d. The exceptions here were follow-up interviews, which usually were conducted by telephone and lasted no more than twenty minutes.

politics? This question remains a mystery to all but those who are privileged to be inside those doors. We can conjecture, but we cannot know what has been said, what has been accepted, or what has been rejected.

Nor can we know what, if any, action a legislator has taken in response to a lobbyist's requests. This is the second unknown. Scholars such as Richard Hall, Michael Malbin, and Frank Sorauf have written about informal (Hall's term) legislative activity.[3] Informal activity occurs behind the scenes, and there is no formal record of it. It includes phone calls, private notes, and one-on-one conversations that beget equally obscure but not insignificant results—a change in the wording of a bill not yet introduced, a decision to withhold an amendment entirely, or, perhaps, a chair's go-ahead to insert new language in a committee report. No political scientist, no regulator, no journalist is there when these communications are made and subsequent agreements are reached. It is the classic black box.

If we accept the premise that lobbyists function as a fourth branch of government, or something akin to that, then penetrating the black box is important work to do. Until we gain improved insight into the myriad variables that color and shape the lobbyist–member exchange, it will remain beyond the reach of political science to establish a convincing database upon which we can construct hypotheses and adequately test them.

But advancement in our understanding of lobbyist–legislator relationships, especially from the perspective of the lawmakers, need not wait until proof can be produced. The information gleaned from this study, in combination with the already abundant literature that examines the exchange from the perspective of the lobbying profession, can teach us much about the art of representing private-sector interests in a venue dominated by public, often very politically motivated, policymakers.

A final observation about the interview-based component of this study: My examination focuses exclusively on direct, one-on-one, *mano-a-mano*, lobbying. This form of lobbying remains for many—including lobbyists, scholars, and lawmakers—the profession's gold standard.[4] A lobbyist explained why it is so important: "It is the only chance I get to make all my points and to answer all of the members' questions. Hearings don't even come close." A legislator representing a district in the Northeast amplified these points: "Now I get to cross-examine. But that's only secondary; I also get to know who I am doing business with. Like [President] Bush with Putin, I get to look into his eyes and see his soul." [e] No other form of lobbying permits such a profound opportunity for member and lobbyist to take the measure of one another.

---

e. President George W. Bush said, after meeting with Russian president Vladimir Putin in 2005, "I looked the man in the eye. . . . I was able to get a sense of his soul."

Certainly, other lobbying techniques—such as grassroots efforts, public relations promotions, electoral and media campaigns, and even strategic use of campaign funds—are necessary; they are often used in conjunction with direct lobbying visits. My decision to exclude them from the present examination is in no way intended to understate their importance or to ignore much excellent scholarship that has been produced on these subjects. On the contrary, the student of lobbying must be conversant with all of these resources.

## Organization of the Book

The next chapter, "The Lobbyist's Professional World," sets the stage for the balance of the book. It is predicated on the belief that lobbyists do not lobby in a vacuum; they must lobby someone, somewhere. Thus, even before we begin to think about what lobbyists do and how they do it, we must know the "territory" in which they operate. That means understanding the professional world of the legislator, including some basics about the organization and functions of Congress. Chapter 2 provides that information.

In chapter 3, "Red Flags," we recognize that lobbying is inherently suspect work. By its nature it is performed in private settings; it is work done "in the dark." Further, lobbyists frequently use what some see as questionable tools to aid in their work (socializing with legislators and making campaign contributions are perhaps the most inflammatory of them), to say nothing about what some view as the questionable image of political people in general. Citizens cannot be faulted for suspecting the worst. But does what first meets the eye tell the whole story?

Chapter 4, "Political 'Capitol'—Gains and Losses," puts the reader into the legislator's mind. If political people are anything, they are calculating. There is no circumstance, no request, and no "opportunity" that they do not test from their own career perspective: What is in it for me? What are my risks? It is the rare member of Congress in the rare situation who will move forward on any project if both of these questions are not answered satisfactorily. How do legislators determine these answers?

Chapter 5, "Inside the Door (and Beyond)," reflects the interview subjects' thoughts about what accounts for good and not-so-good lobbying practices. We begin with the admonition that lobbyists must be trustworthy in every part of their dealings on the Hill. We then discuss value-added functions provided by lobbyists, such as supplementing members' staff and providing "subsidies" in the form of legislative drafts and proposed floor statements. We conclude with a discussion of tactical pluses and minuses.

In chapter 6, "The Lobbyist's Ask," we get to the central point of this book. If a lobbyist does not set forces in motion by asking a legislator to do something, nothing will happen. This chapter recognizes that the shapes and forms of asks are potentially infinite, but that does not mean anything goes. Quite the opposite: The lobbyist's ask frames the mission that the lawmaker is being urged to undertake. It must make sense. Perhaps the number one criterion is that it must be doable.

Chapter 7, "Designing and Executing a Lobbying Campaign," is a brief how-to discussion about how lobbyists operate. Although it does not pretend to address every detail that a lobbyist should consider in planning a campaign, it does give insights into what veteran legislators consider to be the most important features of a well-run campaign, as identified and discussed by interview subjects.

In chapter 8, the conclusion, I draw upon hundreds of interview hours to construct a rough hierarchy of those things members and senior staff believe to be most important for lobbyists to bear in mind as they sell their wares on Capitol Hill. If there is a core message here, it is that lobbying, as done by most practitioners most of the time, requires in equal parts a profound understanding of substance, culture, and process. Quality lobbying is never susceptible to rote, formulaic execution. It requires constant sensitivity and adjustment to the person being lobbied. The art of the lobbyist, as in all forms of sales, is the art of building trust.

## Notes

1. Jeffrey H. Birnbaum, *The Lobbyists: How Influence Peddlers Get Their Way in Washington* (New York: Times Books, 1992), 96–97.

2. Political scientist Richard F. Fenno Jr., in *Home Style: House Members in Their Districts* (Glenview, Ill.: Scott, Foresman, 1978), introduced the term "soaking and poking."

3. Richard Hall, *Participation in Congress* (New Haven: Yale University Press, 1996); Michael J. Malbin, *Money and Politics in the United States* (Chatham, N.J.: Chatham House, 1984); Frank J. Sorauf, *Inside Campaign Finance* (New Haven: Yale University Press, 1992).

4. Rogan Kersh, "The Well-Informed Lobbyist," in *Interest Group Politics,* 7th ed., ed. Allan J. Cigler and Burdett A. Loomis (Washington, D.C.: CQ Press, 2007), 394 (Figure 17.2).

# 2 The Lobbyist's Professional World

Strip away the trappings of self-importance often associated with lobbyists on Capitol Hill—photos with national leaders, membership in the Republican or Democratic National Committee club, preening at inaugural events—and one quickly discovers that lobbyists are sales people. And like other sales people they are well instructed to take to heart the advice offered by Charlie Cowell, one of Meredith Wilson's salesmen in *The Music Man*: "You gotta know the territory."

For lobbyists, the territory is populated by what journalists like to call the inside-the-Beltway crowd. Richard Neustadt called it the "Washington community." [1] Whatever name one chooses, this territory consists of legislators, executive branch officials, journalists, think tank pundits, interest group leaders, a few cab drivers, a bartender or two, and other opinion leaders. These are all customers for the lobbyist, but first among them are the lawmakers and their senior staff members. Other insiders may indirectly affect legislative outcomes; but these are the people who produce them. Without their agreement and support, the lobbyist is nowhere.

Aside from sharing a common professional responsibility as members of Congress, the men and women who occupy the 535 seats in the congressional chambers (100 in the Senate and 435 in the House of Representatives) are an eclectic group: liberals, conservatives, urbanites, country folk, policy wonks, and pure politicians. Like other citizens, each lawmaker approaches her or his responsibilities in a unique manner. A sitting member, a conservative from the Northeast, said of the House: "This ain't no damn army. We don't all move forward or back at the same time or in the same way."[a] A veteran chief of staff who has served for many years on Capitol Hill in several different offices summed it up: "There are 535 congressional offices. They're all different—different levels of interest, different levels of intelligence, different levels of staff competence. Even for us we had to know who we were dealing with. No two offices were ever the same."

The resulting differences are reflected in each member's approach to service in Congress. This, in turn, affects their career goals, their policy perspectives, their level of partisanship, and their commitment to doing the work of Congress—producing thoughtful, internally consistent, public policy. Understanding what drives each member is the necessary beginning point for the lobbyist who is intent upon building effective, on-going relationships with the congressional offices that will control the fate of his own and his client's interests in policy outcomes.

Getting to know a small handful of congressional offices well is not difficult, and for some matters that might be sufficient. In fact, a few lobbyists have been known to make a living off their relationship with one powerful lawmaker.[b] But that is seldom the case, and even when it is, there is some doubt about whether their clients benefit as much as they do. Most often lobbyists are not permitted the luxury of confining their work to one or a small universe of legislators. They must always have in stock a considerable inventory of working relationships. The job of building and maintaining this inventory is not an easy one, given the multiple performance variables discussed in chapter 1.

In this chapter we will focus on the lawmaker, what makes up her professional environment, and what makes her tick as a member of Congress. The reason for doing this is simple: The lawmaker's world is the lobbyist's world. What affects her affects him. It is not enough that he knows his issues; he must know and understand the people and the institution within which he plies his trade.

---

a. Many books and articles that purport to examine Congress virtually ignore the individualism that exists within the institution: In *The Case Against Congress* (New York: Simon and Schuster, 1968), Drew Pearson and Jack Anderson recount many abuses, some legal, some not, by federal legislators. Some of this reporting is quite good, but the book jacket, intended to sell the book, is misleading: "Washington's boldest reporting team tells the full story of the nation's biggest scandal—the misconduct of the men and women sent to write America's laws."

b. Many former staff people for prominent members of Congress leave Capitol Hill and sell their services, sometimes with the help of their former employers, as access providers. Although the words are seldom if ever actually used, their message is clear: "I can get you into see Representative X—if not her, then her senior staff person for the issue in which you are interested." As a second product these entrepreneurs market their knowledge of how their former bosses like to operate, what sorts of provisions they may be open to considering, which ones not, how they like to relate to their colleagues. This is the classic stuff of the revolving door, which will be discussed in chapter 3.

One subsection in this chapter, "The Importance of Committees," is of a slightly different cast than the others. This is an important discussion—lobbyists spend the bulk of their face-to-face time with staffers and members during committee and subcommittee consideration of legislative proposals—but it has no natural place in the text. Considering the nexus between committee operatives and much of the work that lobbyists do, I have placed the discussion just after the subsection on committee staff.

## Types of Lawmakers

Some political scientists have sought to construct typologies that capture lawmakers' overall approach to their jobs. Because every lobbying campaign must be geared to the members (or the member) who control the fate of the legislative matter in question, and because making the right "read" on these members is critical, it is worth taking a few moments to look at some of these legislative types.

Political scientist James L. Payne makes what may be the most basic—though not wholly uncontested—distinction; he distinguishes between the "status" type and the "program" type of legislator. The status type, according to Payne, is "oriented toward prestige, recognition, and judgments of success by society." Priorities for such a member have to do with public image as it is affected by the member's overt responses to policy issues—usually high-profile issues. She is apt to have a low level of concern with making good policy and thus will receive "little satisfaction from the detailed examination of policy." She is not likely to be an important contributor to the development of a bill, amendment, or other policy vehicle. The status type is often referred to as a "show horse" member—all show and little substance.[2]

The program type, or "workhorse," is quite different; she is "preoccupied with substantive policy questions." Payne argues that this preoccupation does not always pay off in publicity and even in reelection benefits. She is willing to run the risk of reelection difficulties because she is "interested in . . . policy examinations that take place in unseen committees." [3]

A midwestern Democrat agrees with Payne: "There are at least two types of members: 'I just want to get reelected,' and 'I am here to make good policy.' " This former lawmaker refers to members of the House of Representatives who qualify as good policymakers or, in Payne's vocabulary, program types, as "the adult supervision of the House." He estimates that this describes 20 to 30 percent of the members.[c] These lawmakers

c. More than 80 percent of the members and staff interviewed for this study placed the range between 15 and 35 percent.

provide supervision because they carry disproportionate weight (in relation to their absolute numbers) among their colleagues. He argues that legislators of this stripe care deeply about the constitutionally mandated role of Congress as the nation's lead policymaking institution; they take pride in discharging their responsibilities with due deliberation and skill; they understand that "the House is what [they] make of it." It is not too much to say that they see themselves as guardians of "their" institution's place among other policymaking bodies. Donald Matthews calls this "institutional patriotism." [4] We will return to this subject later in this chapter.

Other authorities have made related observations—related in the sense that they suggest important distinctions between workhorses and show horses in the context of their effectiveness within Congress. John Kingdon and John Hibbing are among the congressional scholars who have been especially effective in identifying and discussing the relationship between specialization and influence within Congress. Kingdon concludes that federal lawmakers are heavily influenced by knowledgeable colleagues (the workhorses) when deciding their votes—especially on those matters for which they do not sense a strong constituency interest or do not claim personal expertise: "By any measure, fellow congressmen turn out to be highly important influences on votes." Kingdon then adds this: "My interviews are also filled with commentary extolling the virtues of the committee and specialization system and indicating that one reason for turning to a given informant is his expertise." [5]

Hibbing makes an especially valuable observation that bears upon the subject matter of this book. He constructs a template that lobbyists would do well to use as a guide for their work. He sees value in specialization for both the individual member and for the institution:

> Frequently, representatives have become key legislative players not by spending all of their time in the well[d] . . . but by picking their spots, by understanding the process, by developing expertise in a limited subject area, and by knowing what is possible and what is not.
>
> The expectation is that specialization and efficiency of legislators will increase with the passage of years, as members grow to understand the value of specialization within that process.[6]

Knowing process, subject expertise, and understanding what is possible: If there were a bible for lobbyists, these words would be prominently set on the first page.

But all scholars who have studied congressional work styles do not accept Payne's typology. According to Laura Langbein and Lee Sigelman,

---

d. The well is a position on the floor of the House from which a member may address the entire body.

most members do not fit neatly into program- or status-type molds.[e] Langbein and Sigelman hypothesize that when "faced with competing pressures for them to act in different ways, legislators devise complex means of having it both ways. . . . It may be that legislators have become adept at achieving multiple goals through a single use of time." [7]

Most members and staff interviewed for this study agreed with Langbein and Sigelman: Members, while their work might be guided by a dominant trait in their legislative "personality," do "act in different ways" at different times when faced with different needs. For one thing, members aspire to be reelected. As David Mayhew observes, "Whether they are safe or marginal, cautious or audacious, congressmen must consistently engage in activities related to reelection. There will be differences in emphasis, but all members share the root need to do things [related to reelection]—indeed, to do things day in and day out during their terms.[8]

Mayhew notes "three kinds of activities congressmen find it electorally useful to do:" advertising, credit claiming, and position taking.[9] It is not necessary here to discuss these components in depth to understand that they bear a strong resemblance to show horse behavior. What is important to note is that in Mayhew's view even the most issue-oriented workhorse may, from time to time, resort to show horse activity; this simply comes with the political territory. One former staffer was on point, even using terminology similar to that used by Mayhew: "Some showboating always goes on during [a member's term]."

In an excellent analysis of the congressional oversight system, Christopher Foreman describes how legislators, presumably even the best of them, are sometimes willing to sacrifice substance for vote-getting theatrics: "Once laws have been enacted, subsequent congressional supervision of administrative behavior and policymaking tends to be episodic or nonexistent. Both scholarly and popular treatments of Congress generally suggest a legislature that, except for the occasional instance when oversight offers concrete political rewards, remains far more interested in claiming credit for new programs than in the tedious review of old ones." [10]

Thus, notwithstanding the debate between Payne and Langbein and Sigelman about typing members as show horses or workhorses, there is evidence that most lawmakers see themselves as some of one and a little of the other. This shifting in legislators' approach to their work can be subtle, at least to the untrained eye. Richard Hall argues that during the all-important subcommittee and full-committee stages of the legislative process members are driven by their personal policy interests, by constituent interests, and (at full committee) by the desire to support a president of their

e. Langbein and Sigelman use the terms "show horse" and "work horse," which Payne also uses.

party: "At the stage of full-committee action, differently positioned individuals tend to participate because they want to, and what they want is to serve their district interests (service that presumably enhances their reelection chances), pursue personal policy interests or ideological agendas, or promote the agenda of a president from their own party." [11]

Hall also finds that only about 50 percent of the members of the three subcommittees he examined participated actively in the markup of legislation moving through their subcommittee. This observation is surprising as members work hard to get themselves appointed to the committees and subcommittees of their choice. "Even so," writes Hall, "specialization and hard work are hardly universal. Rather, participation is highly selective." [12]

Other scholars have made different sorts of cuts regarding members' interests and participation. Raymond Bauer, Ithiel de Sola Pool, and Lewis Anthony Dexter (following a Mayhew-like view that members are preoccupied with reelection) hold that a member must "do things which will secure for him the esteem and/or support of significant elements of his constituency." [13] They suggest that members must choose from several different professional focus areas at any given time. For our purposes I place these in four broad categories that a member might choose as a focus: (1) program, (2) status, (3) district, and (4) political.[f]

1. Program
    - "He can make a reputation for himself in the field of legislation."
    - "He can seek a reputation as a national leader."
2. Status
    - "He can work at press relations, creating and stimulating stories and an image of activity."
    - "He can conduct investigations and set himself up as a defender of public morals."
3. District
    - "He can become a promoter of certain local industries."
    - "He can be a local civic leader, attending and speaking at community functions."
    - "He can get people jobs and do social work and favors."
    - "He can become a promoter of certain local industries."

f. Some of the activities fit into overlapping categories. The authors also say that a member "can take well-publicized trips to international hot spots." Given the post-Abramoff climate and recent ethics reforms, I have chosen not to enter that option into the text.

4. Political

- "He can be a party wheel horse."
- "He can befriend moneyed interests to assure himself of a well-financed campaign."
- "He can befriend labor unions, veterans organizations, or other groups with a numerous clientele and many votes."

The authors then add: "The one thing [a member] cannot do is much of all of these things. He must choose among them; he has to be a certain kind of a congressman." [14]

The point is this: Each congressional office—or each "congressional enterprise" works in its own way and for its own sets of purposes.[15] These purposes may be fleeting, addressing a momentary priority, or they may be more in line with the member's long-term goals, goals that will flow almost naturally from her decision about the kind of legislator she wants to be.

The extent to which a member falls into one or the other of Payne's classifications, or the extent to which a member chooses to focus on one or more of Bauer, Pool, and Dexter's classifications of activities, should send important messages to the astute lobbyist. Arguably, this is all the more important when a lobbyist is working with members who drive the policymaking process in Congress, legislators who provide the "adult supervision" of the House or Senate. The influential committee member who is highly regarded for her expertise—the workhorse looking to master an issue that is coming before her committee—is not likely to suffer fools. Nor is she likely to be unaware that a lobbyist has spent little time learning about what she expects of petitioners—especially well-paid petitioners in whom clients have invested considerable trust and fortune. A former Republican member from the Northeast described the evaluation process as on-going: "Lobbyists are under scrutiny, consciously or not, by members and staff. 'Is he just another pleader? Or, is he a valuable ally, someone who can help with my constituency and with members of Congress?' "

Typologies that purport to identify and then classify members' work styles based on their level of concern for policy outcomes—in contrast to a self-serving and relatively mindless pursuit of publicity—have some value. But they can identify only general inclinations that may exist in a member's attitude about legislative work. The tendency of scholars and lobbyists alike may be to oversimplify and thus too quickly and incorrectly to pigeonhole members as one type or another.

Although it is probably true that some members are primarily show horses and others workhorses, it is also the case that many if not most members are some of one and some of the other, depending on the issue and circumstance at hand. Just as a member must gauge the quality of the lobbyist who is asking for her support, so too must the lobbyist make an accurate read on the member he is enlisting for his cause. A pure show horse is not as likely to endure the endless give and take of informal behind-the-scenes negotiations and procedural maneuvering as one might expect of the more patient, policy-oriented workhorse. Yet it may also be true that the policy wonk may not have the talent or the desire necessary to do the entrepreneurial activities that call attention to her issue and help to build support among the media and in Congress. There may well be instances in which a little legislative schizophrenia will serve both the lobbyist and the lawmaker well. If the member is Dr. Jekyll, the lobbyist might help to provide a piece—just a piece—of the Mr. Hyde personality.

## The Legislative Environment

Several interview subjects identified, or strongly suggested, factors that they considered as bearing heavily on their day-to-day work environment and, as a consequence, on their potential receptivity to lobbyists' requests for support. I have grouped these into six categories: very busy, pulled in many directions, information starved, reelection aware, defensive, and peer sensitive.[g] A brief description of each of these environmental elements will give insight into what lobbyists must consider when developing their campaigns.

- **Very busy.** Members, especially those who showed strong policy interests, saw themselves as time poor. "You never have enough time or staff." This comment, like many similar comments, was offered in the context of doing what I term "the work of the work" in Congress—in short, writing good law. Amid committee meetings (hearings and markups), meetings with executive branch officials, legislative caucuses, meetings with lobbyists, meetings with staff (personal staff or committee staff), and, in some cases, coalition-building efforts, members involved in program-type work are hard pressed to squeeze all that is necessary for intelligent deliberation into their workday schedules.
- **Pulled in many directions.** Although this item relates to the previous one, it has a different point of emphasis. The previous item has to do with time demands focused on "the work of the work." This item is concerned with the total time demand on members and includes party caucuses, constituent meetings and responses to other constituent demands, activity directed specifically to reelection matters (including fundraising), press inquiries, attendance at evening social events, and some office administrative matters. These are often necessary draws on a member's time, but to the program type they can be unwelcome distractions.

g. The first three categories seem to affect all members at relatively consistent levels; the next three are more heavily influenced by the member's work personality and goals.

- **Information starved.** The business of making policy for the United States is a serious and complex matter. Although some members take their obligations more seriously than do others, few in Congress are not at one time or another awed by the importance of the work they must do to faithfully discharge their responsibilities. There is much to learn and many sources from which to learn. There are also different views on what would be good and not-so-good policy, each with supporting arguments and facts. Even members with long experience or subject expertise do not come to Congress knowing it all. Although their office and committee staffs are helpful, members often feel information starved: "I never get time to just think," complained one northeasterner. It is no wonder that most members welcome new and dependable information sources.

- **Reelection aware.** The essence of Mayhew's thesis is indisputable: Members of Congress must constantly engage in activities related to reelection. One might add that they must not engage in activities that will make reelection more difficult—that is, support legislative provisions that will alienate important constituencies in their districts. Although members might sometimes "suck it up" in support of a party position or of a proposal they believe to be both important and in the national interest, they never make such decisions without careful consideration and much trepidation.

- **Defensive.** Members are defensive in part because they are reelection aware, but this is not the whole story. They are in a give-and-take business—giving and taking with and from political adversaries, potential allies, media outlets, interest groups, and the list goes on. They must be prepared to justify their positions and their actions in support of those positions. There is little that they are asked to do in response to an interest group's request that does not trigger their immediate analysis of potential colleagues' and constituents' reactions and reelection fallouts. A current lobbyist remarked, "It's almost as if I can see their eyeballs starting to spin like slot machine windows as they run through the political fallout possibilities."

- **Peer sensitive.** This item too relates to members' defensive thinking, but there is an important nuance: Members of Congress, like participants in any organization with a job to do, accord special standing to those who do the institution's work. Doctors on a hospital staff know and respect the most competent of their colleagues. Athletes praise the swiftest, best conditioned, and surest footed among their numbers. Academics admire peers for their contributions to the collective body of knowledge. So it is with members of Congress. They know and respect their hardest-working, best-informed, and most competent colleagues, both for their contributions to the institution and to the broader community. These are the go-to lawmakers, the professionals. As a consequence, they are the institution's most influential members. For the program types, this is especially important; it provides the muscle they need to drive the policy process.[h]

The lobbyist must assess which environmental factors are dominating a member's work environment at any given time: Is she obsessed with reelection; packed to the gills with legislative assignments; or emerging as a go-to member and anxious to do all that she can to promote herself to that status. The lobbyist cannot completely separate his assessment from observations about the member's professional personality. Work environment and personality may be split apart for analytical purposes, but as a practical matter they can be so intertwined as to make it almost impossible to fully understand one without considering the other: Environment affects personality, and personality to some degree affects the environment in which a legislator chooses to place herself. Both are dynamic, perhaps not changing much from matter to matter, but not remaining totally static either.

Understanding this is a prerequisite to determining potential levels of interest and flexibility that a lobbyist might expect to find for his cause in a particular congressional office. The last member I interviewed for this study considered it "an insult when a lobbyist has not taken the time or had the interest to find out something about me before coming in to meet." Just as there is no Platonic form for the "good lobbyist," so there is no ideal form for the successful meeting. Generic rules that allegedly account for members' behavior and thus provide recipe-like instructions for lobbyists to follow in deciding whom to approach, and then approaching them, do not exist.

Thus, regardless of whether a particular trait or circumstance is best thought of as part of a member's working environment or as a consequence of her professional personality—or likely both—each of these factors will contribute to shaping the lobbyist's "playing field."

Consider this hypothetical: A lobbyist, in search of a champion for his client's cause, knows that lawmaker X—Payne's program type—is highly regarded for her political and substantive excellence. Because she is a go-to member, and because she is also known for her high energy level, she is frequently approached by other lobbyists who seek her support. Thus the lobbyist must anticipate that he will find himself competing for her time and interest. This knowledge, in turn, should affect his strategic and tactical thinking about how to gain and hold her interest: Does he try to line up strong district support before he goes into her office? Does he strip bargaining positions from his proposal and shape it almost exactly to her known legislative preferences, thus making it more appealing to her and

h. Risk adversity and peer sensitivity may be especially applicable to members who aspire to advancement within Congress.

saving her time? Does he get an advance read on how the administration is apt to react to his proposal and share that information with her?

Although the lobbyist might normally do all of these things during the course of his lobbying campaign, he may decide to frontload these tactics when dealing with this well-regarded, much sought-after lawmaker. In this way an accurate reading of the playing field and the member's role in shaping it will be pivotal components affecting the lobbyist's plan of attack.

## Congressional Culture

Congressional culture is really a subset of the congressional work environment. An important part of knowing the territory is understanding the culture—what is accepted behavior, what is not, what is praiseworthy, and what is considered out of bounds for members of Congress and those who do business with them.

Some lobbyists perform their duties almost as virtuosos. They sense the rhythms of the institution and the cadences of individual offices; they pick up on subtle programmatic and political themes; they know the value of a soft, even understated, presentation; they sense when to perform with gusto and when to be mellow. They also know when to get off the stage. They are, in their own way, artists. In policymaking terms, they are savvy.

Once the lobbyist is inside the office door there is much he can do that signals his understanding (or lack thereof) of "where" he is. With whom does he ask to meet? How hard does he press his point? Does he offer prospects for helping a member achieve her goals? Is he more likely to force a load of new problems onto her agenda than he is to help her solve or avoid problems? Is he asking for what is doable? Is he professional in demeanor?

Other than giving an honest and competent presentation, nothing affects a lobbyist's reputation as much as does evidence of savvy behavior—behavior that signals that he understands and appreciates the mores and work ethic of Capitol Hill. If he gives and receives the right signals, he has a good chance of being accepted as an adjunct resource for the institution, a valued member of the "fourth branch" of government. If this evidence is not apparent—worse, if the lobbyist demonstrates little appreciation for the exigencies of congressional service—he is quickly judged an outsider, a suspect player who may well become a burden on the offices he seeks to influence. (This line of argument will be expanded in chapter 5, under the heading "Presentation of Self.")

Matthews has identified six "normative rules of conduct" that he credits with providing "motivation for the performance of legislative duties that, perhaps [in the absence of these rules] would not . . . be performed." The experienced lobbyist knows that these rules, directed to members of Congress, establish an environment in which lobbyists must practice. Not to be aware of them, and the extent to which a given member adheres to or ignores any one of them, is to risk embarrassment, missed opportunity, or both. These rules, or "folkways," include the following:

- Apprenticeship: showing a willingness to be a back-bencher, to be quiet and to learn.
- Legislative work: performing the essential tasks of the institution.
- Specialization: focusing on the issues and business of one's committees and on matters affecting one's constituency.
- Courtesy: acting civilly and treating one's colleagues with appropriate deference.
- Reciprocity: acting reciprocally, more than simple "logrolling," is a way of political life in which one is mindful that a colleague has been helpful in the past and is happy to return the favor.
- Institutional patriotism: demonstrating a commitment to the legislative body—in the case of Matthews's study, the Senate—and a willingness to uphold and, if need be, defend its place in the policymaking milieu.[16]

Herbert Asher found seven norms at work in the House of Representatives: friendship (among members), forbearance from criticizing a colleague on the floor, importance of committee work, specialization, compliance with House rules, apprenticeship, and logrolling.[17] Others—including Richard Fenno, who emphasized the importance of specialization and hard work—have found similar norms or folkways.[18]

Anyone reading a newspaper, following a political blog, or watching public affairs programs on television, however, must suspect that the increased partisanship now apparent within Congress has diminished adherence to the norms of courtesy, civility, and institutional patriotism. More recently scholars have either debunked the notion of norms altogether or have found certain of them to be no longer operative.[19] Their work has sparked much debate among political scientists. L. Marvin Overby and Lauren C. Bell present a balanced analysis of this debate. After noting the discussion among scholars about the causes of normative behavior in the Senate—Is it driven by a strictly utilitarian, rational-choice motivation to enhance one's own legislative fortunes, or is it driven more by standards-of-conduct issues?—Overby and Bell conclude that "contemporary students of the Congress may have underestimated the importance of norms such as cooperation and reciprocity." But they quickly follow with a caveat: "While there is little doubt that—in a relative sense—there has been erosion of these norms over the past 50 years, it would be a gross exaggeration to conclude that they no longer matter." [20]

The interviews I conducted lend some support for the view that the congressional culture that placed high value on these norms has undergone at least some change. There was a clear consensus among interview subjects that the institution is now more partisan than it has been in recent memory. According to a veteran Ways and Means staffer, "It is very different now. You don't get much by way of bipartisan coalitions." Another committee staffer, alluding specifically to the effects of increased partisanship, complained: "It is not as much fun as it used to be." A pro-labor Democrat, and former subcommittee chair, had this to say: "The K Street Project had an impact.[i] I would hear that some members would say 'you couldn't come in [to my office] with a Democrat lobbyist.' "

A Democrat from a western state, well regarded for his political insights and the quality of his legislative work, thought the effects of the K Street Project went beyond simply determining which lobbyists were welcomed in Republican offices and which were not. He theorized that the project contributed to a diminished concern for "civility" in Congress at both the staff and lobbyist levels. Although he presented no data, his impressions were interesting:

> For many years congressional staffers would serve for a long time. That was because they had a genuine public service ethic. They may have been Republicans or Democrats, but they were also interested in policy. Though I do have to say this was probably more true of Democrats—I think because we tend to have more confidence in government—so they stayed longer. When Republicans took control and after the K Street thing was set up, lots of young people just put in their time [as staffers] just to set up a lobbying career and so they are not as deep into congressional habits and culture. They were never public servants. They never developed a loyalty to the Congress as an institution.

But not everyone agrees that even if Democrats and Republicans are more sharply divided today this necessarily changes the fundamentals of service in Congress or, as a consequence, the lobbying profession. Notwithstanding the K Street Project, and the general sense that House and Senate institutions are more partisan today than in recent decades, the interviews did not produce clear-cut examples of how the overall culture of Capitol Hill has changed to any significant degree. Although it would be too

i. The "K Street Project," allegedly the brainchild of former House majority leader Tom DeLay, R-Texas, was an attempt to force Washington lobbyists to hire former Republican members or staffers. Several sources have reported that sitting Republicans were admonished if they permitted lobbyists with known Democratic ties to come to their office to lobby them.

much to say that every member or lobbyist in every circumstance conforms to the established norms of behavior for the Hill, the interviews confirm that most members and staffers still prize hard work, civility, and the other norms identified by Matthews, Asher, and Fenno.

Perhaps this is because partisan-based distinctions are nothing new in Congress; they have long played a role in how Democrats and Republicans view legislators on either side of the aisle. Writing more than four decades ago, Charles Clapp found that "there are important differences in the way House Democrats and Republicans look at themselves and at each other." Democrats saw Republicans as "tightly bound by adherence to traditional outmoded concepts" and less concerned for the "needs of the American people." Republicans argued that Democrats were less responsible and less "concerned with principle." [21]

It is true that holding these views does not necessarily result in an inability or an unwillingness to work with the opposition, but some of the opinions came close to qualifying as damning the other party. Clapp quotes Democratic House members as believing that their political opposition did not like people: "No matter how they try to hide it . . . Republicans just don't like people."[22] Not liking people! That is pretty strong stuff.

Not to be outdone, Republicans gave as good as they got. One Republican accused Democrats of buying votes with public dollars: "Democrats . . . are interested only in spending on the supposition that this will please more and more groups." Another Republican presaged the message that President Ronald Reagan would make popular decades later: Democrats "tell people what they are going to do *for* them, we tell them what we are keeping government from doing *to* them." [23]

None of this sounds like high praise or an incentive to work with the other party. As if predicting the decades of the 1990s and 2000s, Clapp argued that "A strong sense of partisanship may, in fact, make it difficult for a congressman . . . to adjust to the tendencies for accommodation and moderation which epitomize the activities of the legislative body." Yet Clapp also found that, despite these seemingly contentious views, "compromise and consensus" continued to be important characteristics of the effective legislator.[24]

The interviews suggest the same: Compromise and accommodation, whether across the aisle or within one's own party, remain staples in the lawmaking process. Although there may be momentary aberrations in congressional behavior—aberrations that affect the degree to which one or more behavioral norms are honored by sitting members—there continues to be a prevailing set of values that influences members' behavior and sets expectations for lobbyists.

Perhaps the most instructive, certainly most colorful, statement about the role of behavioral norms in congressional policymaking was offered by a former staffer: "It's like cars; they may be faster and have more bells and whistles, but you still have to turn on the ignition, press down on the gas, hit the brakes, and use the window wipers when it rains." In other words, the basics remain the basics.

## Congressional Structure

To the untrained eye Congress is a single institution with a charge to produce legislation which "shall have passed the House of Representatives and the Senate . . . [and] be presented to the President of the United States." [25] Thus the end product is a single piece of legislation upon which both houses have agreed.

There are clear similarities between the two bodies. They share the Capitol building, each in a separate wing. They both rely on committees to do much of their work. Each is composed of elected representatives, and each must rely heavily on staff people who serve at the pleasure of the elected officials. There are other similarities, but there are also important differences.

Ross Baker quotes former senator John Culver, D-Iowa: "I think the starting point of wisdom on comparing the House and Senate is frankly a very simple but, I believe, critical observation. That's the size difference. Size really explains so much else about those institutions in terms of their organization . . . their rules . . . their accessibility and participation of the members, the committees, the workloads and so forth." [26]

It is true that the House and Senate must each consider and pass the identical bill before it can go to the president for consideration. By that standard their workloads would seem to be identical. But, as Culver points out, that is not the case. There are about as many committees in the Senate as there are in the House, but there are only 100 senators available to do the work of those committees, while there are 435 representatives.[j] The result is that each senator is spread thin. According to Sen. Max Baucus, D-Mont., this becomes apparent when House members and senators square off in conference committees: "The Senators are a lot less prepared than House members. They're spread thinner." [27] And because senators are generally considered to be busier than House members, "contact [by lobbyists] with members [is] typical in dealing with the House. In the

j. Many senators are also considered to be "national figures" and thus in much demand for press interviews and other public appearances. Senators represent an entire state, which, with very few exceptions, means they represent more constituents than does any House member from their state.

Senate one-on-one meetings with Senators [are] unusual. Lobbyist-staff encounters [are] the norm in the Senate and while most lobbyists' meetings on the House side [are] also with staff, there [is] more routine and regular quality to lobbyists' contacts with House members." [28]

The House is also known to be more rules driven than is the Senate, which is more collegial, according deference to each member of the body. In theory, senators are allowed wide latitude for exerting influence across the full spectrum of legislation. House members are generally limited to influencing bills emerging from their committees, and, even then, party affiliation can be a significant factor in determining just how much say a member will have. Senate "rules" permitting filibusters, holds, and nongermane floor amendments also add to the legislative armament that each senator has at her disposal.[k] Christopher Deering and Steven Smith observe that "it is easier for Senate noncommittee members to influence a committee's decisions. This permeability is reinforced by the Senate's more open and flexible floor procedures, which make it easier for noncommittee members to amend bills after they have been reported to the floor." [29] All of these tools virtually ensure that each senator will have an opportunity to be heard on any bill that is moving through the Senate and perhaps to have a chance to modify it. The senator may not win, but at least she can get into the game.

The distinctions between the House and the Senate are often reflected within the lobbying community. Some firms, many in fact, have their "House lobbyists" and "Senate lobbyists." Even the White House has legislative specialists who focus on one body or the other. Much of this specialization has to do with knowing and understanding the rules and folkways of each body, but some of it results from Matthews's "institutional patriotism." Some people are "House people" and some are "Senate people," and none has any desire to change.

## Legislative Staff [l]

Many of the interviews I conducted focused on the roles of congressional staff. In each congressional office, the member's personal staff (or member's staff) performs a wide range of functions. Staffers answer mail, help

k. Filibusters are often attempts to defeat legislation by talking it to death. The Senate, unlike the House, does not limit the time for debate—unless the senators unanimously agree to such a limitation. There is a method to shut down a filibuster, but it takes sixty votes to accomplish. A hold is an informal mechanism by which a senator can have a bill "held" (not acted upon for a short period of time). Nongermane amendments are amendments that have little or nothing to do with the subject of the bill under consideration.

l. Since the subject of this book is lobbying, rather than Congress more generally, only the essentials of congressional staff organizations and functions will be presented here, enough to place lobbying in its proper setting.

constituents resolve their problems with federal agencies (known as casework), handle press relations and scheduling, and assist their boss in her policy-related functions. Our interest here is on the last of these roles, helping the member to participate in the business of the business—writing law. The single exception to this will be a brief discussion about the role of the chief of staff (or administrative assistant). On the committees, the work is heavily weighted toward creating and passing policy in the form of legislation.

There are as many permutations in the way staff is organized as there are members' offices, committees, and subcommittees in Congress. Each House member is allotted a budget that includes provisions for staffing and such items as general office expenses and travel to and from the member's district. In 2007 most offices received approximately $1.3–$1.5 million. Senate allowances are not as uniform. Although they are based on formulas that are similar to the House formula, the wide range in constituent numbers—ranging from California's 35-plus million population to Wyoming's little more than a half-million—results in significant budget differences. The 2006 range was roughly $2.5–$4 million.[30]

## Personal Staff (or "Member's Staff")

*"I am the protector of the flanks."*

The boss beneath the boss in a congressional office is the chief of staff. Often this person functions as a political alter ego for the member. The chief of staff usually plays a major role in hiring, organizing, and managing other staffers. She is often the gatekeeper to the member, deciding who gains access and who does not. In many offices she will play a significant role in setting the member's legislative agenda—often considering what will "fly" in the district. Although she may not be involved in the day-to-day business of developing legislation, she will keep an eye on that function. She does this to ensure that substantive and political objectives are coordinated. Many people who serve in this role are veterans of Capitol Hill, people who have seen it all.

Personal legislative staffers, usually known as legislative assistants, are typically young, a few years out of college, and most often generalists. In the House they may cover three or more committees for their boss. Many offices now have a legislative director (often shortened to "leg director") who serves as the key legislative adviser to the representative and supervises other legislative assistants. Often the legislative director will focus her own efforts on the member's primary committee assignment, leaving the other committees to more junior legislative assistants.

## Committee Staff

*"Representatives and senators . . . cannot handle the large workload on their own."*

Roger Davidson and Walter Oleszek put the matter simply and correctly: "Throughout the three principle stages of committee policymaking—hearings, markups, and report writing—staff aides play an active part. Representatives and senators (to a greater degree because there are fewer of them) cannot handle the large workload on their own and so must rely heavily on the unelected lawmakers." [31]

What distinguishes committee staff from personal legislative staff is their level of subject knowledge, the degree to which they are able to specialize, and their reporting relationships. Many committee staffers have advanced degrees and have had extensive experience in the committee's areas of substantive jurisdiction. It is not uncommon for medical doctors to serve on the health committees, for tax lawyers to staff the tax-writing committees, or for PhDs to serve on these and other committees. These people generally are older than personal legislative staffers, with the exception of the lawmaker's chief of staff, and have had considerably more professional experience. They often are credited with providing much of the advantage that committee members enjoy when considering or defending committee bills: "Committees' specialized staffs place committee members in a better position than others to define issues to their advantage, monitor the activity of their opponents, and respond promptly to opponents' political maneuvers." [32] Although there is a great deal of variation from committee to committee, senior committee staff usually report directly to the committee chair. This is certainly true in the House.

## The Importance of Committees: The Prime Venue for Lobbying

*"Most of the real crafting of bills takes place at the committee and subcommittee levels."*

Jeffrey Berry writes, "With most of the work done in Congress done in the Committees, it's not surprising that most of the work of legislative lobbyists is done there too." He goes further: "Says one corporate lobbyist, 'You have to start at the beginning. You have to start at the subcommittee level.' " [33]

Since the founding era, the role of congressional committees and subcommittees—indeed, their very existence—has changed over and again. In relatively recent times (since the early twentieth century) the pendulum has swung several times, from Speaker Joe Cannon's "King Caucus" [m] and strong party leadership control, to the great committee barons of midcentury, to government by subcommittee, and, finally, back to party control. The relative importance of committee work to policy outcomes has ebbed and flowed with each regime change. Yet, throughout all of these machinations, there have been virtually no periods during which committees have been entirely irrelevant to the process.

Even in today's era of relatively strong party control, there are simply too many issues and too many strong characters with independent political bases to permit a return to anything resembling the King Caucus era. Even when the committee role is limited to the pursuit of objectives established by party leaders, chairs usually find enough wiggle room to assert at least some of their own priorities.[34]

In recent decades, as the issues tackled by Congress have become ever more complex, committees have become an increasingly indispensable part of the legislative process. In the view of one former member, himself a former subcommittee chair, "There is just no substitute for the specialization and the resulting expertise that the long-term focus of legislative committees provides." Scholars agree:

- The continuing importance of committees cannot be gainsaid. If only because they have the first real legislative crack at evolving laws and the edge of expert knowledge, most of the real crafting of bills takes place at the committee and subcommittee levels. [35]
- Committee leaders usually are better informed than their opponents about the politics and policy substance of issues within their committees' jurisdictions, which often allows them to make more persuasive arguments. Their informational advantage also may help them know where to expect support and opposition.[36]

It is no wonder, then, that lobbyists place a heavy emphasis on working with members of the committees that are most likely to consider legislation or policy that is relevant to their clients' interests. The quotes provided above magnify the importance of this "early information" advantage: "[Committees] have the *first real legislative crack at evolving laws*" (emphasis added). A congressional veteran from the Southwest used an apt metaphor to describe committee work: "It is like creating a piece of sculpture; the time to change it is before the clay hardens. Once that happens it is too late. Same for legislation; once it is hardened, it is much tougher to change it. That's why the good lobbyist gets there early."

---

m. "Uncle" Joe Cannon, R-Ill., was the dictatorial Speaker of the House from 1903 until 1911. He was finally contained by a series of reforms passed by the House in 1910.

For this reason, chairs remain focal points in the policymaking process for both members and lobbyists. Some chairs admittedly are stronger and stronger willed than others—for instance, not many people in Congress will try to tell Rep. John Dingle, D-Mich., or Rep. Henry Waxman, D-Calif., how to run their committees. But all chairs—even if not a Dingle or a Waxman—occupy a favored position in the incipient stages of the legislative process. Several former members of Congress commented on the powers available to shrewd and willful committee chairs:

- Members will go to a committee or subcommittee [chair] to ask if she will put a bill on the schedule. This is not done lightly.
- Yes, a member might try to help out a lobbyist by seeing if a chair could delay a bill. But this was pretty rare; I didn't see much of it.
- It all depended on his standing with his committee chair.
- You worried about using up your requests with the chairman.
- Committee members tend to follow their chair and ranking minority member.

The interview subjects saw some chairs as being willing negotiators, though without relinquishing their right to have the final say:

- The chair does negotiate provisions early on. [He] will then have to defend those provisions whether he likes them or not—they are part of his deal.
- [It all] depends on how the chair is working. Sometimes the chair will not seek input from other members; sometimes he will solicit opinions, suggestions, or [members'] positions.
- Often this [sort of thing] is done in the form of a meeting with the chairman and having him approve or disapprove what it is that you want to put into the bill.

All the interviewees who commented on the subject agreed that putting together the initial version of a bill, known as the "chairman's mark," is the province of the committee chair. This is especially true for major pieces of legislation. Two terse observations by former members made the point: "The chair does this [the initial version]; members get amendments." "Bill drafting? This is generally done by [the] chair."

But this is not to say that chairs work entirely without the knowledge and participation of committee members—particularly those of their own party. The task of forming the draft of a bill, the "vehicle," is often a collegial process:

- We would put together what we wanted; then the committee would sit with the chair and go through everyone's interests. Often we could not agree on a bill. Democracy is about the extremes at both ends and then melding something in the middle.

- Often this is done in the form of having a meeting with the chair and having him approve or disapprove what it is that you want to put into the bill.
- The chair would poll the members to see what they would want in the bill.
- Participating in early drafting sessions is very important.

This exchange with a Democrat from New England adds further insight into the options available to committee and subcommittee chairs:

> *Committee chair:* [The process of drafting a bill] depends on how the chair is working. Sometimes the chair will not seek input from other members; sometimes he will solicit opinions, suggestions, positions.
>
> *Author:* Why would he be open one time and not another?
>
> *Committee chair:* Well, I think it probably had to do with how much he wanted to get something done.
>
> *Author:* You mean get out a bill?
>
> *Committee chair:* No. I mean how much he wanted some specific provision. If he didn't care so much, he'd open it up.

Although prenegotiating a legislative provision is a strategy that works to the chair's advantage (he is able to ensure production of a legislative vehicle that will have baseline support when hearings and markups begin), it can also tie his hands early in the legislative process: "The chair does negotiate provisions early on. But then he has to defend those provisions whether he likes them or not. They are *his* deal." For this reason, some chairs in some circumstances will seek to keep their policy options open: According to one staffer: "He would only go so far. He let me know that he'd probably agree to put [an item] in during markup, but he didn't want to be committed so soon."

In addition to the chair's work style, the extent to which other lawmakers want to be involved in early drafting sessions is affected by interest group pressure. An East Coast lawmaker spoke about her efforts to see both public and private interests she deemed important reflected in the chair's mark: "This was mostly done on the big issues: I told the [state] agencies to review provisions and draft changes. Also, the [state] Chamber of Commerce was involved. Then I would sit down with the chairman and see what could be done. This was sometimes done for private interests too, but not as often."

Two former members did not recall that they were frequently involved in early drafting. One said, "This was not that common," and the other saw the process as predominantly a staff function: "I didn't do much of it myself; staff did a lot of that. We'd usually be involved only if there was a strong district interest. Then they'd check in. I'd generally have them run it by whoever it was that was interested. I was the leader of the team, but they did the actual meeting and drafting."

A former counsel recalled that members "almost never" personally participated in the very early stages of bill preparation: "That was my job." Drafting bills was "strictly a staff function." He noted that bills are generated from "many different sources—the administration, interest groups, staff, and members." Whatever the source, he would typically work with legislative counsel to draft or "clean up" a bill from an outside (noncommittee) source. This excerpt from our conversation makes several important points:

> *Author:* Did lobbyists provide helpful language?
>
> *Counsel:* Often, but not always. If I remember, the trade associations and large law firms were very good. If you agreed with their position, you could often take their language almost word for word. Others weren't that good.
>
> *Author:* Why do you think that was? The difference, I mean.
>
> *Counsel:* I think the associations and law firms hire a lot of ex-legislative people. Most of them had drafted plenty of legislation before. They knew how to do it.
>
> *Author:* Did that affect your overall impression of them?
>
> *Counsel:* Absolutely!

Although most former members did not recall being personally involved in the bill-drafting process, many discussed activities that suggested early awareness of and occasional input into the content of bills. For instance, some members reported participating in informal conversations with chairs and other colleagues about what should or should not be included in the initial chairman's mark.

Others had some say in formulating legislative strategies: "We would put together coalitions by designing bills including provisions that other people could be for." By this, the speaker was alluding to the process of "loading the bill" with provisions that were calculated to appeal to enough members to permit the measure to move forward.

Although "loading" may connote the addition of several provisions, not unlike the much-maligned "Christmas tree" bills that are frequently rushed through Congress at the end of a session, this was not always the case. Sometimes just a few key members needed to be accommodated by the addition (or deletion) of a provision or two. Here again, lobbyists' input into early, informal lawmaking processes is evident: "The lower the visibility, the more you can pursue your own beliefs and personal interests, or the convictions and priorities of *other* people." The implication is that lobbyists who are wired into the system and who know what is going to happen before it happens—for example, when a bill will be introduced—are best positioned to accomplish their clients' ends. Getting a provision included in the chair's mark is one of the most effective legislative advantages that a lobbyist can gain for his client.[n]

The clear message is that, in addition to the practical utility of early intervention into the lawmaking process, professional performance is itself of significant value to lobbyists; professionalism adds credibility to their cause. Further, thoughtful involvement at the embryonic stages of legislation often makes the lobbyist a virtual insider—part of the team for a particular bill or amendment.

## Staff–Member Relationships

*"I think there is a pretty good rule of thumb: Good members hire good staff."*

Clearly, there are differences between the House and the Senate in the ways that staff and members interrelate. Ross Baker makes the point that senators must rely on their staffs more than do House members: "The populous House and the tiny Senate must cover the same vast areas of public policy. . . . This results in vast disparities in the breadth and sweep of what senators and members can authoritatively speak out on." [37] The senator, given a more extensive policy domain for which he is responsible, is "stretched thin and must delegate more to his [legislative] aides than is typically the case in the House." [38]

The suggestion, reports Baker, is that "senators are more apt [than House members] to become captive of their staff." [39] For the lobbyist this means that in many instances Senate staff is de facto the senator.

Most members of both houses spoke appreciatively, if not fondly, about the service and loyalty they received from their staffers. But this was not always the case. A surprising number of members revealed that they

n. An important rule of thumb is that a bill taken up by the committee—usually the vehicle or the chair's mark—benefits from a sort of inertia. Once a provision is included in the vehicle, the burden of proof is on its opponents. They must convince their colleagues that the provision should be deleted or amended—usually a more difficult task than merely defending what is already in the bill. Thus early participation in the bill-drafting process often provides a leg up for legislators and lobbyists.

had only limited trust in their staff people. A Republican from a northern state noted that he "liked to have lobbyists meet with staff first. But staff had to be watched; they could have their own career agendas in mind in working with a lobbyist." Even more damning was this statement by a southwesterner: "I found that some staff would commit to a future employer for an earmark; the job was promised, and the earmark was the quid pro quo."

Another southwestern Democrat was "constantly evaluating" the quality of his staff's performance: "I played devil's advocate with lobbyists to see how well they could defend their positions. That was a check on them. But then I would ask staff to speak with adversaries of these lobbyists to check for their information. This was a legitimate assignment—I wanted that information—but I also used it as a means of evaluating my staff."

Evaluations of staff were not limited to legislators; staff colleagues and lobbyists had their own opinions about who was faithful to their member's policy preferences, who was able, who was not so good, and, most important, who had authority to speak for the boss:

- I would never work with her staff. It wasn't that I did not think they were any good, but she never seemed to trust them—so much of my work with them just went nowhere. (Former senior House legislative assistant)
- The staff person may be stating her position, not the member's. That's more common than you think, especially because members don't always have positions . . . when you are speaking [to staff]. (Former chief of staff for an East Coast member)
- I think there is a pretty good rule of thumb: good members hire good staff. (Lobbyist and former member)
- He was a bastard to work for. His staff turned over it seemed like twice each Congress. He could never hire anyone that was any good; so we just stayed clear of that office. No sense wasting our time. (Former legislative assistant)

All of these functions and the various distinctions in work habits and conditions are important for lobbyists to know. Interview subjects freely admitted that they (or their chief of staff or legislative director) would relegate some lobbyists to junior staff. A former legislative director explained that this was often done for people who were lobbying on matters that were not assigned to a committee on which his member served or matters in which she had "little to no interest." She continued, "Of course, there were always exceptions for a constituent; then we would usually have someone with a little more experience handle the meeting."

Experienced lobbyists with long-standing relationships will seldom spend much time with congressional offices that are not interested or involved in the progress of a bill. As sympathetic as the member might be, there is usually precious little that she will be able or willing to do to be helpful. An experienced lobbyist is able to identify the key players for any given issue and then to focus his efforts on them. The ability to make this kind of judgment is, according to a former committee counsel, "one of the more basic decisions a lobbyist has to make. It is a quick indicator if he knows what he is doing or not."

## The Client

There is no official set of criteria for determining what is and what is not quality lobbying. It follows then that there can be no authoritative ranking system for the profession—no top-to-bottom list ranging from the best to the worst. Unlike a baseball fan checking batting averages, a prospective client cannot turn to a page in the morning newspaper to see who is leading the league and who is in last place. Even wins and losses are virtually impossible to tabulate because what qualifies as a win or a loss for a lobbyist is almost always a relative concept: What was the objective? What was possible? Was the sought-for result deferred? Is the goal still alive, and will it be possible to achieve it sometime down the road?

Rogan Kersh explains the ambiguity of the lobbyist's world. He notes that lobbyists frequently have the "ability to influence expectations and, perhaps more important, to account for ostensibly negative results in positive terms." Lobbyists are able to get away with doing this because, according to Kersh, "Most clients know little of Washington activity and decisions, even those directly affecting their interests, in part because of the ambiguous and complex nature of the policy process." [40]

There is another reason why lobbyists are not held accountable: client naïveté. It is often not clear whose interest the lobbyist sees as a priority on any given matter: the client's, his own, or that of some member of Congress whom he is eager to please. These competing interests are not always easily distinguishable. For example, congressional offices generally see quality lobbyists as those who function as adjuncts to the policy processes. Like lawyers who represent clients but are also considered to be officers of the court and responsible for maintaining the integrity of the judiciary, lobbyists—the good ones—are charged with doing their share to maintain the reputation of the congressional policymaking process. Lawmakers expect them to act thoughtfully and honorably, keeping both good policy and client interests in mind as they work toward a policy resolution.

But such meritorious behavior is not always high on the client's list of objectives for the lobbyists he hires or retains. If the company wants amendment X—end of story. That desired outcome is not difficult to understand, but here is where things get complicated. Not all goals worth pursuing in the client's interest are obtainable through one, perhaps immediate, objective. Most clients, certainly the bigger ones, have a diverse set of legislative-related needs and are likely to add to these as time goes by. Seldom is one matter a drop-dead issue, though at any given time the client might see it that way. The veteran lobbyist knows that his best service to the client, whether he is a direct employee on the client's payroll or a lobbyist on retainer, may be to forgo the immediate objective and so live to fight another day.

This set of circumstances is not easy for most clients to understand; in fact, some lobbyists working under the Kersh assumption of client ignorance do not even try to explain their thinking. Even those lobbyists who are direct and intensely loyal employees will often employ a triaging process during which short-term goals are traded off in hopes of achieving more and greater ends sometime in the future. A former Senate committee staffer who is now a lobbyist said almost woefully, "Often my toughest job is to educate and manage the client. Sometimes they are unrealistic in their demands."

Add to all of this that clients come in different shapes and sizes—big, small, progressive, hold-the-line, sophisticated, naïve, with or without an in-house lobbyist, and with or without a CEO who once saw a lobbying segment on *Sixty Minutes*. Larger organizations, the ones most likely to hire or retain a lobbyist, are often horizontally organized in the sense that they have different and largely autonomous divisions or subsidiaries. Each one may have little to no knowledge of what the other one is asking of Congress. What is more, if they did know, they probably would not care very much. The vice president of one division sees her opportunities for career advancement and increased compensation as a function of her division's performance, just as the president of a subsidiary sees his opportunities as being pegged to his own company's profit-and-loss statement. If both executives have need of a lobbyist, and one has reasonable objectives and the other does not, what is the lobbyist to do?

This is not a far-fetched scenario; lobbyists report that it happens "all the time." Many other variables could be mentioned here, but the point is this: It is often wrong to assume that a client is a single entity with a unified set of legislative priorities. One lobbyist bemoaned, "Would that it were so."

Faced with all of these demands, sophisticated lobbyists do the only thing that makes sense for them; they become double agents, as much (or almost as much) creatures of Congress as they are of their clients. They attempt to deal with unrealistic policy demands in a way that is acceptable to their allies in Congress and that, at the same time, is either palatable or understandable for the source of the demand—the client. A liberal northeasterner made this case in discussing the benefits of the much-maligned revolving door of Congress: "Most ex-members are more loyal to the system than they are to their clients. You're not a member unless you have a big ego. So the last thing a former member wants to be known for is sucking up nickels from the Capitol steps."

In other words, a former member who is now lobbying does not want to be seen as having little or no regard for either policy outcomes or the culture of Congress. A former congressional counsel put it this way: "Once having worked in Congress you are not expected to check your interest in making good policy at the company door."

Whether in the context of lobbyists who have moved through the revolving door or of people who have never served in any policymaking capacity in government, the argument is the same: Members and staff appreciate lobbyists who understand and respond to the culture and expectations of those still serving on Capitol Hill. Regardless of client demands, lobbyists are expected to accommodate their requests and their practices to the exigencies of congressional service. Those who do this well will likely succeed in producing benefit for themselves and their clients—maybe not in the case immediately at hand but at some future point. Those who fail will probably not live to fight many more days.

The interest of the lobbyist and the interest of the client are usually the same. The problem for the lobbyist is that the client may not understand this. As we have noted, corporate managers may be more focused on short-term career objectives than on long-term company goals. A member of the Blue Dog Coalition[o] stated the proposition in the form of a question: "If a lobbyist can't get his client to understand what is best for him, how the hell can he expect to convince us of anything?" Perhaps a bit simplistic, but not altogether wrong either.

## Legislators' Incentives

For many members of Congress just getting there is enough; some members are happy to serve in Congress as a rank-and-file representative or senator for as long as their constituents will send them back to Washington. Others are more ambitious; they aspire to achieve a reputation for policy excellence, to chair an important committee, to be in leadership, or even to attain higher elective office.

There is seldom much of a secret about what a political person hopes is in store for the future. Either through observation or through shared confidences, lobbyists are often among the first to know a member's ambitions.

---

o. The Blue Dogs are fiscally conservative Democrats.

This is important intelligence; it helps lobbyists think through their strategies at two levels: Should they approach this member on this issue at all? Can they make a case that their position will help the lawmaker achieve her career objectives?

Of course, the one common denominator for all members is reelection—at least until they are ready to retire from political life or to move on to the next adventure.

## Seeking Reelection

*"Members usually appreciate an opportunity to visit a plant or manufacturing site—lots of people, lots of hands to shake."*

David Mayhew has famously characterized the lawmaker–constituent relationship as the "electoral connection." His observation that members of Congress should be viewed as "single-minded seekers of reelection" is among the most often quoted in political science.[41] Few scholars, journalists, pundits, or other observers have ever disputed this assumption.[p] Political people do not spend years "spinning out political careers" only to risk an early and involuntary retirement by ignoring views strongly held among their constituents. It follows then that the lobbyist who urges a lawmaker to fly in the face of her constituency is running the risk of making himself wildly unpopular with that member and among her staff. Such behavior is deemed acceptable, even admirable, once in a while; but a consistent diet of politically unpalatable requests will cast the lobbyist as ill-prepared or politically naïve. That description does not fit the sort of person to whom a busy, politically pressed lawmaker can afford to give much time.

A Republican from a largely rural district considered knowledge of a member's district to be a "basic" for the well-prepared lobbyist. "I was surprised even to the point of being offended by lobbyists who did not do their homework before meeting with me. What was my district like? Could I do what he was asking and still be back here next year?"

In accord with the view that reelection is the prime focus of most members of Congress, Mayhew found that a number of activities are common to the vast majority of incumbents: credit claiming, advertising, and position taking. The interviews that I conducted for this book provide much evidence in support of Mayhew's observations. The interview subjects, those who served or now serve in Congress, agreed that there is a nexus between effective lobbying practice and activities that members find personally

p. In context, Mayhew was making this assumption to provide a framework in which to evaluate and understand congressional behavior.

beneficial. The lobbyist who successfully marries his client's objectives with what is helpful to the legislator provides a double service, one for the member and one for the client. In so doing, he may provide an even bigger service to himself.

It is not surprising, then, that members of Congress tend to welcome and be supportive of home state and district lobbyists—in other words, lobbyists who represent constituent organizations, interests, and people. These lobbyists and their clients offer a prime forum for accomplishing all three of the Mayhew objectives. A lobbyist-initiated partnership between the client and the lawmaker, one that results in a positive policy outcome, will facilitate an opportunity for credit taking and advertising within the district or state. The lawmaker's own communications resources will likely be supplemented by a constituent organization (for example, a local religious or civic organization) that believes the legislator has served its members well. Several respondents confirmed their preference for in-state or in-district lobbyists:

- I had three screens: The lobbyist had to be good, the issue had to be important, and it helped a lot if they were from my district.
- I always preferred lobbyists from district firms and from organized labor.
- I would certainly see all the interests from my district.
- There might be some local opponents on issues I supported and they would lobby me on [those] issues. I always saw them and was very courteous.

The ability to claim credit and to advertise is not necessarily limited to providing services to constituent organizations. Some lobbyists would go out of their way to bring a positive story back to a member's district. A southwestern member made special note of his appreciation for "lobbyists who go back to the state and tell people what a good job I was doing in D.C." He used as an example a lobbyist who "contacted the local Chamber [of Commerce] and turned them around on endorsing my opponent very early in my career. It was my first reelection campaign."

A former House committee counsel remembered that his boss, a powerful committee chair, felt "deeply indebted" to a health care company for arranging a high-profile district event: "They set up an event with the company and the chairman. It was billed as a town hall meeting sponsored by [the chair]. The boss got to look good; at the same time the importance of vaccinations was brought home to the public. It helped to build support for programs that require kids to get vaccinated. That had to be good for the company."

Even if a lobbyist does not have an issue that he is currently pursuing with a member, attention to the member's need for strong constituency relationships is always welcome. A former Senate counsel made this observation: "Members usually appreciate an opportunity to visit a plant or manufacturing site—lots of people, lots of hands to shake." The southwestern legislator quoted above agreed: "I loved it when they would set something up for me at one of their facilities. It was a great chance to meet people and to learn more about the company. . . . It puts a face on the business."

A current lobbyist, who was chief of staff to several members of Congress over more than two decades in the House, pulled together the benefits of site visits for lobbyists and members alike: "The plant visit serves three purposes: It educates the member about the constituent's business, it makes him very much aware that these voters are out there, and it gives him an opportunity to do a little noncampaign campaigning." And then, as an aside: "We liked that part the best."

## Responding to Political Imperatives

*"Being a team player was something that was held in high regard."*

Less obvious than reelection-related goals are the political imperatives that result from party pressures and personal relationships among members. Here, legislative politics and career objectives come together—and sometimes clash.

In the House most members have a strong preference for being assigned to one or two specific committees. Usually the jurisdiction of these committees dovetails with their district or personal issue interests. Many authorities view service on the "right" committee as pivotal to realizing members' career ambitions.

Two observations, one by Charles Clapp and the other by Richard Fenno, when read together explain why members are so intent upon getting assigned to the committee of their choice. First Clapp: "The committee system is still the crux of the legislative process. . . . Assignment to a committee, therefore, becomes the first order of business for new congressmen." [42] Now Fenno: "Each member of each committee wants his committee service to bring him some benefit in terms of goals he holds as an individual congressman. And he will act on his committee in ways to achieve these goals." [43] Thus committees are a major, if not the primary, vehicle available for members as they participate in drafting legislation.

Because seniority is often a factor in the committee assignment process, junior members frequently do not get selected for the committee of their choice. These members will often seek to change their lead committee once they have gained sufficient seniority. Of course, to do this they will need the support of their party leadership and perhaps the relevant committee chair(s). Gaining support is not always a sure thing—especially not for the occasional maverick. A former member of Ways and Means remembered a tense moment in his quest to be placed on that committee: "Leadership can sometimes demand conformity even if members think they will pay a price in their home districts. On a major bill I didn't go with leadership. One of the whips called up to let me know how 'disappointed' he was. He said that he hoped 'this will not hurt your career.' I got the message; fortunately nothing ever came of it."

A Blue Dog Democrat spoke more generally: "When a member comes to town, he learns that there are different constituencies that have to be accommodated. The home constituency is part of it, but so too are the large national lobbyists and the party members and leaders."

Many senior members harbor hopes of becoming a committee or subcommittee chair (a position that is no longer solely a function of seniority) or to be rewarded with some other position in their party's congressional leadership. Virtually all members at one time or another have lobbied for a rule in the House or for favored treatment on the Senate floor. Party leaders have the power to aid a rank-and-file member in these quests or to turn her down flat. Team play is always a consideration in decisions to reward or punish. Members who defy their leadership do so at their own risk.

This is not to say that members cannot be asked to make the "tough vote" or take other public action that will put them at odds with their district or with the party leadership. It is not always possible for even the most astute lobbyist to create a win-win situation for the members he approaches. But such requests by lobbyists must be rare. Lobbyists should make these requests only after much deliberation and with great sensitivity to the pressures that bear upon the member they are importuning. The Ways and Means member again: "There is a right way and wrong way to do about anything. Being a 'team player' was something that was held in high regard. But I did not worry much about that; I had no interest in trying to be leadership. So if a lobbyist came to me with something that made good sense and he could convince me of that, then I could justify the risk. Well, usually!"

A former staffer, now a lobbyist, added this thought: "You don't have to go in with your tail between your legs, but letting them [the congressional office] know that you understand that what you are asking is very difficult at least signals that you know something about life in Congress. That can make a big difference in how seriously they will take you—even if they turn you down, which they probably will."

The point here is that recognizing the realities of congressional life provides the lobbyist some protection against being perceived as a fool or the proverbial pain in the butt. He knows that he is asking the office to do something that may be unusual and/or unpleasant, and he regrets being the source of this discomfort. In so doing he signals that he is in fact a savvy legislative player—one who should be respected for his efforts on behalf of his client and for his insights into what congressional offices can and cannot do. The congressional office thus has good reason to expect that on other days on other issues he will prove more an asset and less a burden.

## Advancing Within Congress

*"Members do seek to establish a reputation for excellence."*

A Mid-Atlantic Republican made special note of what he considered to be the keys to achieving success in Congress. He called these keys "the Holy Trinity": good information,[q] good policy, and good reputation. The links between these should be obvious. "Knowledge is the foundation for making policy. Members who are both expert and known for their role in writing good law are rewarded with a positive reputation among their colleagues and within the Washington community. "A strong reputation," according to this Republican, "can get people like CEOs to take note of you, to become allies and to raise money. . . . Members do seek to establish a reputation for excellence."

A former Republican leader agreed that good information provided the foundation for "smart" policy. He then discussed the importance of lobbyists asking for "the right things." "The [lobbyist's] position must be good for the country and *good for the legislator;* it must redound to his credit and help to enhance his reputation in Congress." The member then focused on the lobbyist's role: "Everyone you talk to is going to tell you the same thing: lobbyists are measured by their reliability. This means honesty and having the information to support [their] positions. The best idea in the world will mean nothing . . . if he can't support it with facts."

The need for information transcends a member's desire to make good policy. It also helps her to avoid embarrassment at the hands of potential adversaries. Good information and risk avoidance go hand in hand—the former is the means to the latter. There is a saying in football that the best defense is a good offense. You do not have to be a fan to know that this means if your team has possession of the ball it is darned hard for the other team to score.[r]

q. Much more will be said about good information in chapter 5.

r. Yes, I know it is possible, but it is rare and usually hard to do if the other team is at all competent.

Well, that may be true on the gridiron, but for lobbyists interested in winning for their clients and, more important, establishing enduring relationships with members of Congress, football wisdom has it backward. In the lobbying profession, the best offense is a good defense. In this sense, much member activity is driven by what lawmakers see as the defensive prerequisites inherent in their work—certainly, in the work of those who care to be reelected or to advance within Congress. As Douglas Arnold notes, "Legislators need to be concerned with both the positions they take and the effects they produce, and . . . they need to consider both the known policy preferences of attentive publics and the potential policy preferences of inattentive publics."[44]

The reasoning behind Arnold's statement is that members must assume that future political opponents will scour their policy records and make public any positions that appear to be out of sync with the majority of their constituents. In other words, if you are careless with the ball, the other team could wind up scoring—even if they never actually get possession.

Thus what a member wants to know—must know—before she gets on board with a lobbyist's position is not so much "Can I win?"—though that is important—as "Can I explain my position in a way that will make good sense to my constituents, the media, colleagues, and others in the Washington community?" The lawmaker's position does not necessarily need to carry the day; it must be defensible. An East Coast conservative stressed the importance of helping a member protect herself against surprise legislative counterattacks: "A member does not want to get ambushed." Then, after a brief discussion about the relationship between honesty and accuracy, he added, "This is why being right is more important than just being honest."

A sense of rightness on policy matters is important to lawmakers; it is a fundamental in their quest for approval by their district or state and for the esteem of their colleagues. (More will be said about these matters in chapter 4.) But there is another form of rightness that is of near, if not equal, value in establishing a member's reputation for excellence in legislating, and that is strategic thinking. For purposes of this discussion the word *strategic* comprises both procedural and political acumen.

Being able to get elected to Congress is by no means an indication that a member is endowed with the requisite skills for successfully negotiating the arcane world of legislative politics—an entirely different venue from that of electoral politics. The strategic options for advancing virtually any bill or amendment are numerous. Among the most common strategic options that legislative entrepreneurs must consider are determining the right timing and cosponsors (which members to get "on the bill" and which ones not to ask), directing a bill to one committee or another, and seeking a particular rule (in the House) or opting to use a nongermane amendment (in the Senate). We will discuss these and other options in subsequent chapters.

A former member from the Northwest who had served as a subcommittee chair provided this insight: "There are three primary types of legislative contributors: the issues people, the dealmakers, and the strategists. We needed some of each—certainly on the bigger issues we did." When asked if the latter two—dealmakers and strategists—were one and the same, he disagreed adamantly: "No. Not at all. Compromisers (dealmakers) know how to get all involved parties to agree to one bill [or amendment]; they have a knack for sensing who needs what and who can give what." He went on to explain that the dealmakers are "almost always trusted figures" who are perceived as the prototypical honest brokers. Then, as if remembering the story of "Goldilocks and the Three Bears," he added, "They were not too Democrat or too Republican—they were just right."

"Strategists" he argued, "work at both the procedural and political levels. They are masters of the rules of their chamber—House or Senate—and know how to manipulate these [rules] in order to achieve their legislative goals—pass, defeat, delay, amend, other. They can be, and often are, 'into timing, coalition building, and even press relations.' Working at the juncture of politics and substance, they understood how to package and frame a bill."

As will be noted throughout this text, former members of Congress and former congressional staffers were singled out in the interviews for their sensitivity to and understanding of congressional processes and politics. An eastern conservative lawmaker made a compelling case for giving attention to what they say: "Many of these people had been through more than their share of legislative contests. They knew procedures, people, and the mechanics of putting together a winning strategy. They also had a good sense of what could fly [in Congress] and when." Then, with particular emphasis he added, "It's a big mistake to think that just because they no longer work up there [Capitol Hill] they have forgotten all they ever learned or knew."

This same former member then moved the focus from lawmakers to lobbyists, emphasizing the role that knowledgeable lobbyists play in the strategy "business": "What I learned early was that members of Congress had no monopoly on smart strategic thinking." He then made an interesting observation about the content of lobbyist–lawmaker meetings. He held that the common wisdom is that lobbyists spend most of their time trying to convince members of Congress to adopt their (the lobbyist's) policy preferences: "They do do a fair amount of that; that's true. But I found that the best of them could do a lot more. Once you were on board—and many times you were [supportive of] them before they ever walked into your office—they could be invaluable in helping you to think through how you wanted to go from [that point]." In other words, lobbyists were valuable allies in helping members to think through their strategic options.

If being right on an issue is considered to be highly advantageous for purposes of defending one's position with district or state constituencies, then being an astute strategist is equally advantageous in raising a member to the level of "consummate inside player" among her colleagues. This is as true for lobbyists as it is for members of Congress. According to a lawmaker of several decades, both in Congress and in his state legislature, "It doesn't take a legislative pro to understand a policy issue inside and out." Then, mixing metaphors: "But it takes an experienced legislative technician to know how to navigate these minefields."

A Senate staffer—over hot dogs, hoagies, and soda pop in the Senate cafeteria—picked up on the strategic-substance-political nexus. "Part of being a good strategist is to get yourself something that you can sell. I call this *first things first*. . . . If you've done that much, then you can think about how and when you want to start moving forward—but you have got to have the *product* first."

A recent congressional retiree punched his finger at his desk as he agreed with the staffer's remarks and then expanded on them to discuss the importance of compromise as a strategic tool: "He's absolutely right! And let me tell you—you're interested in lobbying, aren't you?—well too many lobbyists over-stand [*sic*] their ground. They don't know when to let it go. They don't get how important it is from day one to have something that enough members will want to be for."

This observation presaged an interview that would take place some months later. In that interview (covered more fully in chapter 5) a former member of the Democratic leadership opined that lobbyists must ask members for only that which is doable. He termed this "the art of the possible."[s] In his mind it is in understanding and working toward doability that the lobbyist has an opportunity to forge binding relationships with savvy members of Congress. If there is a prerequisite to smart strategic thinking, it is spotting potential winners when one sees them and, just as important, avoiding obvious losers: "No one appreciates being asked to run a fool's errand. Actually, it goes further; no member will forget being asked to run a fool's errand."

s. This observation will appear in many places in the text that follows. Whether expressed in these or other words, the message is a recurring theme during my interviews with members and staff.

## Amassing Legislative and Political Assets

*"One thing members try to do is to amass assets—not just money, but a lot of different sorts of things."*

A member who believes in what she is setting out to do, and is confident that she is acting on the basis of good information, whether from a lobbyist or some other source, is free to go on the attack, to push her agenda as far and as hard as she is able to do. If her work is creditable, she will extend her reputation as an effective legislator. She will display her expertise in her chosen subject and gain recognition as a policy specialist. She is capitalizing on the offensive, as opposed to defensive, value of quality information. For the "adult supervision" in Congress, it is what service in Congress is all about. It is why members serve.

During the course of the interviews, specialization and professionalism were mentioned repeatedly—sometimes in the context of lobbyist-provided information, other times in the context of member behavior. A northeastern Democrat gave what amounted to a definition of both professional legislative behavior and professional lobbying behavior; he combined these with concern for two of Matthews's norms: institutional loyalty and legislative specialization:

> When I first got to Congress I was put on the [name of committee], and we had an important bill coming up. I couldn't have cared less, other than maybe seeing a chance to get some money for the district. But I was expected to carry my share of the load. A lot of people were coming to see me, and colleagues were asking me questions. So I dove in and learned a fair amount about [the issues]. It wasn't my idea of why I was in Congress but I saw it as both a responsibility and a way to make a name for knowing what is going on. My staff did a lot of it, but I never could have gotten it done without the [association] lobbyist. He was terrific—right down the middle.

At a later point in the interview this member offered that the lobbyist "was a friend and mentor until he [the lobbyist] retired. He got me off on the right foot. . . . I never forgot it . . . and he never disappointed me."

"Getting me off on the right foot," as used during our discussions, equated closely to "giving me the information I needed to respond authoritatively to my colleagues." (This is my language, not that of the representative.) Given the future accomplishments and reputation enjoyed by this member, it is likely that he would have obtained this information and understood its career value to him with or without the lobbyist's tutelage. This incident permitted the member to establish himself as a go-to person early on. As previously noted, John Kingdon concludes that members of Congress are heavily influenced by colleagues when deciding their votes—especially on those matters for which they do not claim personal expertise: "By any measure, fellow congressmen turn out to be highly important influences on votes." [45]

A northern moderate confirmed the nexus between enjoying a reputation for expertise and exercising influence within Congress: "Colleagues seek out advice if they are not sure about a bill. Members know which of their colleagues are expert on given issues."

Charles Clapp attributed the same sentiment to a House Democrat: "A man can build his reputation as a specialist and eventually become enormously powerful as a generalist. The career as a specialist can carry over into other fields." [46] Clapp then expands on the importance of this relationship: "The structure of the House and the expectations and duties of members dictate reliance on the specialist; congressmen accomplish their business largely by relying on the judgments of others. . . . He should be a recognized authority on the subject to which he addresses himself." [47]

No less a legislative powerhouse than the late Speaker of the House Sam Rayburn, D-Texas, agreed: "A man makes a record in the House the way he does in business or the law or anywhere else. It's hard work that makes the difference. Other members spot the men who attend a committee session where there isn't any publicity, who attend during the long grind of hearing witnesses. . . . There are only a few men who sit there and watch every sentence that goes into the bill and know why it went in." [48]

The interviews support the view that well-informed lobbyists play an important role for members who seek to expand their policy resources and the extent of their political influence. The northeastern Democrat cited above made clear that lobbyists, while they do not have anything close to a monopoly on information flow to legislators, frequently help members enhance their reputations and thus their influence among colleagues: "One thing members try to do is to amass assets—not just money, but a lot of different sorts of things: Yes, money, but also friends, contacts, experts, reporters, relationships with other members and with interest group leaders. Doing these things is one way of helping to amass these assets without necessarily getting over-committed on a particular policy position."

## Conclusion

As the member of Congress at the beginning of this chapter said about the institution's behavior: "This ain't no damn army." Not an especially academic sounding statement, but the message is an important one for academics, journalists, lobbyists, and others who need to think about, or project how, members of Congress will respond to various legislative stimuli.

At first glance it may seem that the structures of the Senate and the House should affect all members of those bodies in the same way. After all, each legislator serves on one or more committees, each has personal staff, and each has at least some access to committee staff.[t] But we know that first glances seldom tell the full stories.

Payne, Langbein and Sigelman, and other political scientists type members by their commitment to serious legislative work. Whatever one thinks of these typologies, this cannot be denied: Some members provide the adult supervision of Congress and others are little more than Mayhew's "single-minded seekers of reelection." For lobbyists who are seeking to do their client's bidding, these two types are very different animals. Members of the adult population stand a good chance of gaining the attention of their colleagues; reelection seekers stand much less chance. Yet it would be unwise to assume that any member can long afford to be oblivious to her district. Washington's K Street is full of lawyers and lobbyists who neglected their districts when they were in Congress.

And reelection is not the only incentive that spurs members to action. Even reelection-obsessed politicos may, after a few terms of service, decide that a "promotion" is in order—perhaps to a committee chair position, a role in party leadership, or even a run for the Senate or governorship of a state. While we're at it, why not aim for 1600 Pennsylvania Avenue? There is a saying in Washington: Every time a senator looks in the mirror, she sees the next president.

Successful lobbyists who have endured for many years know how to match lawmaker to issue at the right time and in just the right way. This skill is a product of experience, innate intelligence, and knowledge of the territory. But for the best lobbyists something more is at work; these lobbyists have an uncanny knack for getting into the heads of their lobbying targets. In some cases even though the issue is right, and the member has the time to spend, something may be amiss; perhaps it's the member's relationship with the committee chair, a problem with the administration, or a feeling of disaffection with the client's trade association. The intuitive lobbyist does more than learn that such obstacles exist. He combines intuition with intelligence and a firm grasp of the institution to anticipate the member's response to these problems and then to tailor his own course of action.

Back to the theater and Willy Loman's advice to his son Biff: "The man who makes an appearance in the business world, the man who

t. This is somewhat of an overgeneralization; leadership usually works with a different staff structure.

creates personal interest, is the man who gets ahead. Be liked and you will never want." The popular image of the lobbyist is probably not far from Willy's image of himself—at least the image that he wants to convey. We do not know what product Willy sold. Arthur Miller never tells us that; nor does he tell us much about Willy's customers. But we do know some of these things about lobbyists. They sell concepts to sophisticated, well-staffed public officials who have earned the trust of hundreds of thousands, if not millions, of voters. Each of these "customers" has her own set of incentives, but nothing says these will remain constant. Times change, the institution changes, and so do congressional leaders and ordinary members.

For these people, and maybe for Willy, his advice does not go far enough. Making an appearance is fine, and being liked is usually a plus, but the true genius in selling is matching product and presentation to customer. That means understanding the customer and all that influences her—colleagues, culture, and dreams for her own future. Knowing the territory is the essential starting point for the lobbyist or the salesman, be he Willy Loman or Tommy Boggs, a highly regarded lobbyist now practicing in Washington.

With these ideas in mind, we now move on to consider how lobbyists use this knowledge to shape their relationships with individual members and staff.

## Notes

1. Richard Neustadt, *Presidential Power* (New York: New American Library, 1964), 64.
2. James L. Payne, "Show Horses and Work Horses in the United States House of Representatives," *Polity* 12 (Spring 1980): 454.
3. Ibid., 455.
4. Donald R. Matthews, *U.S. Senators and Their World* (New York: Vintage, 1960).
5. John Kingdon, *Congressmen's Voting Decisions* (Ann Arbor: University of Michigan Press, 1989), 85.
6. John R. Hibbing, *Congressional Careers: Contours of Life in the U.S. House of Representatives* (Chapel Hill: University of North Carolina Press, 1991), 119–120.
7. Laura I. Langbein and Lee Sigelman, "Show Horses, Work Horses, and Dead Horses," *American Politics Quarterly* 17 (January 1989): 92.
8. David R. Mayhew, *Congress: The Electoral Connection* (New Haven: Yale University Press, 1974), 49.
9. Ibid.
10. Christopher H. Foreman Jr., *Signals from the Hill: Congressional Oversight and the Challenge of Social Regulation* (New Haven: Yale University Press, 1988), 3.
11. Richard L. Hall, *Participation in Congress* (New Haven: Yale University Press, 1996), 174.
12. Ibid.

13. Raymond A. Bauer, Ithiel de Sola Pool, and Lewis Anthony Dexter, *American Business and Public Policy* (New York: Atherton Press, 1963), 406–407.
14. Ibid.
15. Hall, *Participation in Congress,* 128. Hall actually attributes the term "congressional enterprise" to Robert H. Salisbury and Kenneth A. Shepsle, "Congressional Staff Turnover and the Ties-that-Bind," *American Political Science Review* 75 (1981): 381–397; and "Congressman as Enterprise," *Legislative Studies Quarterly* 6 (1981): 559–576.
16. Matthews, *U.S. Senators and Their World,* 92–102.
17. Herbert B. Asher, "The Learning of Legislative Norms," *American Political Science Review* 67 (June 1973): 513.
18. Richard F. Fenno Jr., "The House Appropriations Committee as a Political System: The Problem of Integration," *American Political Science Review* 56 (June 1962): 316.
19. See Hall, *Participation in Congress,* 52–55, for an excellent discussion on this point.
20. L. Marvin Overby and Lauren C. Bell, "Rational Behavior or the Norm of Cooperation? Filibuster Behavior Among Retiring Senators," *Journal of Politics* 66 (August 2004): 921; see also 911.
21. Charles L. Clapp, *The Congressman: His Work as He Sees It* (Garden City, N.Y.: Anchor Books, 1964), 19–20.
22. Ibid., 20.
23. Ibid., 20–21.
24. Ibid., 24.
25. U.S. Constitution, Article II, section 7, paragraph 2.
26. Ross K. Baker, *House and Senate* (New York: W. W. Norton, 1989), 57.
27. Quoted in ibid., 64.
28. Ibid., 158.
29. Christopher J. Deering and Steven S. Smith, *Committees in Congress,* 3d ed. (Washington, D.C.: CQ Press, 1997), 80–81.
30. Ida A. Brudnick, *Congressional Salaries and Allowances,* Congressional Research Service, RL30063, August 30, 2007, update, http://assets.opencrs.com/rpts/RL30064_20070830.pdf.
31. Roger H. Davidson and Walter J. Oleszek, *Congress and Its Members,* 11th ed. (Washington, D.C.: CQ Press, 2007), 222–225.
32. Deering and Smith, *Committees in Congress,* 203.
33. Jeffrey M. Berry, *The Interest Group Society* (New York: Longman, 1997), 163.
34. For a thorough discussion of the development of the congressional committee system, see Smith and Deering, *Committees in Congress.* See also Congressional Quarterly's *Guide to Congress,* 6th ed. (Washington, D.C.: CQ Press, 2007).
35. Edward V. Schneir and Bertram Gross, *Congress Today* (New York: St. Martin's, 1993), 381.
36. Deering and Smith, *Committees in Congress,* 10.
37. Baker, *House and Senate,* 50, 51.
38. Ibid., 92.
39. Ibid, 93.
40. Rogan Kersh, "Corporate Lobbyists as Political Actors: A View from the Field," in *Interest Group Politics,* 6th ed., ed. Allan J. Cigler and Burdett A. Loomis (Washington, D.C.: CQ Press, 2002), 234, 236.

41. Mayhew, *Congress: The Electoral Connection,* 17.
42. Clapp, *The Congressman,* 207.
43. Richard F. Fenno Jr., *Congressmen in Committees* (Boston: Little, Brown, 1973), 1.
44. R. Douglas Arnold, *The Logic of Congressional Action* (New Haven: Yale University Press, 1990), 82.
45. Kingdon, *Congressmen's Voting Decisions,* 105.
46. Clapp, *The Congressman,* 26.
47. Ibid., 27.
48. Quoted in Sherrod Brown, *Congress from the Inside* (Kent, Ohio: Kent State University Press, 1999), 35.

# 3 Red Flags

Lobbying is the subject of much myth and even more paranoia. Why shouldn't it be? The potential risks and rewards for stakeholders are high; much of the work of lobbyists is done behind the scenes in private meetings for which there is no public record; many lobbyists and members of Congress have been chummy for several years; many of these people were at one time or another colleagues on Capitol Hill; and campaign money flows like a gushing river through our national political landscape. If we did not harbor suspicions about the lobbyist–legislator exchange, it would certainly seem that we should. But there's more than first meets the eye.

In this chapter we will examine what the interview subjects had to say about the five most troubling, most widely discussed, red-flag items that signal to many scholars, journalists, and government officials areas in which our political system has either been corrupted or is in serious danger of being corrupted:

1. The covert nature of virtually all lobbying.

2. The degree to which members of Congress and lobbyists socialize.

3. The extent to which former members and staffers swing through the revolving door of Capitol Hill.

4. The use, by deep-pocket clients, of the "marquee" names of the lobbying profession.

5. The use of private campaign contributions in congressional campaigns, often in the form of largesse from political action committees (PACs), and the extent to which these funds may be used to influence votes in Congress and decisions about who gains access to congressional policymakers.

In each area, with the possible exception of campaign money, we will see that a majority of the interview cohort, while understanding the problems associated with negative perceptions, believe that none of the flags identifies a widespread or deep flaw in our politics. Yes, those things to which the flags draw our attention must be taken seriously, but in the final analysis most are either benign or even beneficial to our policymaking processes.

Low-profile or covert activity, the subject of the first section of this chapter, is inherent in the practice of lobbying. It cannot be any other way; if one is to lobby, one must work where legislators work, which is frequently in low-visibility settings. Doris Kearns (now Doris Kearns Goodwin) provides some insight into President Lyndon Johnson's appreciation for dimly lit policymaking forums: "The public, Johnson reasoned, would only hurt itself by knowing too much. Democracy demanded good results for the people, not big debates." [1] A retired member from the Northeast agreed with this line of reasoning: "I think sunshine has done at least as much to encourage [bad] policy as it has been a plus [for] good policy." [a]

But, the quest for efficiency notwithstanding, the very thought of powerful politicians huddling in secret with large corporate interests—especially when some of those meetings are held in upscale social settings—makes many observers nervous. Do they have good reason for alarm?

The first section of this chapter is a precursor to chapter 6, "The Lobbyist's Ask." Whereas that chapter will concentrate on the *what,* including a look at the specific acts that lobbyists urge members to do in support of their client's policy objectives, this chapter will focus on the *how.* How do legislators and lobbyists work behind the scenes?

The second section, "Assets for Hire," looks at the marquee names of lobbying. These big-name professionals are among the most sought after practitioners in Washington. They are not for everyone; only clients with the deepest of pockets can afford their exorbitant rates. But are these elite lobbyists the best at what they do? Are they worth their price?

And while many of the marquee names are former members of Congress or former senior staff, Capitol Hill veterans who do not reach marquee status are still in high demand by K Street lobbying firms, trade associations, and large corporations seeking to fill out federal lobbying teams. These "formers" are thought to enjoy an inside track to their ex-colleagues, some of whom are among the most influential political actors in Congress. But does being a former really improve one's opportunities for success when one comes trudging up Capitol Hill, hat in hand? In "Assets for Hire," we learn

---

a. In the 1970s Congress adopted "sunshine" rules requiring that all policy sessions—primarily hearings and markups—be conducted in public unless a motion was made and carried to close the meeting.

what lawmakers and staff think about the marquee names and their revolving-door expatriates.

No authoritative book on lobbying would be complete without a discussion of what one interview subject called the 800-pound gorilla—campaign finance. The topic under investigation is lobbying after all, and as money and lobbying are so frequently mentioned in the same breath, at least some attention to the matter is warranted. The third section of the chapter looks at campaign finance, a subject that academics have had much to say about. Political scientists have produced countless studies to analyze the effects of campaign contributions. A sampling of these will be offered here. Lawmakers, of course, also have much to say on the subject; they are the ones after all who must raise the money and ultimately determine if and how much this work will affect their policy decisions.

## Covert Activity

The very words "covert activity" send shivers up the backs of some democratic theorists; their mere utterance taps into a reservoir of mistrust that purists (and some who are not so pure) harbor about policy deliberations that are conducted in a private forum. But the low-profile, behind-the-scenes nature of the policy process is not unique to the dealings of lobbyists and legislators. Every day people in all walks of life arrange private meetings for the purpose of persuading others on matters of both substance and strategy. And even if private meetings play on the element of surprise, this particular form of competitive advantage does not equate to a lack of ethics. Only when the objective is to procure an unfair advantage for one class of citizens, or to accomplish some goal that is patently harmful to the greater good of the commonweal, should there be any objection to secret negotiations.

Among the more inflammatory forms of low-profile activity are social meetings—meals shared and recreational activities enjoyed. The definition of "low profile" includes more than just secret encounters; the term encompasses any outings that a member would not want publicized in his state or district. Lobbying in such venues—whether consisting solely of initial relationship building or carrying over into serious negotiations—has been the subject of impassioned debate for well over a century. The scandals surrounding Jack Abramoff, noted in chapter 1, is just the latest incarnation of an old problem, once again bringing such activity into public focus.

The subject merits a full discussion on multiple grounds: (1) It is both timely and important; and (2) many of the interview subjects provided strong, sometimes conflicting, responses to questions about the issues.

Indeed, several of the more involved responses seem at first to defy reason, but after due deliberation have merit. For this reason the discussion about socializing will provide some historical context—some older and some recent—but all of it germane to achieving an understanding of what is at stake in lobbyist–member relationships and what is necessary for maintaining a civil and effective working environment among policy elites.

## Working in the Dark

*"As little as the public may not 'be there' when 'specialty issues' come up for votes . . . still less is it there in the crucial formative stages of legislation."*

Issue specialization and subject expertise are among the most broadly recognized benefits that accrue to legislators as a result of committee assignments. In addition to the advantages afforded by participation in the initial stages of the lawmaking process—getting one's provisions into the early drafts of a bill—having the right committee assignment vastly improves legislators' opportunities for having their provisions carried into law.

The information advantage enjoyed by committee and subcommittee members is compounded by the relative degree of privacy available at the early stages of legislative development. Richard Hall and Frank Wayman argue that important legislative work is frequently done in relatively confidential settings. Highlighting the importance of nonpublic legislative activities,[b] they conclude: "Only a small fraction of the decisions that shape a bill ever go to a vote, either in committee or on the floor. The majority are made in authoring a legislative vehicle, formulating amendments, negotiating behind the scenes, developing legislative strategy, and in other activities that require substantial time, information, and energy on the part of the member and staff." [2]

A committee counsel expanded on this idea: "I would not say that we intentionally avoided doing our work in public; some of it had to be done that way. But most of the real work was done on the phone and in the office. . . . I suppose it is true that public sessions were more or less ratifying sessions."

Hall uses the term "in the dark" to describe this subsurface activity.[3] For members and lobbyists alike, this environment affords an opportunity to win big—or to stumble badly. It is here that each legislator has the greatest opportunity to influence the shape and progress of legislation, because

b. By "legislative activities" or "legislative acts," I refer to those things that legislators do to move forward, retard, amend, or in any other way affect the content or progress of a policy proposal in Congress.

of the flexibility afforded by confidentiality and the consequent absence of external influences.

A former member from the Deep South, after apologizing for using "one of the oldest truisms still around," had this to say about making laws: "[It's] like making sausage; if you like them, never watch them being made." The retired lawmaker then leaned forward to emphasize his point, very much in the Lyndon Johnson style: "Well, you oughtn't to watch law being made either. It's not always so pretty, but that doesn't make it bad."

As the former congressman suggests, while the very thought of "clandestine activity" is fraught with sinister overtones, could it be the overtones, not the legislators, that are actually misleading? Throughout the course of my interviews, former members consistently discounted the extent to which informal negotiations are a catalyst for inappropriate behavior. One former member emphasized: "I never wanted to be asked to do anything I might not normally do. . . . As far as I could tell that was true of [other members] as well. . . . It didn't matter how obscure or confidential the situation was." Likewise, a former committee counsel, now a prominent lobbyist, spoke of his relationship with his former boss: "I have had a long relationship with him, and I will never abuse it. He trusts my judgment. I can't ask him to take a position that is against what he stands for—no matter who knows or does not know about it."

Political scientist Diana Evans supports the view that work done "in the dark" does not translate into work done corruptly. Evans's research allowed her to examine "interest group participation in committee decisions that do not come to a recorded vote. . . . Rather, [she looked at] deals [that] were negotiated behind-the-scenes in settings that were not visible to the general public until well after the fact, if ever." Specifically, she analyzed the disposition of two bills in the House of Representatives and found that, "Even under the decision-making conditions expected to be most favorable to interest groups, virtually complete public invisibility, interest groups did not always get their way with congressional committees." [4]

As members see it, "in the dark" describes a situation in which they are able to make difficult decisions free from what they regard as unwise positions held by their constituents. Although lawmakers may fairly be criticized for not coming clean with voters in their states and districts, their goal is seldom personal gain or campaign enrichment. Their motivation, consistent with Lyndon Johnson's thinking, more often derives from a conviction about what is or is not good public policy and what is needed to achieve the right policy. As one interviewee put it, "[Working behind closed doors] gave me elbow room. Sometimes, in this business, you need that to do the right thing."

Frank Sorauf, well known for his academic work on campaign finance, agrees that behind-the-scenes activity is critical to the development of legislative policy. He argues that the nature of influence in the legislative body involves much more than roll call votes. "[Interest groups] exert influence . . . in initiatives not taken, in committee amendments, or in special rules affecting floor consideration. . . . Political scientists . . . have long shared reservations about the exclusive reliance on roll calls." [5]

Policy elites are well aware that lawmakers spend comparatively little legislative work time doing public acts (such as voting, cosponsoring legislation, or speaking on the floor and in committee). Offering an amendment, for instance, is a public event. It is a matter of public record easily accessed by any person caring to make the effort. Drafting an amendment, on the other hand, is almost always a private event, rarely if ever done in a public forum.[c] "Back room deals" and legislative negotiations—including classic tradeoffs—are the necessary stuff of the amendment-writing process. Consider this exchange with a former ranking committee member:

> *Committee member:* We would instruct staff to come back to us with a draft. They—well, my people—would find out who else was interested and then they would sit down and work it out.
>
> *Author:* Was it bipartisan?
>
> *Committee member:* Yes. Well as often as we could work that way. . . . We were in the minority; so it was always a big help if we could get some people from the other side.

Michael Malbin, executive director of the Campaign Finance Institute, notes the relative lack of accountability attendant to these low-visibility activities and other, seemingly minor issues. His findings suggest that there may be some reason for worry. "As little as the public may not 'be there' when 'specialty issues' come up for votes . . . still less is it there in the crucial formative stages of legislation, whether in open committee sessions or in closed private meetings that produce the agendas and bills on which committees act." [6]

Dan Clawson, Alan Neustadtl, and Mark Weller raised the ante still further: "Most corporations and government relations units focus only a small fraction of their time, money, and energy on the final votes on the big issues. So-called access-oriented approaches have a different purpose. Their aim is not to influence the public vote on the final bill, but rather to make

---

c. Members will sometimes spontaneously draft an amendment during an open markup session. Often this is done to perfect or substitute for an amendment that has met with some opposition in the committee but that might be salvageable in a slightly different form.

sure that the bill's wording exempts their company from the most costly or damaging provisions." [7]

This is classic "in the dark" work. Clawson et al. well understood that the combination of a low-visibility issue (one in which few people would have an interest) and a low-profile legislative venue provides lawmakers and lobbyists with considerable legislative freedom not otherwise available to them. They continue: "In fact, most [low-visibility issues] are not 'issues' at all in that they are never examined or contested. . . . Members don't usually have to make a stand on these matters or face public scrutiny."[8]

## Building Trust Through Friendship

*"Socializing is important; friendship breeds trust."*

"Friends don't screw friends." This message, from a veteran lawmaker, conveys an undeniable truth about social interaction among lobbyists and members of Congress. The lawmaker continued: "We are overly afraid of people, especially lobbyists, getting to know members. This is not good. We suppose the worst about principles and ethics. People can be friendly but still make tough choices. It is good to have people come together. Friendship and ethics are not mutually exclusive—even in [policymaking]."

These remarks closely parallel the view of another former representative: "Friendship matters. You will do things for friends that you will not do for others, in part because you believe in your friends." Employing the same colloquialism used by the first legislator, he added, "They won't screw you."

Another ex-lawmaker provided a different reason for accepting, even encouraging, lobbyist–lawmaker friendships. He felt he "could size a person up at a social function, like having dinner or even a quiet lunch." [d] And the result of this sizing-up process was by no means always favorable: "If [the lobbyist did not make a favorable impression], I would just make sure I had something else to do if they invited me again. They'd get the message after a while."

Private meetings between lobbyists and lawmakers, even if not conducted in social settings, have long been the subject of suspicion. Margaret S. Thompson, in *The Spider Web,* discusses an 1875 bill that "was destined to become the first lobbying registration initiative ever to win

d. "Socializing" can take many forms. But, in the lobbyist–legislator context, it is most commonly done over a meal. Certainly there are other forms—hunting and fishing outings, evenings at the theater—and some of these might approach the excesses of the Abramoff–DeLay golf outing in Scotland. Without question, though, lunch or dinner is the most common and likely among the least expensive venues in which members and lobbyists socialize on a one-on-one basis.

endorsement from either chamber. . . . Among other things, [the bill] would have addressed what many . . . contemporaries believed to be the most obnoxious aspect of outside advocacy: the secrecy with which it supposedly was conducted." [9]

Distrust of "special interests" and lobbying are nothing new in our political heritage. Indeed, the very word *lobbyist* has always carried with it at least some connotation of nefarious deal making conducted in pursuit of interests "adverse to the rights of other citizens." Slightly more than a century after James Madison made this observation in Federalist 10, Lord Bryce, a British historian and diplomat, noted that while the term *lobbyist* "does not necessarily impute any improper motive or conduct . . . it is commonly used in . . . a *dyslogistic* [uncomplimentary] sense." [10]

It is understandable then that suspicion of lobbyist–lawmaker relationships would intensify, perhaps in geometric proportions, as social intercourse between petitioners and lawmakers has become the subject of television and newspaper exposés. For many people the Abramoff–DeLay scandals provided proof that journalists have had it right all along: Lobbyist–lawmaker relationships are inherently corrupting. Abramoff's golf outing to Scotland and other forms of lavish entertainment heaped upon Republican congressional leadership—leadership that claimed a moral high ground—were the last straw, the required proof that something was rotten in St. Andrews.

Early in 2008 an article in the *Washington Post* juxtaposed the historic fears with the new by highlighting Abramoff's indiscretions:

> When people think of lobbying, they generally envision shadowy operatives and their bought-and-paid-for members of Congress sneaking self-interested giveaways into law. That still happens, of course. Witness the Jack Abramoff scandal. The disgraced lobbyist pleaded guilty in 2006 to arranging all kinds of expensive outings for government officials including free parties in skyboxes and a golf trip to Scotland in a private jet, in exchange for legislative favors.[11]

Democrats played the Abramoff–DeLay card to near perfection; the scandal contributed mightily to their 2006 off-year election victory—a victory that returned them to control of both houses of Congress after a hiatus of twelve years. A former Republican member, one who had voluntarily retired just before the Democrats took over, quipped: "That was one hell of an expensive golf game." The golfing scandal, and other revelations of Abramoff's outrageous behavior, reignited a series of debates that had brought about modest reforms nearly a decade earlier. The focus of these 2007 debates was, as it had been in the 1990s, on giving better definition to the line between proper and improper social interaction among lobbyists and lawmakers.

Although the accompanying debates were usually cast in ethical terms, there was also a practical aspect to them: How much reform would prove too much reform? Said another way, was there a possibility that unintended and negative consequences could result from lawmakers' zeal to restore confidence in Congress? Would lawmakers over-regulate to the point of chilling legitimate give-and-take between lobbyists and members? Some say that is exactly what has happened.

The legislative response to the Abramoff scandals has been to proscribe most lobbyist–member opportunities for socializing. Rep. Rahm Emanuel, D-Ill., a former senior White House aide to President Bill Clinton and a prime architect of the Democrats' return to majority status in Congress, set out his party's objectives in a statement posted on his Web site early in 2007:

> Like you, I am concerned about the integrity of our government. Recent scandals have created an ethical cloud over Congress and the Executive Branch while focusing attention on the relationships between lobbyists and lawmakers. On the very first day of this new Congress, we introduced sweeping ethics standards to sever corrupt ties between government and special interests by banning lobbyists from giving gifts such as meals and private travel to lawmakers.[12]

Sen. Russell Feingold, D-Wis., known for his campaign finance reform efforts, placed particular focus on lobbyists' ability to buy meals for members of Congress and their staff. He saw this practice as creating a "subculture of lawbreaking." As much as any issue that was raised during the lobby reform debates of the 108th, 109th, and 110th Congresses, the "meals issue" highlights the questions posed above: What is proper social interaction between lobbyists and lawmakers, and how much regulation is too much regulation?

Senator Feingold came down hard on the gift-meal issue and did not appear to be concerned about the possibility of over-regulation. He offered the following statement on the floor of the Senate:

> Mr. President, first of all, I commend my friend from Connecticut and also the Senator from Pennsylvania for their amendment on meals that was offered before the recess, and also the Senator from Mississippi, the chairman of the Rules Committee, for accepting it. If we are going to have a lobbyist gift ban, it clearly has to include meals. The provision in the underlying bill that allowed for Senators and staff to continue dining at the expense of lobbyists as long as those meals are disclosed on the Senator's Web site would have been an administrative nightmare and

> also created a subculture of lawbreaking just as, unfortunately, the $50 limit has done.
>
> I am obviously not going to stand here and say that any Senator's vote can be purchased for a free meal or a ticket to a football game. But I do not think anyone can say that all lobbyists are buying these meals out of the goodness of their heart. At this point, no reform bill is going to be credible that does not contain a strict lobbyist gift ban. And no one has ever explained to me why Members of Congress need to be allowed to accept free meals, tickets, or any other gift from a lobbyist. If you really want to have dinner with a lobbyist, no one is saying that you cannot. Just take out your wallet and pay your own way.[13]

This view found favor among some editorial writers. In December 2006 the *New York Times* praised House Speaker Nancy Pelosi, D-Calif., for her stated intention to propose reforms that would ban "gifts, meals, and travel money from lobbyists" and would put "the brakes on lawmakers' borrowing corporate jets for regal-class travel." [14]

The *Milwaukee Journal Sentinel* advised: "Lawmakers ought to use a little common sense and operate under a few simple principles. Live on your salary. Pay your own way. Buy your own meals. If you want to travel, go at government expense." [15] This may appear to be good advice, and for some lawmakers it may make sense. But it is not likely to be very practical. Most senators and representatives are not members of the "Millionaires Club"; they can ill-afford many meals at Washington prices. It is not unreasonable to assume that the meals ban, now effectively in place, will virtually eliminate the lunch and dinner options as practical means for socializing between members and lobbyists.

Several former legislators questioned the need for any reforms. The essence of their position is reflected in the view of one former member: "The whole thing is really overblown." Several interview subjects agreed, some noting that they have enjoyed socializing with lobbyists:

- A [member] is not usually won over in casual conversation. This takes more directed, more intense conversation. So selling a position is not usually for social conversation alone.
- I tended to socialize with people I liked, with people with whom I had long and comfortable relationships, not so much with relative strangers.
- Socializing with lobbyists? If I had professional friends, maybe a lunch or a dinner. But these were not real social or personal friends. I did not see those people on weekends.
- I did not socialize a great deal; my family was in town. So friendship did not affect my views of lobbyists or how trustworthy they might

be. . . . My friendships were mostly professional and not very social . . . no theater, no golfing. Though I did have some lobbyist friends and we might go to lunch. But that was mostly it.

- I did not generally care to socialize with lobbyists. Mainly because I wanted to get home to the district and family and so worked long hours. There's nothing wrong with it, I just didn't do it.

Another member agreed that the matter has been taken well beyond its true significance: "The image of the lobbyist as a winer-diner, a social animal, is wrong. Most are very substantive and good. I think most—and I stress 'most'—did not care to do much socializing with us."

Overall, the interviews produced strong counterarguments to the positions held by Emanuel, Feingold, and media observers—certainly to the extent that they suggest that barring lobbyists from footing the bill for modest meals with legislators would reduce incentives for unethical favors. As noted earlier, the idea of a member of Congress pulling out his wallet and paying his own way is not realistic.

The interview subjects overwhelmingly supported moderate forms of socializing. They argue that socializing poses no threat to the integrity of the policymaking process. In fact, virtually all who commented on the matter saw these encounters as a plus for the system. Two former members, each with eight or more years of experience in the House, summed up the views expressed by the strong preponderance of former members and staff. Note that the word *trust* appears in each quotation:

- There is an overreaction on travel and meal restrictions. Socializing can be a benefit. To discourage it altogether could hurt the ability to arrive at compromises—to bring people together. Members can be effective as brokers if they and lobbyists are comfortable with and trust each other.
- Lobbyists and organizations that you've worked with and that you've learned to trust are often your most important sources of information. I wanted to go into meetings well informed. And that is what they did [for me]—sometimes it was in the office; sometimes it was over lunch.

The second speaker argued that friendships could help a legislator discover mutual interests where he thought that none could exist. He remembered that "on at least a couple of occasions" he had learned from "listening to various lobbyists and learning that there were potential compromises and joint efforts that could be made" between organizations that "were not used to seeing each other as potential allies." Because he was in a position to see the whole picture, he could put "the necessary pieces" together and bring the interested parties to the table: "The lobbyists' information was at the root of this. In the end they made each other—lobbyists and members—look good. A win-win. None of this would have happened if I had not spent some down time with [each of] these groups."

Lobbyists can also serve as sounding boards for members' legislative ideas and strategic plans. Members will share thoughts with these confidants that they will not share with comparative strangers. A Mid-Atlantic conservative pointed to the potential benefits that this sort of open exchange can produce: "Good friends, the kind of people that you feel you can really talk to—and, sure, that can include lobbyists too—help you [think] something through. . . . [They] surface ideas and problems. They can help expose the details of a proposal or a problem. . . . You know the story—a friend might tell you something that a stranger won't."

Synergies that flow from lawmaker–lobbyist friendships often work in the reverse direction—from lobbyist to lawmaker—with a legislator acting as a sounding board for the lobbyist. This was the view of a former Senate staffer turned lobbyist: "When you have a friend, someone you can spend time with, you can learn from them. This helps sharpen everyone's thinking about how ideas—yours and theirs—can be made better." For her, the byproduct of this give-and-take is the extent to which it can result in a perfected "action request." As she noted, "This helps everyone; you have a viable proposal and that is good for the member, me [the lobbyist], and the public." [e]

Socializing, with all of its potential benefits, is not a slam-dunk tactic for lobbyists. Like access generally, it presents opportunities for failure as much as it does prospects for success. It can be done tastefully or inappropriately: "Some lobbyists try to overdo the friendship stuff." This former legislator was specific about what he found most disagreeable: "I did not care much for lobbyists who were superingratiating. . . . I did not like it when people came on too strong—tried too obviously to become my friend. Friendships happen naturally and are usually the result of a long relationship." He closed with this piece of wisdom: "They [friendships] are not mass produced like some lobbyists seem to think they can be."

The not-to-worry view, however, had its detractors among the interview subjects, some of them among the most prominent members to sit in recent years. One such legislator worried that there was "too much money in the system, and I don't mean just campaign contributions. . . . We would be better off with no meals. They just are not necessary." Although this

---

e. This lobbyist made an interesting observation related to an important side benefit of permitting lobbyists and legislators to socialize. She noted that members from "opposite sides" (Democratic and Republican) would often be included in a small social gathering. This informal contact enabled them to get to know each other and, perhaps, to see each other more as fellow lawmakers than as partisan adversaries and even, if only upon rare occasion, as potential allies.

member was not troubled about friendships per se, he did show concern for the asymmetric availability of social opportunities.

Another former member—also one of the most highly regarded people to serve in Congress in recent decades—addressed the same concern: "I worry about the imbalance. Some people can do this; most cannot. I am not sure that Congress gets to hear all it needs to hear. They hear from people with lots of [resources]; they do not hear from the rest." Although his words were neutral and seemingly understated, the expression on his face as he spoke was intense.

Other former members shared these concerns:

- There is just too much money involved.
- I worry about too much socializing.
- Lobbyists do not want just access; they want influence.

Naturally, there was a counter to the counters. When told of these remarks, a corporate lobbyist who had served briefly as a chief of staff in the Senate argued: "Even Ralph Nader can afford the price of a lunch. You don't have to play golf in Scotland for people to get to know each other. That's a bunch of crap!"

Hyperbole and temper aside, the mainstream view was that "excessive" socializing can be "dangerous," but moderate socializing and genuine friendships often result in "candid and constructive information flow and idea swapping." Although there might be some risk of undue influence, the risk was viewed as minimal.

A West Coast liberal summed up the optimists' view: "Socializing is important; friendship breeds trust." Again, the emphasis here was on the professional candor that flows in both directions when members and lobbyists come to know each other and are relaxed in each other's company. The thrust of this message, repeated over and again, is that for members and for lobbyists mutual friendships and the ability to trust one another are often synergic and positive relationships. Socializing together should not be discouraged without considerable thought.

## Assets for Hire

Many organizations, companies and associations among them, decide to "go to the outside" for lobbying support on key issues. The practice is common, even if these organizations already have a full complement of in-house lobbyists on their payroll. Why do they do this? Why do they opt to increase their already significant costs for government relations (the corporate euphemism for "lobbying") by retaining an independent, usually very expensive, lobbying organization?

In a sense this is a trick question but one with a sensible answer. There is probably no such thing as a "full complement" of lobbyists. No matter the size or the wealth of a corporation or association, it is unlikely to have one of everything on its lobbying staff. A health care company, for example, will employ lobbyists who are familiar with health policy. These lobbyists will know which congressional committees have jurisdiction over health services and payments legislation and which government agencies implement programs related to health care. Such a company may have a tax person and a foreign trade expert on staff, though that is not likely except for the largest companies, and even those may not have specialists who are able to cover these peripheral policy areas.

For most matters this in-house coverage, even without the peripheral disciplines, would be adequate. But most is not all, and some important issues may arise for which the organization has no in-house legislative expert. For such matters outside lobbyists may provide much-needed services. Many independent lobbying firms—in fact, practically all—feature a full roster of legislative pros, among them retired (or defeated) members of Congress and former senior staff people.

In some cases there is an additional bonus—star power. A few lobbyists can match their inside-the-Beltway celebrity status with virtually any U.S. senator. In fact, some of them are former U.S. senators. Does this help the people they represent? That will be discussed in the next section.

## The Revolving Door

*"These revolving-door people sometimes gave predigested advice. They had already anticipated and factored in policy concerns and political problems. . . . These were legislative pros."*

As senators and representatives, senior congressional staffers, and members of the executive branch spin in and out of the private and public sectors, so too do their privilege, power, access, and, of course, money. It is little wonder that lobbying firms sign up people who have established connections in the federal government and whose résumés are powerful draws for potential clients.

The revolving-door phenomenon has become a red-flag issue among legislators, academics, and journalists. Critics say that big companies and other major lobbying entities have an advantage not available to ordinary citizens and less well off interest groups that cannot afford the expensive price tags that come with these insiders. This is an undeniable fact, but is it a legitimate criticism? Public Citizen's Congress Watch, a Ralph Nader watchdog organization, claims that it is. What is more, Congress Watch alleges that many members of Congress seek to serve their financial ends at least as much as they attend to their constituents' concerns: "Congress is no longer a mere destination for those seeking a seat in one of the world's most famous legislative bodies. For many lawmakers, it has become a way station to wealth, a necessary period of job training and network building so that after leaving their public service jobs they can sell their influence to those with deep pockets." [16]

The practice of moving from a congressional seat to the lobbying world, now widespread, raises some concerns that relate closely to the friendship–information complex of issues. And—like the matter of socializing among lobbyists and lawmakers—journalists, some public interest groups, and many academics view it with suspicion. Most of the interview subjects expressed a different view, many emphatically—though there were some important caveats.

Although the interviewees generally found the "formers" to be among the most competent lobbyists, they had varying opinions on this point; former staff people were consistently viewed as more competent on the issues than were their former bosses. Two former lawmakers were perhaps the harshest critics of ex-members who had become lobbyists:

- I would always see a former senior member but found generally that former senior staff were more competent—more knowledgeable about their issue and more broadly informed. I'd say only about a third of the former members were really effective and worth meeting with.
- If I were an executive recruiter, I would be interested in recruiting only a small number of the former members who wish to lobby. Most former members do not have the right mind-set—they just do not want to get into the details of an issue, do not want to do the hard work of becoming truly expert.

One interview subject made this observation: "Many former members were horrible lobbyists. Some were just not credible because they were taking positions that they had opposed when they were in Congress—or that they could have well been expected to oppose." Another interview subject described many of the former legislators as "almost pathetic." Other respondents joined in giving less than ringing endorsements:

- I would always see a former member if I could, but that was no guarantee that I would help him. Some of these were better than others. Some simply traded on their past relationships. Frankly, I saw no difference between experienced lobbyists and those who had been in

Congress. Some former members could never get over being a member. It was sad; they weren't very good. I saw them as weak.

- Many of these people abused their privileges. Many of them just relied on old friendships; that was fine. But sometimes they came onto the House floor or even into the gym—most members did not like this.[f]

Observations about former staffers who had swung through the revolving door were considerably more complimentary:

- Because former staff has been lobbied more than most former members, they bring a better perspective on what is expected of a good lobbyist. Generally, former members have better access; former staff have better information. But this is a very general observation.
- Former staff have their own networks of staff people just like former members do. Here they can have access and considerable credibility on the Hill and in the executive [branch] as well.
- The most fundamental thing is competence. He [the lobbyist] must know what he is talking about. . . . Former staff people are especially good at this; usually, but not always, better than former members.
- Former members do not always have the depth of knowledge that a former staff person will have.
- Former staff know what is good lobbying and what is bad lobbying. . . . They have a good sense of what a member is looking for. . . . They also tended to be very sensitive to the other side. That was often a big help; it is as though they would slip back into their staffing mode—providing a full briefing.[g]

One legislator was more generous than others had been when speaking about former members who returned to the Hill as lobbyists. In part, he said, this was because he tended to see "people with whom I had had long and comfortable relationships—not so much with relative strangers. I think that made a real difference in how I looked at them." A former colleague had much the same view: "I had a soft spot for some former members. If you know them, and they were straight shooters when they were in Congress—or even better, if they had helped you, then you'd be happy to see them. And, of course, some of them really do know the subject that they are talking about."

---

f. This speaker did not mind former members using the gym, but he did object to their using that access as a lobbying opportunity.

g. Note the speaker's indirect support for the notion that good information and subject expertise are the most important assets provided by lobbyists. When discussing the comparative benefits of former staff and former members, the interview subjects went directly and spontaneously to the matter of issue competence.

This same former member also recognized the special value of former staffers: "Some long-time relationships were those I had with staff people. I learned to trust their competence and their integrity, and from this professional friendships grew."

Perhaps the most encouraging remark came from a former member of his party's congressional leadership: "I think that, as a general matter, former members are getting the message that the old boy network is just not good enough anymore." He continued: "The revolving door is now different than it used to be. The new breed understands that you have to work at it and that the welcome mat is not rolled out just because you are a former member of Congress."

Overall there was a consensus that the revolving door provided many more advantages for congressional policymaking than disadvantages:

- Revolving door people have paid their dues. . . . You must have lived it to understand it.
- The vast majority of these people really respected the institution. They were truthful and had a solid understanding of the system, and they came with an institutional memory. That was especially valuable.
- When I first came to Congress, one particular former member was extremely helpful to me; he gave me advice on whom to talk to on the committee.
- I never had a problem with it [the revolving door]. Former members could sometimes be very effective in educating other people. Also, some of these had strong institutional memory and substantive knowledge in policy areas.

Perhaps the most compelling argument in support of the revolving door came from the former party leader quoted above: "These revolving-door people sometimes gave predigested advice. They had already anticipated and factored in policy concerns and political problems. They had accounted for these in putting together their positions. Not only was that welcome information, it also emphasized the point that these were legislative pros and worth paying attention to."

## Marquee Names

*"This town is more and more about star power."*

There is one class of lobbyist for whom reputation among Washington elites is a virtual necessity. These are variously known as the super-lobbyists, roll-arounds,[h] or marquee names. They are also known by the less colorful appellation "big independents."

As the word *marquee* suggests, these lobbyists have star power. Their reputation may mean more to them than it does to most lobbyists because their fame, even if well earned, is what propels them to an elevated status within their profession. In the Washington pecking order they often outrank and are reputed to have more influence than many members of Congress. Often junior members—and probably some senior lawmakers as well—consider a visit from such a person to be an honor, a status symbol to be casually mentioned during cloakroom conversations with colleagues. Tommy Boggs is probably the preeminent of the marquee names practicing today. In recent decades such notables as Clark Clifford, J. D. Williams, Charlie Walker, and Gerry Cassidy have enjoyed larger-than-life status, though many others qualify for mention.

Why do these people become household names inside the Beltway? Why do they obtain top billing? A quick glance may surprise even some Washington pros. Many of them are not former lawmakers or executive branch officials. Boggs qualifies for the revolving door in only the most technical sense. Although he is the son of two lawmakers, he never served in Congress, and he put in only a relatively short stint as a staff person for a nonlegislating committee, and that was almost four decades ago.[i] Gerry Cassidy served as general counsel to an important Senate committee, but that too was long ago, more than three decades past. Not more than a handful of members now sitting would recall working with either Boggs or Cassidy during their respective times on the Hill. So why are they so successful?

Is money a factor? Most interview subjects who addressed the point said that it is. One former member interviewed for this book was somewhat scolding: "Your book may not be about campaign money, but you have to at least acknowledge that it is almost always the 800-pound gorilla in the room." Other members agreed:

- Money plays too big of a role.
- I am very concerned about the lobbyist–fundraising nexus.

Those involved in the congressional "money chase" will concede that, at a minimum, campaign money buys access to congressional offices.[17] Thus a well-founded reputation for "shaking the trees" is a decided advantage for the lobbyist and client seeking to have their case heard. The

h. "Roll-arounds" because they allegedly move around town in chauffer-driven limousines.

i. True, his father, Rep. Hale Boggs of Louisiana, was the Democratic majority leader in 1972, when an airplane accident claimed his life.

marquee lobbyists and the firms they work for (or own) have just such reputations: "The super-lobbyists help raise money, lots of it."

If votes are not readily affected by campaign contributions, then the access provided by the marquee names must provide their clients with some other form of policy-related benefit. But, beyond the ability to get inside the door, the exact nature of that benefit is not entirely clear—certainly not to the interviewees. The set of observations that follow suggest that something other than fundraising may be at work in giving superstar lobbyists the advantages that some say they enjoy:

- This town is more and more about star power. The big clients want the big lobbyists [to represent them], and the members like being seen by the big lobbyists. It is status for both [the client and the member].
- I don't think they have any more success than any other lobbyists. But the press [and clients] sure thinks they do.

Other interview subjects, while not quite so cynical, nonetheless had doubts about the superstar lobbyists' track records for delivering results. A Republican from a western state hypothesized: "The high rollers' reputation has more to do with the kind of issues they lobby—higher profile, big money issues. It is a function of lobbying the more high profile committees. It is not so much a function of how good they are."

It is by no means a given that every member is awed by celebrity lobbyists. In fact, some claim that retaining the marquees may have hurt some clients at least as much as it helped them:

- If they didn't need [a big-name lobbyist], why would they spend so much money for this guy? It seemed to me like hiring him was a desperation move. . . . Hiring these high-profile lobbyists was like raising a red flag.
- I didn't see too much of them [marquee names], but I have to say that when I did it made me a bit suspicious of their client's motivation.
- Many of them were arrogant and dealt almost exclusively with the majority. Remember, what goes around comes around.

Some former members were more impressed by the marquees: "Better than the eat-what-you-kill types, but that was about it." Others were more aggressive in their praise for the big-name independent lobbyists. One interview subject had this to say (parts of this quote are paraphrased):

> It was sometimes noticeable to me that association and company lobbyists and some of the smaller independents had to take the issue that affected their client whether they liked it or not. Also association people had to clear their positions with their membership. This meant that they had to water things down to something that everyone could agree with.

> That was not especially helpful to me. I did not like being fed a bunch of pabulum. . . . The good thing about the big independent lobbyists is that they can take what they want and reject what they don't want. This is why I felt that the big-time independents had already done some pre-screening before they visited me. . . . The big guys would not take [on] a foolish, unwinnable issue; it's not good for their reputation.

On another point, the same member argued: "I know a lot of people say that you can't go over the heads of staff. Well, I don't fully subscribe to that. Sometimes you have to go to the principal; and that was something the big names could always do."

Only one member attributed super-lobbyist status to superior skills:

> These people are experienced, and they know how to present a case. They school their clients to be quick. Boggs is especially good at front-loading his arguments. This is a time saver. . . . Many of them are with full-service [organizations]. They have good lawyers and experienced legislative people. They may raise money, but it is usually a lot more than that. Say what you want, some of these people are good—very good!

Although the interview subjects showed a diversity of views about the marquee names, there was no consensus other than that as a general rule these lobbyists

- have star power;
- play active and productive roles in contributing and raising campaign funds;
- can virtually ensure that their clients will have access to congressional offices, especially senior offices (e.g., chairs of committees), for whatever the reason; and
- for the most part are competent at what they do and are supported by highly competent staff teams.

Whether the marquee names produce a positive result for the client is another matter. There is an old joke: A rabbi and a priest are watching a prizefight. The rabbi notices that one of the fighters has crossed himself before coming out for each round. The rabbi: "Father, do you think that helps?" The priest: "Not if he can't fight." One is tempted to say of the super-lobbyist: Not if he can't lobby.

## Campaign Contributions: The 800-Pound Gorilla

Now for the 800-pound gorilla in the room: campaign finance. For researchers and political practitioners the $500 million questions are these: Does campaign money buy anything of value, that is, votes or services? If so, how much of what and where?[j]

In a cover blurb extolling Phillip M. Stern's book *The Best Congress Money Can Buy* (1988), journalist Daniel Schorr wrote: "Stern's book packs a wallop that should wallop a PAC. It is a cogent and coherent account of the corrupting influence of political money on Congress. It is must reading for anyone concerned with resuscitating the democratic process."

Stern and Schorr no doubt reflect what, for many Americans, is the *going-in view* about the effects of political money. The book and the blurb are provocative, but do they square with the best evidence that is available? This may be one of those "you pays your money and takes your choice (of answers)" questions. This is because, like everything else that is even remotely related to lobbying and the tools that lobbyists use, the influence of money is dependent on the member, the relationship, and the situation. There is no right answer.

Evidence, pro and con, empirical and anecdotal, abounds. The following sections draw upon studies by academics as well as personal recollections of those who have given, and those who have received, campaign money. The first discussion focuses on money and votes; the second on services, including access.

### Money and Votes

*"Members must raise a ton of money. We all raise some of it from people we are not especially comfortable with. You don't want to give these people policy, but you might be able to do other things for them."*

There is a considerable body of political science literature examining the effects of campaign contributions on members' voting—on the floor of their chamber, in committee, and in subcommittee. While one can find a study to support virtually any point of view, the consensus seems to comport with Janet Grenzke's findings about campaign contributions: "The results . . . provide little support for the claim that money maintains a pattern of pro-PAC behavior in Congress. . . . The interviews corroborate the statistical

j. The amount of money raised by congressional candidates in 2007, a nonelection year, was $507 million.

evidence. All the officials insisted that 'our contributions are too small to change a vote' [United Auto Workers]. They behave as they would anyway, and the money comes after [National Education Association]." [18]

Grenzke ultimately concludes that the organizations she examined were able to exert influence, as she says, "Not because their PACs give campaign contributions. Rather, they are large organizations with widespread support in members' districts and consequently have a variety of resources." [19] Thus the causal factors influencing votes have more to do with grassroots-type leverage and perhaps monetary resources other than campaign contributions—among them skilled lobbyists and access to research vehicles.

W. P. Welch arrives at a similar conclusion in his examination of the "exchange model"—a system through which interest groups give value (money that can be converted into reelection votes) and receive either votes on issues or value in other forms from members of Congress: "The influence of contributions is 'small,' at least relative to the influences of constituency, party and ideology. . . . Money was to reward a legislator for his past voting without regard for whether he truly did the group a favor or whether his future behavior was likely to be influenced by the contribution." [20]

More recently Matthew C. Fellowes and Patrick J. Wolf produced a more equivocal finding: "Our empirical results show that aggregate business campaign contributions do influence macro-level pro-business tax and regulatory policy votes—much more [than they do] access into the policy process or an occasional low-profile vote." [21]

The Fellowes–Wolf study is in at least one important way similar to anecdotal evidence produced by the interview subjects: It produces a mixed result. No interview subject admitted to casting a vote with the specific intent of pleasing a political contributor. Of course, this is not unexpected; what person smart enough to be elected to Congress would admit that money had purchased her vote? Nor did any interviewee provide hard evidence that other members had been influenced by money. But some got close:

- Members from swing districts always find money to be important.
- Low-profile issues offer the member a great deal of flexibility. If reelection prospects are not at issue, then that's a no-brainer; the member will go with the contributor.

Al Wilhite and Chris Paul provide empirical support for suspicions raised by such remarks: "Corporate PAC contributions affect legislative voting. . . . As corporate contributions comprise a larger share of a candidate's campaign chest, there is an increased probability that the legislator will support pro-business legislation."[22]

The majority of interviewees (81 percent) who commented on the subject were in line with the preponderance of these studies.[k] One ex-legislator eschewed moral and legal arguments. He argued that the decision not to be excessively influenced by campaign contributions when voting was, in political science terms, the decision that one would expect of rational political actors. In his view, selling a vote would be "just plain stupid. . . . Why would I sell a vote if I would only have to use the money to buy it, plus many more votes, back. It doesn't make any sense?"

A former House Ways and Means member confirmed that even in low-profile venues that produce no public record members would not stray far from their core beliefs or their constituents in providing favors for campaign donors:

> It really is a glass bowl down there and everyone knows it. I don't think that you can ever think in terms of total confidentiality—not on the kinds of things we're talking about, the kinds of things that make a bill or amendment happen, or that get the executive branch to do something. You always have to figure that someone is going to find out—once one person finds out, everyone finds out.

Other interview subjects agreed that exchanging votes for money would not be productive, even if one were inclined to do so:

- The money thing is way overblown. You will always make someone unhappy on an issue. Sometimes both sides are supportive of you. You might as well go with what you believe; that way you can defend yourself if you have to. . . . I've been here for a while and I know how important that is.
- But you [the legislator] seldom have all of the stars lined up—the House, the Senate, all relevant committees in both houses, powerful interest groups that want in, and the administration. Money usually does not buy all of that. So you may get part way with all of what you want or all the way with part of what you want, but you almost never can get all the way with all of what you want.
- People who contribute try to establish a personal relationship, and sometimes they do. Money may be what brings you together—you get to know each other at fundraisers and other events—but it's not what gets you to vote with them, certainly not on any major stuff.

---

k. Interviewees were told that campaign money and its effects were not the subjects of this book. Thus only a relatively few—slightly less than one-third—raised the subject in any context. For this reason the response universe is very small here.

There was one point that all interviewees but one agreed upon. That is the point made by the ex-member quoted earlier in this chapter: "There is too much money in the system." A former colleague added, "If nothing else, [accepting money] looks bad. I worry more about that than what actually happens."

## Access and Other Services

*"It is indisputable that for a certain segment of members—probably by far and away the majority of members—money translates into access."*

Although members of Congress do not concede that money buys votes—certainly not their own votes—most are willing to agree that contributions are a factor in deciding who gains access to congressional offices and who does not.

One of the most definitive studies on this subject is Laura Langbein's "Money and Access." Langbein concludes that "overall . . . PAC contributions appear to significantly influence access." She places a dollar figure on the value, to the legislator, of access. She finds that one could predict a twenty-five-minute meeting for each contribution of $6,390 (in 1986 dollars).[23]

Langbein's finding suggests a causal relationship between the amount of a contribution and the predisposition of the recipient to meet with the contributor for a given period of time. The logical inference is that the better off the contributor is, the more likely he is to gain a substantial audience with policymakers. This strongly suggests that the access playing field is slanted in favor of more highly organized contributors—those who can bundle contributions and provide support over a sustained period—in other words, the marquee names and those who can afford them

Later work by David Austen-Smith disputes the idea that contributions and access necessarily go together like spaghetti and meatballs. In fact, Austen-Smith finds that in some circumstances legislators may disregard a pleader's contribution history entirely: "The more like the legislator the lobbyist is, the more valuable the lobbyist will be to the legislator on informational grounds. . . . Consequently, if legislators know the preferences of the prospective lobbyists, they will, *ceteris paribus,* choose to listen to those lobbyists whose underlying preferences most closely reflect their own; and this will be true *irrespective* of any campaign contribution."[24]

Some legislators may act as Austen-Smith predicts if timeframes are short and if immediate answers are necessary. But the interview subjects tended to agree with Langbein that money does purchase access:

- It is indisputable that for a certain segment of members—probably by far and away the majority of members—money translates into access. In some instances, it [money] will get you more than access. It will get you some sort of support. The member will actually do something for you.
- Money will get you access.
- Access is the main thing. But you really do not get a lot else for money.

Voting, the most public act that legislators perform, is only a piece of what members of Congress do to affect policy outcomes, and by many accounts it is only a small piece. As Welch points out, members' voting is constrained by "constituency, ideology and party." [25] Thus the opportunity for a lobbyist to affect a lawmaker's vote is limited before his hand ever opens the client's wallet.

This is not the case for work done behind the scenes. There are untold numbers of unrecorded legislative activities that first form and then advance, retard, pass, or defeat legislation. They are an integral part of a process that may take years to complete; they are conducted in private meetings, over the phone, in staff-level discussions, and through internal memorandums. There is evidence that here, in the shadows of the Capitol dome, mischief does occur.

Some investigators have found direct, though not necessarily frequent, links between money and policy for low-profile issues or issues considered outside the public realm. "Contributions appear to have the greatest predictive power when there is low visibility." [26] Low visibility can be a function of issue salience, legislative venue (e.g., subcommittee versus the full chamber floor), and the nature of the act being preformed (e.g., voting versus trying to shape a committee agenda). It is a reasonable assumption then that where no record is established the temptation to sell a favor will be the greatest.

In a study of low-visibility settings—common to committee deliberations—Woodrow Jones Jr. and Robert Keiser provide evidence that there is reason for concern, that money can buy support: "Issues which draw headlines and television coverage are likely to be the ones where there are stronger pressures for members of Congress to vote on the basis of ideology, party, or constituency interest. . . . Those who receive campaign contributions are likely to support the interest group giving them money on less visible issues." [27]

Finally, John Wright finds that while there is little evidence "in support of a direct link between money and voting" an indirect link does exist. More specifically:

- Representatives' voting decisions in committee, particularly the Ways and Means Committee, are best explained by the number of lobbying contacts.
- Campaign contributions [were] useful predictors of groups' lobbying patterns.
- Lobbying is significantly related to previous contributing; the political and technical information representatives receive from groups is shaped to some extent by campaign money.[28]

The interviews bear out the academic findings: Money, twilight, and policy favors do mix—if not very often, then often enough to cast a huge shadow (pun intended) over our national politics:

- Members must raise a ton of money. We all raise some of it from people we are not especially comfortable with. You don't want to give these people policy, but you might be able to do other things for them—things that make them look good to their constituency [group members, etc.] but don't really matter very much. And, yes, asking a question or two at a hearing might be one way to do that.
- Some things you do can be as much for show as for anything else. But if you helped someone in doing that, say asking a question at a hearing or even lining up cosponsors for a bill that is not going to go anywhere, that's a nonevent that got someone a few kudos and helped you get a future ally.
- Normally, for a member from an eastern state to encourage enforcement of environmental conservation standards against a midwestern utility company is easy. It would be no skin off my back. But if the midwest utilities have contributed a fair amount of money to the member, then he might not go on a letter demanding that they bring themselves into compliance.
- If your constituency does not care, and no one really knows—why not?

All of this smacks of a cavalier what-you-don't-know-won't-hurt-you mentality on Capitol Hill—not particularly reassuring. But Hall and Wayman found some small reason for hope: There is "solid evidence [that] moneyed interests are able to mobilize legislators already predisposed to support the group's position."[29] This finding is consistent with the view of a southeastern Republican interview subject: "Yes, members will do favors they might not otherwise do for groups that have given/raised money. But this is never something that they personally disagree with; it is simply something that without the organization's support would not rise high enough on the member's scan for him to agree to work on it."

It is for the reader to decide whether this equates to being only a little bit pregnant.[30]

## Conclusion

The red flags in this chapter point to what many citizens claim to know about the lobbyist–member interface. We might express their presumed knowledge as an equation:

Secretiveness + special-interest money + election-obsessed politicians = corruption

The various studies and interviewees' comments seem to confirm much of what we know—or, better said, want to know—about professional politicians and wealthy donors (many of them big corporations). Can there be two more suspect creatures than these? Not likely.

Many authors, journalists, and some academics add to these worries by treating suspicion as fact—correlation as an established causal relationship. Look at some of the titles of their work: *Pigs at the Trough, Money Talks, Dollars and Votes,* and *The Best Congress Money Can Buy.* One need read no further than the title to deduce the message that follows.

Yet the best information we have does not support the inevitability of the equation's result. Nor does it come even close to confirming the correlation-based accusations. Some of this information, the empirical studies, is grounded in reasonably neutral, verifiable fact, but much of it is not. For the reasons set out in chapter 1, we must rely on first-person reporting for virtually everything that we know about what transpires in face-to-face lobbying contacts. Without being in command of this information, we cannot make unimpeachable connections between money, interests, and the subsequent acts of politicians.

Congress has begun to lower the red flags by restricting opportunities for socializing between lawmakers and lobbyists, creating more transparency in campaign fundraising processes, and enacting other campaign finance reforms. On their face, these reforms seem sensible, and to a large extent they may be. But they may also beg an important question: Is transparency in fundraising and contributions activity enough to ensure against possible negative effects of campaign money in our political system, or is more needed?

On the one hand, our imperfect information-gathering tools do not uncover massive vote-buying schemes or unprincipled favor-doing. On the other hand, the qualitative evidence (and some empirical evidence) indicates that some of this underground activity does occur. Even to the extent that grateful beneficiaries of campaign largesse take action in support of a measure with which they agree—not because they necessarily want to take that action but because they are eager to please a contributor—money has purchased something. Is that not corruption? Maybe it is only "corruption light," but it is still a favor done in return for money, and that *is* corrupt behavior.

Are there ways in which "in the dark" activities—those that might provide the most likely opportunities for corrupt behavior—can be made more transparent? If so, would that be a wise thing to do? Might such transparency put a chill on the use of legitimate legislative bargaining tools?

It is against this backdrop—suspicion and a negative public perception of their work—that lobbyists, the fourth branch of government, operate. Nonetheless, the point made in chapter 1 stands: Regardless of the tools lobbyists use (campaign money, social gatherings, etc.), the kind of lobbyists they are (revolving-door veterans or K Street glitterati), or the settings in which they operate (light or dark, high or low visibility), it is the members of Congress who have the ultimate say about what is effective lobbying and what is not. Thus, if we are prepared to take these public officials at their word, red flags notwithstanding, there is still an important place for lobbyists who understand the rules and the legitimate needs of policy-committed lawmakers to ply their craft.

## Notes

1. Doris Kearns, *Lyndon Johnson and the American Dream* (New York: Harper and Row, 1977), 297.
2. Richard L. Hall and Frank W. Wayman, "Buying Time: Moneyed Interests and the Mobilization of Bias in Congressional Committees," *American Political Science Review* 84 (September 1990): 814.
3. Richard L. Hall, *Participation in Congress* (New Haven: Yale University Press, 1996), 41.
4. Diana Evans, "Before the Roll Call: Interest Group and Public Policy Outcomes in House Committees," *Political Research Quarterly* 49 (June 1996): 289.
5. Frank J. Sorauf, *Inside Campaign Finance* (New Haven: Yale University Press, 1992), 168.
6. Michael J. Malbin, *Money and Politics in the United States* (Chatham, N.J.: Chatham House, 1984), 248.
7. Dan Clawson, Alan Neustadtl, and Mark Weller, *Dollars and Votes* (Philadelphia: Temple University Press, 1998), 66.
8. Ibid., 68.
9. Margaret S. Thompson, *The Spider Web* (Ithaca: Cornell University Press, 1986), 64.
10. James Madison, *The Federalist* (New York: New American Library, 1961), 77; James Bryce, *The American Commonwealth* (London: Macmillan, 1888), 1: 674.
11. Jeffrey Birnbaum, "Mickey Goes to Washington," *Washington Post National Weekly Edition,* February 25–March 2, 2008.

12. Rep. Rahm Emanuel, "Lobbying and Ethics Reform," www.house.gov/emanuel/lobbyingreform.shtml.
13. Sen. Russ Feingold, "Statement of Senator Feingold on the Ethics and Lobby Reform Bill," March 29, 2006, www.feingold.senate.gov/~feingold/statements/06/03/20060329 lobbying.htm.
14. Editorial, *New York Times,* December 18, 2006.
15. Editorial, *Milwaukee Journal Sentinel,* January 22, 2006.
16. "Congressional Revolving Doors: The Journey from Congress to K Street," *Congress Watch,* July 2005.
17. Laura Langbein, "Money and Access," *Journal of Politics* 48 (1986): 1054–1062.
18. Janet M. Grenzke, "PACS and the Congressional Supermarket: The Currency Is Complex," *American Journal of Political Science* 33 (February 1989): 8.
19. Ibid., 20.
20. W. P. Welch, "Campaign Contributions and Legislative Voting: Milk Money and Dairy Price Supports," *Western Political Science Quarterly* 35 (1982): 478.
21. Matthew C. Fellowes and Patrick J. Wolf, "Funding Mechanisms and Policy Instruments: How Business Campaign Contributions Influence Congressional Votes," *Political Research Quarterly* 57 (June 2004): 321.
22. Al Wilhite and Chris Paul, "Corporate Campaign Contributions and Legislative Voting," *Quarterly Review of Economics and Business* 29 (Fall 1989): 83.
23. Langbein, "Money and Access," 1061.
24. David Austen-Smith, "Campaign Contributions and Access," *American Political Science Review* 89 (September 1995): 566.
25. Welch, "Campaign Contributions and Legislative Voting," 490–491.
26. Jean Reith Schroedal, "Campaign Contributions and Legislative Outcomes," *Western Political Quarterly* 39 (September 1986): 387.
27. Woodrow Jones Jr. and Robert Keiser, "Issue Visibility and the Effects of PAC Money," *Social Science Quarterly* 68 (1987): 175.
28. John Wright, "Contributions, Lobbying, and Committee Voting in the U.S. House of Representatives," *American Political Science Review* 84 (1990): 433–434.
29. Hall and Wayman, "Buying Time," 814.
30. Many scholarly studies examine why people and organizations make political contributions and consider what effects this money may have. The following are only a handful of what is available: Alan Neustadtl, "Interest-Group PACsmanship: An Analysis of Campaign Contributions, Issue Visibility, and Legislative Impact," *Social Forces* 69 (December 1990): 549–564; Thomas Stratmann, "Campaign Contributions and Congressional Voting: Does the Timing of Contributions Matter?" *Review of Economics and Statistics* 77 (February 1995): 127–136; Gregory Wawro, "A Probit Analysis of Campaign Contributions and Roll-Call Votes," *American Journal of Political Science* 45 (July 2001): 563–579; Frank L. Davis, "Balancing the Perspective on PAC Contributions: In Search of an Impact on Roll Calls," *American Politics Quarterly* 21 (April 1993): 205–222.

# 4 Political "Capitol"—Gains and Losses

In June 2003 the *New York Times* referred to President George W. Bush as the "lobbyist in chief." [1] The *Times* was not the first news outlet to use this tongue-in-cheek but very descriptive and accurate title for the president. Like all other high-powered lobbyists, presidents cannot compel Congress to do anything. Their sole power, as Richard Neustadt has famously written is "the power to persuade." To dramatize his point, Neustadt offered this hypothetical anecdote:

> President Truman used to contemplate the problems of the general-become-president should Eisenhower win the forthcoming election. "He'll sit here . . . and say, 'Do this! Do that!' And nothing will happen. Poor Ike—it won't be a bit like the army." [2]

Presidents do not have because-I-said-so authority—not when it comes to moving members of Congress in one policy direction or another. Legislative power for presidents resides in their ability to successfully employ the impressive array of influence tools at their command. Although marquee lobbyists, corporate vice presidents of government relations (a euphemistic term for lobbyists), and public interest group executives have their own share of influence assets, none compares to the president's array of armaments. Among them are patronage, campaign support, grants, and contracts for organizations within a member's congressional district.

The presidential analogy can be taken further: Each year the president delivers to Congress a State of the Union address, which is followed by a message, or series of messages, laying out the administration's agenda for the upcoming congressional session. These are his "asks." If the chief executive is to be taken seriously, his proposals must make sense, either substantively or politically or, in the best of circumstances, in both ways.[a]

Again Neustadt: "Despite his status [the president] does not get action without argument." [3] In other words, the president must be able to support his positions with cogent facts and viable policy designs. Like all other lobbyists, he must be mindful of a rule propounded by a former member of the Democratic leadership: Lobbyists must use as their standard "the art of the possible" when making requests of congressional offices. Members and staff do not have time to tilt at windmills. Lobbyists foolish enough to suggest such adventures will find future appointments hard to come by.

This chapter provides a foundation for chapters 5 and 6. It gives insights into the "power stakes"—the political and substantive gains and losses—that most members of Congress seek to maximize or protect when they are making policy and determining political choices. It frames the context in which members evaluate lobbyists' requests and their (lobbyists') strategic and tactical suggestions for pursuing those requests. As we will see, members almost habitually ask two questions: First, What is in it for me? And, second, What are my risks if I get involved in this enterprise? It behooves the lobbyist to be certain that what he plans to ask of a member will satisfy her "me first" scrutiny. He must anticipate her concerns for potential political gains and losses, and he must have engaged in at least some preliminary strategic thinking.

## Anticipating Gains and Losses: The Key Questions[b]

Members of Congress seek to acquire, husband, and then wisely invest political capital, often measured in goodwill, respect, IOUs due to other members or to themselves, and election day returns. Thus, when members are asked by a colleague or a lobbyist to perform a legislative act, the question "What is in it for me?" almost always plays a role in their deliberations. (This is probably not much different from what concerns most people in most careers.) It is not likely that a lawmaker will ask this question aloud, nor is it necessary for a petitioning lobbyist to address it in any direct way.

---

a. Sometimes presidents will send to Congress a bill that they know will go nowhere. The hope is to elicit a thumbs-down rejection by congressional leaders (usually of the other party) that may then be turned to political advantage for the president and the president's party. The request amounts to more of a dare than a serious legislative initiative.

b. The cost-benefit variables are presented here in rough order of importance as disclosed by the interview subjects. Although I made no effort to establish a formal ranking system for these variables, the ordering presented here is, I believe, a fairly accurate reflection of the subjects' thinking.

What is necessary is that the asker should anticipate the question by making sure that the lawmaker will be inclined to give the right answer: "Yes, this will be a good thing for me (the member) to do." Lobbyists who ask members to do foolish things—things that will cost them capital without returning a commensurate return—will quickly find much of the cost passed back to them in the form of allies lost, objectives not accomplished, and reputation for skillful lobbying practice diminished.

A former chief of staff, now serving as a member of the House, gave this description of how a congressman for whom he had once worked evaluated legislative "opportunities":[c]

> A member of Congress is bombarded daily with dozens of good ideas—opportunities, suggestions, recommendations, etc., any one of which can drain time, take you off course, and steer you away from achieving your master plan. We always operated with a set of strategic values and goals. The "screen" was a way to measure whether these "good ideas" or spot "opportunities" were really worth the time, manpower, and cost when measured against our broad office goals. It was a way to follow Goethe's saying, "That which matters most must never be at the mercy of things which matter least." As I recall, we weighed every idea against whether it had value on several fronts:
>
> - Did it help advance our legislative agenda?
> - Did it have any press or media value?
> - Is it consistent with our philosophy?
> - How much effort, manpower would be involved?
> - Was there any cost involved?

Each of these questions reflects an item of political capital that the office sought to protect.

A Senate counsel advised that lobbyists should be sensitive to the importance that legislative operatives attach to this accounting process and the results it produces: "To be effective a lobbyist must start with a genuine concern for the person being lobbied. . . . I don't care if he is staff or a member; he cannot afford to waste his time or other assets on things that will go nowhere." In other words, congressional offices, aware of their power stakes, will not willingly (or knowingly) squander political capital. The extent to which a potential asset or debit is important to a targeted office is the extent to which it must be important to the lobbyist.

c. This interview subject was kind enough to follow up on our conversation with an e-mail that laid out the process recounted here. I have shortened and paraphrased the items in the list.

Douglas Arnold provides a highly instructive example of a gain versus loss analysis within the framework of electoral politics—almost always the deciding factor for a member of Congress:

> The first thing to realize is that legislators are not beginning with a blank slate. All have a sense of who their consistent supporters are, who are consistent opponents, and who occupy the spaces in between. . . . Most legislators play a conservative game and follow the preferences of their most consistent supporters rather than those of their past opponents. . . . It is far easier to alienate one's longtime friends with a few very wrong votes than it is to transform one's most steadfast opponents into reliable friends with an equal number of pleasing votes.[4]

Arnold's comments reinforce an idea presented in chapter 2: Members are defensive. Note the tip-off language: "play a conservative game;" "follow the preferences of their most consistent supporters"; "easier to alienate one's longtime friends . . . than it is to transform one's most steadfast opponents." Taken together, these observations suggest that attentive legislators are able to employ multiple stratagems to preserve their political power stakes. Arnold argues: "Wherever they turn, legislators see opportunities to make themselves look good or to make their parties look good." He also argues that even if the party seems to go astray legislators are able to "avoid direct electoral retribution for producing displeasing effects" and "simply refuse to join in any actions that might produce large and traceable costs." Thus legislators can continue to be responsive to their own political base.[5]

Even for the legislative workhorses, the program types who take pride in their policy leadership roles, maintaining one's power stakes among colleagues and other Washington policy elites is a strategic imperative. Effective policy participation depends upon successfully building and then nurturing these stakes over an extended period of time.

This is where revolving-door lobbyists have a noticeable advantage over most other lobbyists. They are in a unique position to anticipate how members will match up a lobbyist's request with a legislator's interest—even an interest that is limited to maintaining efficient office operations. Former members and staff have the advantage that comes only with hands-on experience in judging what is a cost and what is likely to be seen as a benefit.

In the two observations that follow, the first by an independent lobbyist who had been a Senate legislative staffer for more than a decade; and the second by a former member of the House, we see how important these insights can be:

> At the end of the meeting [the client] pulled out a report that must have been the size of the federal budget and handed it to me. [Name of lobbyist] turned white. I guess he had no idea this was coming. He quickly jumped in and said very casually, "Of course, we know you are very busy and don't have time to read this, so we'll get up a one- or two-pager and get that to you in a day or so.

A small point? For sure, at first glance. But the lobbyist's quick action, action based on having been on the receiving end of too many tomes, ensured that the key portions of his client's argument, once submitted in condensed form, would be read by someone in this Senate office.

The second observation:

> [The client] was nervous because we were going to ask [the member] to phone around to some other offices to see if he could firm up a few leaners.[d] I let him know that it wasn't such a big favor. I told him, 'That's what they [members of Congress] do. If they do not do that, they are not doing their job.'

Here the former member, now a prominent Washington lobbyist, remembered how he was able to put his client's mind at ease. Few people other than those who have served on the Hill know that importuning other members for votes is common among members, and, although some avoid the practice, many see it as part of the legislative territory.

On the following pages are eleven questions relating to political capital that were most frequently mentioned by the interview subjects.

## 1. Is this good policy? (Rightness)

*"If you believe the [position] is right, then you go full steam ahead."*

Members of Congress take positions for a variety of reasons. On different occasions they seek to support policy positions, their colleagues, district or state interests, party initiatives, committee leadership, the administration, and financial interests and other constituencies. Their reasons aside, however, nothing is as liberating for them as is the belief that the position they are supporting is the right one. One member called this the "am I right?" test. Another former member, one who had served in his party's leadership, used an especially descriptive metaphoric phrase: "Believing you are right is like an inoculation." This mind-set permits members to be

d. When projecting legislative vote counts, members of Congress and lobbyists frequently employ a five-point system: solidly for, leaning for, totally undecided, leaning against, and solidly against. In the example given, the "leaners" are those leaning the lobbyist's and member's way.

proactive and to explore legislative and political territory that may be new to them and not necessarily "in line with their district interests."

According to a former subcommittee chair, members do not mind "using up a chit with other members in these cases. . . . If you believe the [position] is right, then you go full steam ahead." This former chair believes that members will not worry about harming their reputation in Congress—a factor that he mentioned several times during our conversation—by working for a well-reasoned and supportable objective. He went further to describe the liberating force of conviction: "Members have different portfolios. Some things you do for the good of humanity—things that strike a chord with you; things that you really care about. On things like this you can pursue the press and do a favor for a group you think is right, for a reporter, and for yourself. You can wind up with a lot of positive coverage for doing something that you believe."

The sense of rightness was also seen as providing an exception to David Mayhew's "single-minded seekers of reelection" thesis, discussed in chapter 2. This was the view of a Democrat now associated with a prestigious think tank. He noted that some members "get a satisfaction from pushing the limits on the right thing. . . . Some members are not as reelection-obsessed as others." For these members, he argued, "rightness on the merits may preempt rightness as defined by political imperatives." Thus the basic premise holds: Members are more willing to take chances when they believe they are right on an issue.

A former majority counsel took a slightly different tack; he spoke in terms of the "quality of policy" and tied this idea to the "am I right?" test. In his view, this necessarily meant something more than a mere calculation of support or opposition. Some policy initiatives "interest members and staff more than others. Some may be more important, more sophisticated, more noteworthy, and more compelling; members can be intrigued by these."

Here, lobbyists find an opportunity to tap into a legislator's thirst for peer recognition as well as constituent approval. The combination of issue salience and a conviction about the quality of a policy proposal may well motivate a member to take risks that she might ordinarily consider not worth the effort.

Of course, all of this is dependant upon matching lobbyist and member interests. A former House legislative assistant emphasized this point. He noted the importance of

> finding someone who is going to be comfortable with what you want him to do. The less selling you have to do the better it is for everybody. . . . You [the lobbyist] have to find someone who thinks it's the right thing to

> do or convince them that it is. It's not that hard to get a member to do something she believes in. What is more difficult is if the member is less convinced or is unconvinced. Then you have to convince them, but you are also at greater risk if things don't turn out.[e]

Another lobbyist was faced with a different, perhaps more difficult, problem. His chief ally in the House worried that the position he had urged upon her, and that she believed to be right for her district, was "beyond the sophistication level of the vast majority of [her] constituents. It would not likely fly in the district." In essence, this was her view:

> Some issues may have had a small direct effect on my district, but they had the potential to affect how well I could serve them in the future. So constituents or contributors who were looking for support for an issue or for a vote may, in my mind, have been competing with another member whose vote or help might sometime in the future be very important to the district. I knew that how well I could represent my constituents had to do with how effective I could be overall. So I saw it as my duty to respond to other important members who may have needed me on an issue even if it meant selling out in the short run.[f]

This member easily qualified as one of Payne's "workhorses" (see chapter 2). Although she was decidedly an entrepreneurial member—"I always wanted to own the issue"—she was also considered to be one of the most effective legislators, in the most complimentary sense of the word. And she usually enjoyed large majorities on election day. For her, the possibility of an electoral cost was tolerable; she could trade off a small piece of short-term constituent loyalty for a longer-term investment that she knew (even if her constituents did not) would eventually yield a positive result for her district. Thus she forged ahead with the lobbyist at her side. For another member, perhaps a show horse or a member from a marginal district, the cost-benefit calculus could render a very different result.

This distinction is important: Members interpret what is a cost or a benefit in different ways because of different motivations and conditions. The way each member will do the math should be a core component of the lobbyist's own calculations. What he might ask of one lawmaker, he should not consider asking of another. The criteria an individual member will use to evaluate potential risks and rewards must inform the lobbyist's decisions about whom to ask, for what, and when.

---

e. There is much in political science literature that suggests that lobbyists tend to lobby their friends—those who already agree with them. Perhaps this observation supplies part of the reason for this preference.
f. Small portions of his comments have been paraphrased.

## 2. What would my constituents think? (Constituency)

*"If it's right for the district, it's right."*

But rightness is itself a relative term. When a member acts in good faith to represent her home constituency, her motivation equates to being "right" in the congressional mind-set. A northeastern Republican emphasized the importance of constituency in members' thinking and advised that the most effective lobbying technique "is to make an issue or a position relevant to the people in my district. And then if things work out, let them know about it." (This quote will appear again in the discussion of salience and visibility.)

A former staff person linked the definition of "right" to constituent interests: "If it's right for the district, it's right. . . . That provides the member with a sort of blank check." This thinking gives a legislator broad leeway in seeking her legislative objective as long as it is for the people back home. She can justify almost any action in pursuit of what is good for her district.

Interestingly, she qualified this response by noting that if a member "feels [she] is in good shape," and has "trust with her constituents," she will be able to "take more chances" than can a lawmaker who is less politically secure. According to this logic, it is at least possible that senior members from safe districts will give the political views of their constituents less weight in defining "rightness" than will a less politically secure member—perhaps an argument in support of the large percentage of return rates normally enjoyed by congressional incumbents.

## 3. Is this an important matter—especially for my constituents? (Salience)

*"It is important to match up the lobbying presentation with the member's district needs."*

A moderate Republican former member agreed that district interests should be read into the "am I right?" standard: "Defensibility of the position was an essential prerequisite for me. . . . I think it was for everybody." She continued by linking defensibility to constituent perceptions: Would doing the act, "if it became public in the district" enhance or diminish "my standing among my constituents?" Would she be seen as "more or less trustworthy, more or less *faithful* to the people who had elected [her]?"

This observation is notable for what it does not say as much as it is for what it does say. Although one might deduce a nexus between "defensibility" and reelection concerns, the former member did not actually say that. Given her choice of words and the context of her observations, it is likely that she spoke exactly as she intended to do. As a member with a solid hold on her district she spoke in terms of trust and faithfulness. Her emphasis was on not letting down the people who had placed confidence in her, not on being returned to Congress.

A former colleague, in discussing an off-the-record act in which he had been deeply involved, expressed the same idea: "If this [act] became known to others, I would be concerned [that] friends, other members, groups, constituents, and financial supporters would be disappointed in me." These were people and interests that likely were part of his base inside and outside of Congress. He was willing to run some risks with them because he believed in the policy imperative at issue. He felt he could afford to stray a bit if he could defend his action were he called upon to do so.

The difference between concern for letting one's supporters down and worries about reelection prospects might appear to be slight, and not fully knowable in any given circumstance, but it is an important distinction for lobbyists to have in mind when they are presenting to legislators. The former requires an assurance that the requested act supports what is, in the member's mind, her duty to do—to represent faithfully and with trust constituencies she deems to be most concerned about the issue at hand.

The latter begets a more politically oriented justification on the part of the lobbyist. A veteran chief of staff agreed:

> The district impact [of a position] is paramount because it is just another way of describing its effect on reelection. . . . You have to know that when you say something like "public visibility" to a member of Congress, he thinks "district visibility." That's the only public that exists for him. . . . The effects on our constituency mattered insofar as they were the effects on voters who knew about these things and our role in bringing them about.

A former member, as if offering an addendum to this comment, stressed the importance of issue salience: "The district means who votes; relevance means what matters to them. Doing something on a noncontroversial issue is always easy—no one really cares much. But doing it for a very controversial matter [among constituents] can have major electoral consequences."

Four former members concurred in these constituent-centered definitions of salience:[g]

---

g. A northeastern Democrat and former subcommittee chair modified the definition still further. In his view, a view that tracks almost word for word with that of Richard Hall, "constituency" did not always "equate to a majority of people in the district." Sometimes there is a "small well-informed and intensely interested group—I think you political scientists like to call them stakeholders—and they're the only ones that know or care." In these cases this small subset of constituents is the one "that a member will feel he needs to listen to."

- The most effective technique is to make an issue or a position relevant to the people in my district. And then, if things worked out, let them know about it.
- The lobby organization that paid close attention to getting support for me on an issue back in the district was always welcome.
- The ability to make a point resonate in the district is always a key. . . . Make it relevant to a member's interests in Congress or to getting reelected, or both.
- Visibility did not matter much if it was something you believed in. It might have some value if it was good for the district.

Several interviewees stressed the importance of visibility without alluding to issue salience in the district. The following conversation took place during a follow-up telephone interview with a former member:

> *Author:* Does visibility matter if the issue is not considered to be important by voters?
>
> *Member:* Absolutely. Even if the issue itself is not, your actions might be [important to them].
>
> *Author:* In what ways?
>
> *Member:* Well, are you doing something that people will see as double-dealing?
>
> *Author:* Double-dealing?
>
> *Member:* Yes. Are you promoting a position that does not square with what you have said or with how you have taught these people to think about you? [h]

Thus, even if members are not pursuing a matter that means much to their constituents, visibility (or in more contemporary language, transparency) matters. It is a tool that conveys messages about legislators to their constituents. If constituents have no knowledge about what a member is doing (or has done), the electoral consequences of legislative activity are nil. A lobbyist who had served for only three years as a legislative assistant used a well-worn riddle to make this point: "If a tree falls in the woods where no one can hear it, does it still make a sound? Well, if no one knows about an issue or what the member has done about the issue, can it still be important? No!"

A former member, clearly alluding to a first-person experience, reinforced this idea. He hypothesized that a member's decision to become involved in a regulatory matter "may be affected by the extent to which the

---

h. See the discussion in question 4 on consistency.

matter is or is not likely to become public." He continued: "Some of these matters may not be popular [among] the general public, but [the lobbyist's] position might be right. The lack of visibility might just give a member the room he needs to help out a major constituent." Here again is the idea that "sunshine" might not always be a positive in the arcane business of policymaking.

Every now and again an interviewer gets lucky. An interview subject, a legislator who by his own description had "seen it all," laid out, as if preparing for a classroom lecture, the variables that members will factor into their thinking before agreeing to support lobbyists' requests. Note that he too adopts a constituent-centered and therefore reelection-oriented focus:

> The first thing is that visibility is measured primarily in terms of visibility to the constituency you are concerned about.[i] The decision is based on district attitudes, the intensity of importance to the district, contribution profile of requestor, members' sense of good policy, and a sense of his past policy positions.

As if enjoying the role of professor, the interviewee went further with his lecture notes:

> By measuring, I am thinking about the congressman's general sense of how his district is inclined to think about a given issue. Often, it is more gut feeling than anything else. . . . Intensity is defined by how much a member suspects that many voters care a great deal about an issue. Some things people tend to forget or not to hold against you. Other things stick with them.

"Visibility," according to a former Republican member, "is a crosscutting factor. It affects how members will react to numbers of different circumstances. . . . I don't agree that we always thought that everything would become public; or, even if it did, that it would matter to anyone but us." He then repeated a now familiar message: Sometimes, under cover of darkness, a member will opt to help a lobbyist knowing that his actions, should they become public, would not meet with constituent approval.

## 4. Is this position consistent with my past policy positions and my overall ideology? (Consistency)

*"I felt strongly that I needed to be seen as being consistent and not vacillating."*

---

i. Here he seemed to be referring to geographic, policy, interest group, colleague, or financial constituencies. As he continued, he clearly limited his thinking to the district constituency.

Consistency matters at both the lobbyists' and the lawmakers' ends of the lobbying exchange. Neither will have much credibility if they are perceived as dancing from one side of an issue to the other, motivated only by what is most convenient for present circumstances. One interview subject came down hard on some of his former congressional colleagues: "Many former members are horrible lobbyists. Some are not credible because they were taking positions that they had opposed when in Congress or that they could well have been expected to have opposed."

In the present discussion our focus will be on the other side of the exchange, the members' side. Members of Congress must protect their own record of consistent behavior. Remember, elected officials live in a glass bowl. Life under the microscope is the norm for them. Deviations from past or expected behavior—especially in the positions they champion—will be noticed and subjected to strict scrutiny. An occasional change of mind is not uncommon and can usually be justified on the basis of newly discovered evidence—to borrow a term from the law. But frequent alterations are not as easily rationalized. Offending members could pay a price in diminished influence among peers and in a loss of confidence by their constituents.

Again, the former chief of staff: "They [lawmakers] worry about being seen as a waffler." Other respondents agreed. When discussing what tests they employed to determine if a policy position was one that they could "go with," two former members of the House said that they would ask themselves:

- Is this in line with my past policy positions? I felt strongly that I needed to be seen as being consistent and not vacillating?
- Is it consistent with our philosophy? Could I be accused of not standing for anything?

A former Republican member thought that consistency in position taking was one of the most important traits that legislators must exhibit. To his thinking: "It is necessary if they [legislators] are to establish and maintain respect from constituents and peers." His staff was "always instructed to be certain that my past positions were consistent and that I would not be vulnerable to charges of catering to special interests—whatever the hell those are supposed to be." And later, "Consistency is very important; it is necessary if you are going to demonstrate that you are trustworthy. . . . [It] is an integral component of trust."

Some interview subjects volunteered that on rare occasions they, or one of their colleagues, might veer from an established policy direction. They recalled working behind the scenes with either colleagues or lobbyists to achieve an objective that was not congruent with past behavior; nor was it in line with what appeared to be constituent preferences. Speaking in the third person, and with guarantee of anonymity, a legislator gave an example:

> They may not go so far as to covertly push a position that was inconsistent with their district's wishes or with their own past performance, but they might have done some low-level services: arrange a meeting with another member and maybe even say nice things about the lobbyist in attempting to arrange the meeting. That, it seems to me, was sometimes done for interest groups that [these legislators] knew well and wanted to help out even if they couldn't vote with them.

On rare occasion a member might agree to perform a more aggressive sleight of hand. A former subcommittee chair, possibly recalling his own past actions, revealed that "members may do this. A chair might schedule a bill for a hearing even if he will not support it. Sometimes this is done out of a sense of fairness, sometimes as a result of pressure from members who want to appease an interest group, and sometimes for a group that you want to help."

The former chair added an important caveat: "I might schedule a markup but tell the supporters of the bill that I would vote against it." He went further to explain that in these cases the bill's supporters, including some of his colleagues, made convincing arguments that the matter in question deserved full consideration by the subcommittee; even if he could not personally support the measure it was his duty to his colleagues to ensure such an airing. For this chairman the decision to go to markup was, in its own way, entirely consistent behavior. He had built a reputation for even-handed administration of his subcommittee and was justifiably proud of that. Through his actions he made this important point: Consistency can be a function of policy positions or of one's philosophy for doing legislative business. In other words, it can be a matter of substance or of style.

## 5. What will my colleagues think if I do this? (Visibility within Congress)

*"The more members [who will know] . . . the more important it is to do it right."*

For legislators the word *public* has at least two definitions. Most often it refers to the general public, what elitists sometimes dub the masses. But for members of Congress it can also refer to their fellow legislators—for example, "If this becomes public the chair will be very angry." Of course, the two definitions are not mutually exclusive.

Very little that happens on Capitol Hill remains confidential for very long. Members and staff are constantly talking to each other and to other offices. Some of the content is gossip; some of it is business; and some of the gossip *is* business. A former Senate staffer confirmed the loquacious nature of the legislative personality: "You wouldn't *even* ask someone to keep quiet. It just isn't part of the culture. If it serves their purpose to [reveal] a confidence, they'll do it." A former member who had risen from the ranks of congressional staff was more entertaining. "The legislative beast" he said, "is born with its mouth open and tongue wagging."

Most things that occur in the course of legislative dealings are not news. Asking a colleague for a vote or to cosponsor a bill is daily fare. So too are negotiating provisions for an amendment, asking another member to meet with a valued constituent, or attempting to have a person or interest group placed on the witness list for an upcoming hearing. These are the sorts of informal activities that were discussed earlier. They are routine activities; it is not likely that other members will talk or care much about them.

The most notable exception here, according to several interview subjects, is the "bad news stuff." Circumstances in which one is perceived as a double-dealer, ideologically inconsistent, disloyal, or in any other way untrustworthy will likely cost a member some of her political capital and thus diminish her opportunities to function effectively. The loss, in order to do damage, need not be especially widespread in terms of the absolute number of lawmakers who become aware of an indiscretion. A small subset (for example, the members who sit on a subcommittee with her) are all that is needed to render her suspect where it counts the most—her key legislative platform.

There are also instances in which a member, not necessarily a show horse, actively pursues a high-profile legislative strategy. Aggressive legislators will make a conscious decision to elevate their visibility among congressional colleagues by assuming the role of legislative entrepreneur for a particular issue. This work requires that they publicize their work by wooing media attention—often by conducting high-profile hearings, conducting press conferences, and seeking media interviews. Here the members consciously opt to place their legislative wares up for public and congressional scrutiny, a high-stakes risk-reward proposition. Rep. Henry Waxman, D-Calif., and Sen. Edward Kennedy, D-Mass., are masters of this process. They also have impressive records for producing important legislation.

For a southern Democrat one's level of exposure within the institution "is an important matter. . . . The more members [who will know] . . . the more important it is to do it right." The inference is that a member's reputation for competence and integrity is at stake when her activities become broadly visible among House or Senate colleagues. A former fellow legislator agreed: "How well you are perceived is important." She alluded specifically to the diminished importance of seniority in selecting House committee chairs: "For members who want to be chairs they have to show their caucus that they are skilled legislators. Just being able to hang around doesn't do that." Thus a member must prove herself worthy of her colleagues' respect in order to advance within the committee structure. This is in line with the thinking expressed by a Republican: "Visibility always ups the ante. You can either look good or bad—smart or stupid. Smart is better than stupid."

Another legislator dotted the *i* when discussing the relevance of projected exposure to the viability of a lobbyist's action requests: The importance of "visibility [in the House] depends on the member's ambitions." Beyond this he thought it was not much of a factor in determining the extent to which a member might, or might not, pursue a lobbyist's request.

As might be expected, some former lawmakers categorically disagreed: This statement by a Blue Dog is representative:

> Sure [visibility is] important. It had nothing to do with the lobbyist; I would have thought the same thing about an idea from my staff. I always wanted to know who and how many [members] needed to be involved.[j] The more visibility the more chance of [another member] wanting to get involved. . . . Sometimes that was helpful; other times it could be a problem.

There is an additional subset of colleagues (beyond fellow committee members) that is important to legislators. These are colleagues who have become their personal friends. Political scientist Barbara Sinclair notes the importance of personal relationships in the business of legislating: "Even before geography and committee is a personal relationship. . . . Do I know [her] well enough to talk to her about this issue?"[6]

Several interviewees acknowledged the role of personal relationships: "Your allies [in Congress]" are frequently "the people you know best." And those, according to a midwesterner, are likely to be drawn from one or more of three sources: "The people that you came in [to Congress] with, . . . the people who have helped you in the past with committee assignments and by introducing you to other members . . . [and] those you socialize with—in the gym for instance." Another former member recalled the first time he had lunch in the House dining room: "They sat me at a table where I didn't know a soul. I guess that was what the table was for because no one knew anyone. We started to talk, get to know each other, and

j. In context, this lawmaker was clearly thinking as much about general exposure within Congress as he was about potential allies and adversaries.

some of those people became my best friends for the entire time I was in the House."

Making friends with congressional colleagues, and through that process adding to one's inventory of working relationships, is an integral part of the job of becoming a legislator. It is frequently a conscious act, something not left to chance—not for people accustomed to evaluating others for their potential utility as allies and, yes, as fundraisers:

- I had been very aggressive in getting to know other members, particularly in my class.[k]
- Members do things to position themselves to do business with other members. But nothing is more important than developing personal friendships.[l]
- Much of the work that is done revolves around these relationships.
- The [name of trade association] went out of their way to help me meet people that they knew would be important to me at some point. . . . Then I would follow up, and sometimes a real friendship would develop.
- They [name of company and lobbyist] put together an event for some members of our state delegation before I even took office; it was a big help.

A former subcommittee chair considered friendship to be a prime motivating factor in determining members' legislative activities (for example, votes and decisions to cosponsor bills) when there is no substantive, moral, or political imperative at stake: "On many issues there is no clear right or wrong. It can be a matter between two powerful interest groups—with no real difference in policy outcome that you care about or that matters to your district. Friendship with a colleague or with a lobbyist can make the difference. You might try to help out a friend."

Because friends are potential political assets, they must be treated with special care. Members "need to consider the effects of their own acts on their friends" for fear of alienating and thus rendering useless some portion of these prized assets: "The effect that something I might do could have on one of my friend's [legislative] projects may have serious consequences on that relationship." In other words, supporting or opposing a good friend in Congress could bear directly upon one's store of political capital. Certainly,

k. By class, he meant the members of Congress who entered as freshmen during the same year he did.
l. Many members join legislative caucuses (such as the Republican Wednesday Group), special-interest organizations (the Congressional Black Caucus), and congressional social societies (the Marching and Chowder Society) in order to build relationships with other members. These groups provide opportunities to share information and perhaps even to begin building an influence base. A former member likened this sort of positioning to "asset building."

some bumping and chafing among friends "happens on a regular basis," and members understand and accept that. But, said a former subcommittee chair, "You can't help but ask yourself if it will [alienate] one of my best friends and allies—especially if he serves on your committee; that's where it matters most."

Lobbyists should take care to know as much as they can about these relationships. We will see in chapter 6 that lobbyists frequently attempt to tap into friendships between members by asking one of them to intercede with the other. A former legislative director agreed that this happens "often enough" and noted its relevance to the highly personal nature of legislative politics: "The member-to-member remains a staple. Congressmen build relationships. . . . They tend to talk to friends and to people who think like they do regardless of their party, though usually they . . . stay within their own party. Members build relationships through social arrangements. Sometimes they anticipate that they will need certain colleagues so [they] seek them out for friendship."

But there is an important caveat here: When a lobbyist attempts to piggyback on congressional friendships, the stakes for providing good information and making intelligent requests are heightened. If the rationale and information put forward in support of a request proves faulty, or if the policy assumptions turn out to be incorrect, the lobbyist runs the risk of having led two lawmakers—the member he has importuned directly and that member's colleague and friend—into a blind alley. Double-dip damnation!

Of course, if the lobbyist's position proves to be well advised, he will have done himself and the lawmakers he has attracted to his cause a favor. This is especially true if their combined efforts succeed. In these cases all involved will benefit from the project that the lobbyist set in motion.

Calculating the costs and benefits that are derived from close personal relationships is its own art form; it is not always subject to a straightforward analytical process. In fact, the calculus can be both complex and chancy. Members sometimes have hybrid relationships with their congressional colleagues (for example, personal friends may not share a similar political ideology). No rule is written that prohibits a liberal from befriending a conservative: "It happens all of the time."[m]

Louis Frey, a moderately conservative former Republican member from Florida, recounted his efforts to pass safety regulations for mobile homes in 1972. "The original sponsors were close personal friends whom

m. Although they have nothing to do with Congress, two members of the U.S. Supreme Court provide such an example: Washington scuttlebutt has it that Justices Antonin Scalia and Ruth Bader Ginsburg are great personal friends—despite their frequent, sometimes intense, differences on jurisprudential matters.

I could talk into giving me a chance to build support for the legislation. The group included people like [Congressmen] Larry Coughlin [R-Pa.], Walter Flowers [D-Ala.], Bill Gunter [D-Fla.], Peter Kyros [D-Maine], Bill Lehman [D-Fla.], and Ron Sarasin [R-Conn.]." [7]

In this instance Frey realized an immediate benefit while assuming the risk of incurring a cost at some point down the road. He achieved legislation that he very much wanted, but he also exposed himself to a cost by giving IOUs to members with whom he often disagreed. At some later time he might be faced with the sort of conundrum that Douglas Arnold suggested—pressure to repay a debt that, if satisfied, would alienate key constituencies among colleagues and voters.

### 6. If people find out about this, will I look foolish or, worse, dishonest? (Visibility among the general public)

*"They are always worried—some even paranoid—about stuff getting out to the press."*

We looked indirectly at the significance of public visibility (as opposed to visibility limited to congressional colleagues) for lobbyists and legislators in chapter 3, in the section entitled "Working in the Dark." The focus there was on the covert nature of lobbying activities that take place before and concurrent with formal lawmaking processes. But, as important as such activities may be, they do not produce the final word in policy development. For this to happen the fruits of subsurface legislative bargaining must be brought to light prior to enactment, if for no other reason than that our Constitution demands it.

But legislative work becomes public for reasons other than constitutional mandate. The congressional press corps, always thirsting for a leak, is large, skilled, and indefatigable. Much of the time reporters benefit from controlled leaks engineered by entrepreneurs or their adversaries. The former was frequently the case for an East Coast legislator: "Taking an issue to the media is sometimes helpful. . . . The press is an important tool for members who want to gain support for an issue. We'd leak a potential story to an editor or producer; the trick was to make it sexy. [Name of lobbyist] had a real talent for this. He was fun to work with."

At one point this member was mentioned as a possible candidate for the U.S. Senate and even for governor of his state. Press alliances established by providing leaks would have been helpful in these pursuits had the member not ultimately decided to retire from politics.

A New Englander followed a similar strategy:

*Member:* Policy is media driven. Sometimes the most important thing you can do to get something going is to get a reporter interested.

*Author:* Do members actually initiate contact with the press?

*Member:* Absolutely! Sometimes we would do it; other times we would advise an interest group that it should be done and give them some ideas about how to get it done. That helps you, the interest group, and your issue.

Leaking in the hopes of attracting public support for a legislative proposal sometimes creates the potential for negative consequences. A former administrative assistant who had been promoted from legislative director remembered that the senator he worked for would spend "hours being briefed" before going to the media, especially if the issue was complex: "Some issues are too dry for the media. But getting coverage can be very important. [The senator] cultivated reporters; this was critical but it can be difficult. Members stand a chance of looking bad if they are not knowledgeable about their issue. They must be able to answer the questions that will come. Good press can turn sour—fast!"

Of course, proactive legislators run risks beyond being caught short on key facts while promoting their policies. For one thing, they cannot always control the timing or the content of press coverage. Sometimes opponents decide it is in their interest to "get there first and control the story." This member continued: "We hear a lot about spin. It's very real. . . . Some lobbyists were very helpful in planning [press strategies]." This member went on to explain that "many lobbyists or their clients" had large and sophisticated public relations offices that could offer some good advice."

Aside from its possible effect on the course of legislation, going public—either through the media or through some other high-profile mechanism—reinforces the importance of the "am I right?" standard: "Members will not perform an act or service for a lobbyist if they believe it is wrong. Don't forget, members seldom act alone. They have staff and colleagues that see what they're doing—at least, what they're trying to do. Also they are always worried—some even paranoid—about stuff getting out to the press; then you are before your constituents and everybody else."

Score one for the advocates of sunshine!

President Lyndon Johnson may have been right: The public would only hurt itself by knowing too much. But to the thinking of the nine-term veteran just quoted, the threat of broad public exposure may have a prophylactic cleansing effect. Another member concluded: "We [members of Congress] are all political people. If we thought we had pissed off somebody in Bulgaria, we would start wringing our hands."

## 7. Who will oppose this and with how much intensity? (Opposition)

*"What has occurred previously? Has there been major opposition by important groups? If so, which ones?"*

Few proposals, whether in the form of a bill, an amendment, or a procedural motion, move through Congress without some degree of opposition. Whether consciously or instinctively, political people are always sniffing the air: "Is there danger out there?" "Where is it?" "How strong is it?" As a former congressional counsel observed, "You always figure who's going to be for it and who's going to oppose you. That's routine." A midwesterner indicated how important this information could be to a legislator: "If some groups were strongly against it, I would have a hard time being for it."

Opposition has many faces. It can be in the form of a counterproposal, a parliamentary delaying tactic, an all-out lobbying campaign, or a broad public relations effort. It can come from one or two interest groups, or it can be generated by a large coalition of organizations that are in cahoots with their own set of legislative allies: "I found the trade association people [to be] especially good at that kind of intelligence; they had a good handle on where the opposition would come from." This sort of heads-up "was valuable in helping us get ready for hearings and markups."

Beyond merely identifying potential opponents, lawmakers and their allies in the private sector must assess how hard these organizations will be willing fight. Will they offer only a token rebuttal and then move on, or will they dig in and fight every inch of the way? A northern Democrat: "Labor was great. They were always there until the end—winning or losing you could count on them." According to a Blue Dog Democrat: "The more, and the more important [the] opposition that is anticipated, the more intensity that is needed and, perhaps, the more members that are needed to be involved." Another former member warned that some organizations "take names." When a lawmaker decides that she will take on one of these groups, she "runs the risk that someone [or] some organization will want to get even." Thus opposition, depending on its source and intensity, can have long-term political effects.

Here, as in so many other instances, good information has a special value. Members need to make accurate assessments in order to weigh potential benefits against likely costs. In doing this, they must be in command of all relevant facts—substantive and political. The Blue Dog laid out the operative questions: "What has occurred previously? Has there been major opposition by important groups? If so, which ones? Have members wrestled over this in the past? Who were they? Has it passed [this] chamber before?" Again members rely on colleagues and trusted lobby organizations for the necessary information. A former ranking minority member, speaking of a trade association, gave a detailed example: "They tell you who is for it and who is against it; they don't send you out there thinking it's all just apple pie. They let you know the Heart Association is against it, and so are some of your best friends in the House. Then you know where you stand. Surprises are nice for parties, not for legislating."

It is this kind of information that protects against the blind alley that is so dreaded by defensive-minded lawmakers. It may not be possible for lobbyists to present supporting data or otherwise prove every point that they make. That is fine; members can live with that. But to the thinking of a twenty-two-year veteran of the congressional wars, it is the duty of the lobbyist, as much as is feasible, to protect the member against blindside attacks, especially those that have merit: "Just don't get me screwed. Let me know where I could take a hit. Then I can decide [what I want to do]."

## 8. Does my party have a strong position on this issue? (Party and committee chair position)

*"Neither party core can pass squat."*

During the mid-twentieth century much was written about the diminished importance of political parties in the work of Congress. Several factors were found to be at work. Among them were the increased effects of primaries in the candidate-selection process, the focus on "candidate centered" elections, and the growing importance of interest groups as sources of both information and campaign funding. These changes combined to create an environment in which individual members were able to rely upon their own resources; they did not have much need for their party or for other forms of campaign resources.

This trend began to reverse in the late 1970s. The Republican Party, still reeling from its post-Watergate collapse, initiated a "variety of programs aimed at . . . increasing the [campaign] committees' electoral presence, and providing candidates with campaign money and services." [8] The Democrats put similar reforms in place at roughly the same time. Together the two parties reasserted themselves as electoral forces on a national scale.[9] The parties were also becoming more effective in providing policy leadership. As Roger Davidson and Walter Oleszek were able to say: "By any test one [could] use, congressional parties [were] flourishing." [10]

Sinclair found that Democratic chairs in the postreform era looked to party leaders for help in passing legislation: "The Lone Ranger brand of policy entrepreneurship that was prevalent in the 1970s [was] much less feasible. . . . Faced with a much more difficult legislative context, members were not only willing to allow their leaders to use aggressively [their considerable] powers and resources to help pass the legislation those members wanted, but insisted that they do so." [11]

A southwestern Democrat agrees that parties are now major policy players. He places them among "several important constituencies" that a member must factor into the policymaking equation. "When a member comes to town, he learns that there are different constituencies that have to be accommodated. The home constituency is part of it, but so too are the large national lobbyists and the party members and leaders."

In the House, party leaders are now granted considerable powers to aid them in winning the prized 218 votes needed for an absolute majority. Among these powers is control of the Rules Committee and of the committee-assignment process. The latter can be used to exert significant pressure on individual members, particularly on junior members: "Not only is the fate of most legislative proposals determined in committee; to an important degree the fate of individual congressmen may be decided there too. A person's congressional career may rest largely on the kind of committee post he is given." [12] Thus party leaders whose success or failure as leaders depends on party cohesion are also key players in affecting members' careers.

A similar point pertains to committee chairs, especially the most senior and powerful of them. Christopher Deering and Steven Smith argue that these legislators remain people to be reckoned with:

> The full committee chair is the most powerful member on the vast majority of committees. He or she benefits from years of experience in dealing with the policy problems and constituencies of the committee, exercises considerable control over its agenda, schedules meetings and hearings, . . . normally names conferees, controls the committee budget, [and] supervises a sizable staff. . . . Consequently, the support of the full committee chair can be critical to bill sponsors. This is as true today as it was thirty and forty years ago.[13]

And, like the broader congressional party leadership, many chairs are well positioned to affect individual legislative careers. They are seldom reluctant to let colleagues who stray from the party line know this. Remember the promising East Coast moderate (chapter 2) who chose not to support his party's position in committee and heard about it from the chair. "On a major committee bill, I didn't go with leadership. The chair called up to let me know how 'disappointed' he was. He said that he hoped 'this will not hurt my chances to get on the [name of committee] next term.' "

Although the parties have a strong incentive to see their incumbents reelected, chairs have offsetting priorities. In addition to furthering their own legislative agendas, they are charged by the leadership with producing results. Their job can be made easier or more difficult, depending on who serves on their committee:

- A powerful chair can veto members he does not want on his committee; same for ranking minority members.
- Sometimes a chair likes getting someone on his committee because it helps to assure him votes. Certainly the new member will owe much to the chair.

Attempting to influence committee assignments is among the most important and most sensitive matters that lobbyists face. The default position is to steer clear of the process: "That is members' business," a veteran Republican said with a distinct bite in his voice. "I didn't expect to hear from anyone else on this." By the word *expect,* he clearly meant "did not want to."

Other former members left the door open for *some* input from *some* lobbyists. "I would listen to someone I knew for years and who had a good reputation. But generally I saw this as a family matter that we [members of Congress] had to work out."

Constituent interests, not surprisingly, often play a role in the lobbyist–member exchange on committee assignments. A legislator from the Northwest observed: "The exception [to not wanting to hear from lobbyists on this issue] was for constituents. If you have a major industry in your district [or state], then you will certainly listen to them and maybe try to help."

A former member of the Senate Finance Committee spoke about the importance to lobbyists of "picking up on" these situations. He placed great value on "practical experience" gained by working in or with Congress. Once again, note the favorable mention of revolving-door lobbyists: "Here is where you see the value of experienced lobbyists and congressional veterans. These people understand what is going on and know when they have to lay off. Too much pressure at the wrong time can turn someone off."

Not all members are convinced about the rebirth of parties as players in the lawmaking process. An author of several provisions that are now in the tax code gave the parties low grades for their roles in policy development. He was especially harsh (and colorful) in his assessment of party caucuses:[n] "[Caucuses] are forums for a handful of activities, but they do not

n. The party caucus is a meeting of all party members sitting in either the House or the Senate. The caucus's function has changed from time to time as has its effectiveness. Generally, though, it is a mechanism for attempting to create party unity and for permitting members to be heard in a private setting.

seem to accomplish much. . . . The caucus affects only the party core and neither party's core is big enough to control a House outcome. Neither party core can pass squat."

Other interview subjects took similar positions; they agreed that party was not the most important factor in determining their policy decisions. These observations are consistent with John Kingdon's finding: "Party leaders and staffs turn out to be the least important of the potential influences on the [voting] decision. . . . Fellow congressmen and constituents are the most important actors." [14]

Several comments made by interview subjects reflect the uncertain role of leadership in enforcing party discipline. The consensus was that party allegiance matters to members, but more as a background or secondary element in their calculations than as a primary consideration: "The party can be a political asset; it was certainly a natural resource for developing political and legislative alliances. I would certainly support leadership whenever I could—but sometimes other things were just more important to me."

Interview subjects had varied views about how party mavericks—Blue Dogs, RINOs (Republican in name only), and others willing to chart their own course on a particular issue—should be approached by lobbyists. The following observations represent the two poles, though most members who addressed the subject were closer to the first:

- I know some lobbyists would come in that would never go to someone they considered more in the party mainstream, but I certainly was not squeamish about that. If they saw me as a potential ally, that was just fine.
- I did not like some business people who would come in just assuming that I was going to be their mole. . . . I wasn't going to do that. People who knew me knew that wasn't my style.

In context, the latter member's point fits squarely in the "do not take me for granted" category. He did not like bucking his party and did not appreciate lobbyists who simply assumed that he would do that. Nor did he like lobbyists who acted as surrogates (with or without portfolio) for the party leadership: "I did not care for lobbyists that came in preaching party loyalty. I did not think that was their place."

Lobbying upstream against party or committee leadership is a perfect example of the highly personal nature inherent in lobbyist–member encounters. In these instances it is extremely important that lobbyists be aware of the individual member's attitudes and work styles. Some are true party people; others see themselves as more loosely affiliated with their party—more a relationship of convenience than one of common ideology.

In all, a mixed picture of party control in Congress is presented, especially in the House, where policy control on major issues is now relatively centralized (as compared with the 1960s through the early 1990s). But it is selective centralization; leaders do not attempt to call the shots on all issues. They save their muscle for the top agenda items. And even on those matters leadership often leaves considerable substantive and managerial discretion to committee chairs. A former subcommittee chair cautioned: "Any lobbyist who thinks he can just bypass a chair is flirting with real danger."

Thus lobbyists who are attempting to work through congressional allies in pursuit of a legislative goal should take the advice of a southern conservative: "See to it that the chair is approached with great care. Don't do anything that seems like you are trying to short-circuit him."

Chairs may not be the unrivaled potentates they once were, but the consensus of the interview subjects was in line with the view of this fourteen-year veteran: "I [don't care] about the reforms you mentioned. If you're thinking about challenging the chair, think again!"

## 9. Is the president taking a strong position on this matter? (Administration's position)

*"I have never been afraid to ask a member to buck the White House. If I can make the case that it is in the member's interest to do this, then I am doing him a favor."*

From obscure departmental bill reports[o] to major White House initiatives, the president, through his administration, is a player in the legislative process. The executive branch brings at least two critical assets to legislative deliberations: subject expertise and presidential prestige. Although political actors may argue about the quality and possible bias of information generated by the executive agencies, there is seldom a want of data and expert opinion from "downtown." The president is able to get out front on just so many issues at any one time, but the minions of the White House and departmental legislative agents who represent the administration on the Hill carry some degree of authority by dint of the president's alleged interest in seeing his positions prevail.

For these reasons the president is always a potentially formidable foe or a highly valued ally. Few in Congress underestimate the political force of

o. Bill reports are summaries and analyses of bills in which an executive branch department has an interest, usually because the bill would affect a department program. They may play a role in helping the administration determine whether it will support or oppose a bill.

1600 Pennsylvania Avenue when that force is unleashed. This is especially true for members of the president's party. As Barbara Hinckley notes, most members "feel more comfortable voting with [their] party than against it." But like many other observations about the use of power in Washington, this idea can be overstated. Many scholars reject the notion of the president as the hegemonic leader of even his party in Congress. William Leuchtenburg recounts this poignant observation by President Lyndon Johnson: "When [Franklin D.] Roosevelt reached the summit of his power, he took on the gods of Olympus [Congress] and got rolled back, and he never reached those heights again." [15]

The interviews indicate that the White House has significant—though something less than hegemonic—influence over members' policy positions. A Rocky Mountain Democrat touched on the "bully pulpit," pegging the president's influence to his ability to get his message out to the public. This member discussed the president's media advantage in the context of partisan and constituency influences: "The administration's position might make a difference in how an opposition member would vote if the president is using his press advantage. . . . The president's leverage will vary based on how partisan a member is. Members who are not especially partisan do not have much trouble supporting the opposite party downtown, especially if that is where their district is (i.e., how their constituents feel about the issue)."

In other words, the legislator's vote would be influenced to the degree that the president is able to generate support in the member's state or district. The member's decision would not be based on the power of the president's argument; nor would it be determined by her desire to be supportive of the administration per se. Rather, it would be because she was anticipating, or responding to, constituent opinion. The controlling influence, then, is consistent with all that has been said about the force of the reelection incentive.

A GOP staffer agreed with this and then noted that some of the members she had worked for were given a "pass" by presidents of their own party [p]: "We always got low White House support ratings. We had to; [otherwise] my bosses would never have been reelected. The Reagan and Bush people knew that and were pretty good about leaving us alone. . . . Sometimes our congressional leadership was a problem, but not usually too bad."

p. The majority party in Congress controls many important organizational matters, such as the ratio of majority to minority lawmakers that sit on a committee or subcommittee, scheduling for committees and the chamber floor, and overall staffing advantages. Thus each party has a strong interest in obtaining a majority position in the House and in the Senate. Consequently, they generally tolerate mavericks within their own party if they believe that member can hold her seat for the party.

A former Republican member claimed that he exercised independent judgment, basing his decision on the merits of an issue: "I was pretty loyal to [the administration], but I had no trouble making up my own mind even if that meant not [voting] with them." Another member said that he was "conditionally loyal" to the White House (if in the hands of his own party). By that he meant he would support the White House "if there was no good reason not to."

These views make clear that lobbyists need not abstain from approaching members of the president's party even if the White House has staked out an opposing position. As is the case with congressional (and committee) leadership, some members are more inclined to be loyalists than are others. And, of course, a member's mind-set and district attitudes must be factored in as well. But, given the right result of these calculations, the opinion of a Democrat now serving for an East Coast district is worth noting: "You can always come in with your best argument. If you can convince me that the administration is wrong for my constituents, I will want to know that; that could be doing me a good turn."

A revolving-door lobbyist laid it out in almost identical terms: "I have never been afraid to ask a member to buck the White House. If I can make the case that it is in the member's interest to do this, then I am doing him a favor. It's the executive branch that is trying to screw him." A former committee chief of staff, now a Democrat serving in the Senate, agreed: "Only the zealots think 'my party right or wrong.' We'll listen to any argument that makes sense, no matter where the administration is. We may not buy it, but a lobbyist will not hurt himself for his effort."

Further conversation with this Democrat reinforced much of what has been said in prior chapters about the importance for lobbyists of appearing to be savvy. The thrust of his message was that lobbyists should not assume that a member will impute knowledge of congressional systems and culture to the lobbyist—not if the relationship is a new one. Thus the lobbyist should make clear that he knows the administration is taking a different position from his but that he would like the member to consider his position anyway: "This lets him know that you understand what is going on, and it gives you more credibility with him."

Most party leaders in Congress, including committee and subcommittee chairs, on most occasions, will do whatever they can to be helpful to *their* president. It is expected that the executive branch will attempt to coordinate its efforts to move or retard legislation by strategizing with its party leaders in Congress. A former committee chair provided an example: "We would sometimes work with them on the timing and content of hearings—witness lists, questions, etc. Even when we were in the minority [in Congress], if [our party] had the White House, we would cooperate with them."

The process may lock in a chair and so indirectly lock in party loyalists on the relevant committee. But this does not mean that they are all duty bound to a code of silence. (Of course, in Congress, this is a duty that is often not so binding.) Lobbyists are still free to approach congressional offices to seek information and to solicit advice even if they are on the other side of an issue: "That was always how we could do something for people we liked."

The gist of the interview content was that the administration's positions were perceived to be more of a background influence, albeit sometimes a powerful one, than a deciding factor when members were making up their minds on an issue. But there are important exceptions here, most notably when the White House and its congressional party leaders stake out a strong, unified public position. In these circumstances, congressional leaders working in concert with the administration are able to bring "real pressure to bear if they think that your vote is necessary [for a party win]."

But the motivation to support the president and party is, again, not attributable to blind loyalty or to a conviction that party leaders have it right. Instead, it is based largely on a first-person-centered analysis: Can I weather reprisals if they come? Will the rewards be adequate? The idea of taking one for the team is not high on members' lists of motivating rationales. Members do not especially care to take one for anybody if they can avoid it.

## 10. How much time will it take to do this? (Time and other resources)

*"Something that takes longer to do is tougher."*

Members are usually able to limit the amount of time they invest in meetings with constituents and lobbyists—often one and the same. If they do not have enough time to host someone in their legislative office, they may step off the floor of the House and into the Rayburn sitting room (adjacent to the House floor) or into the lobby just off the Senate floor for a brief chat. Another favorite time-saver is to tell a lobbyist, "Walk me to the floor. We can talk about it on the way over." None of these meetings need take more than a few minutes.

Not so with the sort of work that is required to prepare amendments, to lobby senior members on agenda items, or to prepare to defend positions at subcommittee markups. These are likely to be time-consuming events that require extensive preparation and follow-up.

Follow-up, in fact, was a recurring theme during my interviews with former members and staff. A southeastern Republican believed that "being dogged" was the "most important" characteristic of a successful legislator—and doggedness translates into a significant commitment of time: "Overall, the best thing a member can do for a bill is to be persistent, to stay on top of it every step of the way. This means time, and it takes its own sort of energy."

The work of political scientist Glen Krutz supports this view: "Effort matters. The degree of intensity of a sponsor in pushing a bill is important in determining which bills move forward. . . . If you work hard, you can get results." [16] Successful members then are those who are willing to invest time in their legislative projects. Because the time needed to do things in Congress is not infinite, the corollary assumption is that time must be budgeted by legislatively active members.

A former legislative director elaborated: "It all came down to time—his [the member's] and ours. If we had the time, we could have seen everyone we needed to and done everything we should have. But, no chance! We didn't even have time to do things we [thought to be] necessary. It was by far the greatest source of tension in our lives. Everything was done half-assed—just not enough time."

The decision to expend time is thus weighted to reflect the member's interests and priorities:

- As I recall, we weighed every idea against whether it had value on several fronts [including] how much effort and power [were needed]. . . . Even small things took time, and we needed to prioritize. We learned to say no.
- How much time would the staff or the member have to spend on the matter?
- Timing and the amount of time are big. Is he [the member] busy with other work? Is he in reelection trouble?

The amount of time available to a member is also affected by exogenous circumstances. An East Coast Democrat and former subcommittee chair discussed the conditional nature of time: "At the end of session, time is more scarce—there's just less of it. What you might agree to do earlier in the session you would not do later. This is especially true if there has been a referral [between committees] or if the Senate is not expected to act." This former subcommittee chair made clear that neither he nor his party's leadership wanted to waste time working on a bill that was "going to go nowhere." Thus, according to this line of thinking, short-run viability becomes a component in the calculation of available time.

In a subsequent interview a former committee counsel disputed this logic: "Not right! Not always! I remember many times that we wanted [to get] a bill through the House even if we knew nothing [would pass] the

Senate. It might set us up for next [term]." The point here was that time might be wisely spent on accomplishing a strategic, as opposed to substantive, objective. The counsel confirmed this: "My boss [the committee chair] would certainly see that as worthwhile. In fact, I would say that it was usually the approach that he preferred."

Another former staffer, now a successful association lobbyist, believes that not all time is equally valued on Capitol Hill: "Members do distinguish between their own time and their staff's time. They may not be especially aware or worried about how much staff time is needed to get something done. The new breed of member will spend staff time pretty freely." Still another staffer-turned-lobbyist agreed with her former colleague: "Time is its own thing. Lots of time, especially the member's time, would rate as pretty expensive; though on most issues requiring staff time and maybe only some of the member's, then time wouldn't be as costly."

Perhaps the best indication of the importance of time is the frequency with which it was mentioned, almost reflexively, when interview subjects were discussing other elements of cost or a particular unrecorded activity—nineteen times in addition to those just noted. A few of these observations follow:

- The more important [the] opposition that you can expect, the more time that is needed and, perhaps, the more members that are needed to be involved.
- We were always careful not to waste the chairman's time.
- Bill drafting takes a lot of time and effort.
- Becoming involved in putting together a bill or an amendment can be very important. Time and IOUs might become involved.

Clearly, for the congressional office, the time it will take to pursue an objective is carefully computed in the cost-benefit calculus that has as its focus the member's professional objectives. Thus it is reasonable to argue that in the well-run congressional office the value of time, like the value of money, is a relative matter: One would be willing to spend more of it on goods that have significant potential for providing assets to the legislator.[q]

A moderate from the Northwest gave his view of the members' perspective: "Something that takes longer to do is tougher—it always is. . . . It has to be important enough." His observation is disarmingly simple, yet it provides an invaluable insight into the weighting process members employ when deciding whether or not to pursue a lobbyist-generated request for proactive support.

q. Members are also willing to spend more time with lobbyists with whom they have established personal relationships. See the discussion on building rapport in chapter 5.

This observation conflates the two most important time-related variables: How much time must be expended, and how much value will be returned for the outlay. A former member of the House Science and Technology Committee pulled no punches: "Time is scarce for a member. If there is nothing in it for him, he is not likely to do what you're asking. It has to promise a payout." A former House Banking Committee member was equally blunt: "It had to be good for me." [r]

## 11. Will I be asking the member to contract a debt to another member or to some other person? (Incurring IOUs)

*"Does the other member keep track of the IOUs? Some members do. That makes it more costly to go to that member."*

Members contract debts to other members in at least two ways. First, is the explicit exchange (sometimes known as logrolling): "I will vote for your bill if you will vote for my bill." And, second, is the indirect exchange in which no quid pro quo is mentioned, though at least one of the participating members (usually the lawmaker doing the favor) makes a mental note of the transaction and then seeks to redeem the note at some later point. Regardless of how it is assumed, the respondents viewed this sort of debt to be common among legislators, but they did not regard it as an especially important factor in determining their legislative positions or other lawmaking activities:

- [IOUs] are not such a big deal. They are the way the system works.
- Using up a chit with other members is not [so important] if you believe you're right and really want it.
- IOUs did not play much of a role. There were too many other things going on. It is sort of unanswerable for that reason. "You do not care about this, so vote with me." How much is that worth as an IOU? How much do you have to pay back for another vote that [your colleague] does not care about? Some IOUs are more expensive than others.

The "more expensive" IOUs usually result when a ledger-keeping colleague is involved. Payback is almost certain to be demanded:

r. It should be remembered that the thinking behind "what's in it for me?" and "what's good for me?" is not necessarily purely selfish in nature. Members are motivated, as we have seen, by such incentives as desire to be respected by their colleagues and to make good policy. Such objectives serve public policy ends as well as members' concerns for reelection and status among policy elites.

- Does the other member keep track of the IOUs? Some members do. That makes it more costly to go to that member. Other members do not care about these things.
- Members do remind each other of this.
- Becoming involved in the drafting of a bill or an amendment can be very [expensive]. Trade-offs might become involved.

The following exchange with one of the interview subjects is relevant:

*Member:* You can ask whatever you want to as long as it makes sense. But if you are expecting me to ask favors of [other members], it's not a bad idea to show me that you are sensitive to that and will understand if that is farther than I am willing to go. . . . Giving [members] a graceful way out is never a bad idea. Believe me, it is noticed.

*Author:* And I assume appreciated?

*Member:* Oh, yes!

Notwithstanding different points of view on the subject, the Capitol Hill wisdom seemed to minimize the importance of IOUs as a concern for lobbyists. For example, one interview subject thought IOUs are "way overrated." Another member considered them to be "my business; I never expected a lobbyist to raise that with me."

## Conclusion

After the schmoozing is done, relationships are in place, strategizing is complete, and the client is "on board," lobbyists are left with the task of convincing lawmakers to take action in support of their policy objectives. A midwesterner put it this way: "You must ask the member to do something. Seek a concrete result from the meeting. Don't just present a general concept. . . . What are you asking me to do?" In other words, what is the "ask"?

The ask, which is the subject of chapter 6, is what a lobbyist requests a member to do in order to further his client's agenda. In presenting his ask, the lobbyist seeks to elicit a response from the member in the form of a legislative act that will affect, directly or indirectly, a legislative objective that is important to his client.

Asks may vary widely in intent and content, but in every case the lobbyist must analyze how each importuned member will weigh her capital gain-loss prospects should she accede to the request. On this point Neustadt's commentary on the presidency is once again instructive. Although Neustadt was writing about the executive, he provides excellent advice for all those who would maximize their influence among members of

Congress, not the least of whom are lobbyists. Neustadt observes, "To ask how he [the president] can guard prospective influence is thus to raise further the question: What helps him to guard his *power stakes* in his own acts of choice?" [17] (Emphasis added.)

The best that a lobbyist can do—and some do it better than others—is to anticipate how his ask will match up with the lawmaker's perception of her power stakes. To the extent that the ask and the stakes are compatible, business may be done. To the extent that they are not—well, time to move on.

## Notes

1. Robert Pear and Robin Toner, "President Leads the Roundup for Votes to Add Drug Benefits to Medicare," *New York Times,* June 23, 2003.
2. Richard E. Neustadt, *Presidential Power* (New York: Mentor, 1964), 22.
3. Ibid.
4. R. Douglas Arnold, *The Logic of Congressional Action* (New Haven: Yale University Press), 83.
5. Ibid., 64, 63.
6. Barbara Sinclair, *Legislators, Leaders, and Lawmaking: The U.S. House of Representatives in the Postreform Era* (Baltimore: Johns Hopkins University Press, 1995), 232.
7. Lou Frey Jr., "Legislative Entrepreneurship: Different Strategies for Different Issues," in *Inside the House: Former Members Reveal How Congress Really Works,* ed. Lou Frey Jr. and Michael T. Hayes (Lanham, Md.: U.S. Association of Former Members of Congress and University Press of America, 2001), 252.
8. See Paul S. Herrnson, "The Revitalization of National Party Organizations," in *The Parties Respond: Changes in American Parties and Campaigns,* ed. L. Sandy Maisel (Boulder: Westview Press, 1994), 51.
9. Ibid., 52.
10. Roger H. Davidson and Walter J. Oleszek, *Congress and Its Members,* 11th ed. (Washington, D.C.: CQ Press, 2007), 189.
11. Sinclair, *Legislators, Leaders, and Lawmaking,* 48, 50–51.
12. Charles L. Clapp, *The Congressman: His Work as He Sees It* (Washington, D.C.: Brookings Institution Press, 1963), 207.
13. Christopher J. Deering and Steven S. Smith, *Committees in Congress,* 3d ed. (Washington, D.C.: CQ Press, 1997), 131.
14. John Kingdon, *Congressmen's Voting Decisions* (Ann Arbor: University of Michigan Press, 1989), 21.
15. William E. Leuchtenburg, *In the Shadow of FDR: From Harry Truman to Bill Clinton* (Ithaca: Cornell University Press, 1993), 148. (Leuchtenburg was quoting from an interview with Bill Moyers, November 18, 1965.)
16. Glen S. Krutz, "Issues and Institutions: 'Winnowing' in the U.S. Congress," *American Journal of Political Science* 49 (April 2005): 313–326.
17. Neustadt, *Presidential Power,* 63.

# 5 Inside the Door (and Beyond)

For lobbyists, nothing is more important to success than personal credibility. That credibility and lobbying should be so closely linked may seem almost too obvious to merit elaboration. But not to elaborate would be a mistake, especially in a book given entirely to the lobbying profession. Credibility has special importance in the lobbyist–lawmaker context because of what it is that lawmakers do: They make policy. In the case of Congress they make policy that affects more than 300 million U.S. citizens and, frequently, citizens of other nations as well. Making policy is a daunting task, to be sure, and one that lawmakers take seriously, often calling it "a truly humbling experience." Thus the subject merits its own discussion.

At the outset we should understand that credibility for a lobbyist is a trifurcated concept; it consists of components that are based on honor, reliability (as in being right), and tactical competence. Members of Congress cannot afford to waste their time with pleaders who come up short in any of these three areas. Providing good information (the subject of a full discussion later in this chapter) and a sophisticated understanding of how the system works are the hallmarks of a professional lobbyist. There can be no compromise on the first and very little on the second.

There are three primary justifications for the special status accorded to credible outside (that is, noncongressional) performers in federal lawmaking processes:

- As we have said, writing law is serious business; the stakes are high and the consequences of failure can be catastrophic—much more so than in most private transactions. Lawmakers are generally aware of these risks.
- Lawmakers need information to do their work—lots of it. They do not control sufficient resources to supply all of the facts, figures, and projections they need

to write foolproof policy. So-called neutral sources (including government agencies, think tanks, and universities) are not without their biases and self-interest; nor are they infallible.

- Lobbyists are frequently sole-source providers of key arguments and supporting data.

But lobbyists also represent vested, often economically driven, interests. Their incentive to fudge is significant. Political scientist John Wright cites E. E. Schattschneider: "Schattschneider was surely correct in observing that misrepresentation can be an important source of interest group influence." [1] Indeed, this is the central claim of Wright's book. The Wright–Schattschneider thesis is undeniable: Lobbyists do have incentives to misinform. Yet the interviews I conducted produced little evidence of this behavior. Why?

Although members frequently need to supplement the resources available to them to create policy, they are by no means impotent. They have their own legislative staff people and committee staffers, and, perhaps most important, they can always find lobbyists and other sources with a view that is different from the one they have already heard. In other words, although lawmakers' ability to go on the offensive is often wanting, their resources for defending themselves are substantial; policymaking is seldom an uncontested process. Thus the chances of an errant lobbyist getting found out are very good.

In the words of a former Blue Dog member: "Trust is where it starts and where it ends. Nothing would happen without it; not for me." Of course, lobbyists cannot afford for nothing to happen; clients do not pay for "nothings" or even "almosts." The lobbyist's job is to make things happen, even if some of those things include blocking or preventing bad (from the client's perspective) legislative action.

For all of the key Capitol Hill players—lawmakers, staffers, and lobbyists—there is strong incentive to demonstrate that they are in the know and dependable. By some standards the incentives for lobbyists are the strongest: Members and staff belong on the Hill; that is where they work. Lobbyists in a sense are interlopers; although they ply their trade in congressional offices, they do not actually work there. Thus they must constantly renew their credentials for belonging.

This chapter looks at the office meeting—the epicenter of the direct lobbying process. It is here in face-to-face conversation with members of Congress (and sometimes with staff) that lobbyists establish, and attempt to renew, their credentials as trustworthy policy players. In this relatively private setting they have an opportunity to share important information and to demonstrate that they are savvy in the ways of Congress. And it is here that they sow the seeds for victory or defeat.[a]

The first section of the chapter, "The Office Meeting," discusses important principles applicable to direct lobbying and lobbyists' on-going quest for credibility. I resist the temptation to organize the discussion chronologically—this happens first, and that happens next, and so forth. Although some patterns are obvious and common to most in-office visits, there are too many variations to render a roadmap-type approach effective. Remember, this is not a how-to manual.

Instead, I present observations—some broad, some more focused—offered by legislators and staff as they considered my overarching question: What makes for a good or bad lobbyist? From these observations—opinions, if you will—one may derive the principles for effective lobbying identified as paramount. In some cases the principles were broadly accepted among the interview subjects; in others, widely divergent views were expressed. The conflicting views create a playing field riddled with gopher holes and beset by other hazards. Recognizing these obstacles is part of what goes into being a quality lobbyist.

The next two sections, "Tactical Best Practices" and "Tactical Missteps," admittedly have something of a manualish, how-to cast to them. But they make points that were clearly important to the interview subjects. To ignore them would be to deprive the reader of insights into what the lobbied view as good or poor lobbying practices. These sections reflect the responses of the interview subjects; they are not the products of my own thinking. Again, we will see that unanimity is sometimes hard to come by.

## The Office Meeting

The office meeting—usually consisting of legislator, lobbyist, and staff—is *the* prime venue for direct lobbying.[b] This may be truer today than ever before; lobbyist-sponsored trips by members of Congress and their staff have been tightly regulated, and pricey meals on lobbyists' credit cards have all but been eliminated. Lawmakers and lobbyists can still break bread together, but now the lawmakers (or staffers) must pay for their own share of the food and drink. Needless to say, the office visit has become more important than ever before. No food—true! But no bill either.

Some interview subjects applauded the new limitations. The reason? For them the office meeting was the right setting: "I preferred the office

a. One caveat: If there is an epicenter of the epicenter, it is found in those specific acts that a lobbyist asks a member to perform in pursuit of a client's cause. I call these the "ask," which is the focus of chapter 6.

b. Executives representing the client and experts (usually selected by the client) frequently attend these meetings as well.

meeting. I liked having my staff at meetings with lobbyists. Look, I never made any bones about it; they knew the issues better than I did and were in a better position to ask the right questions and say the right things." Another former member sounded a similar note: "I always had staff with me during lobbyist meetings; I would have a committee specialist with me. I wanted them to ask questions and to hear answers without them being filtered though me."

One staffer, still serving on a congressional committee, recalled a late-evening conversation with his then boss, who expressed regret: "I think I just blew it. I may have committed to too much." The staffer assured his boss that he would " 'uncommit' him tomorrow." He did.

Other legislators had decidedly different views. Some argued that it was easier and more efficient to do business "over a cocktail and a decent meal." Another went further, perhaps literally: "I liked to meet outside of D.C.—maybe in the district. It was more relaxed, more time, better focus."

But even these legislators understood that the cocktail hour with dinner and in-district scenarios could accommodate only a fraction of the lobbyists who could claim legitimate reasons to seek an audience with them. The office meeting is and will remain the site of the quintessential lobbying presentation. During these sessions, presentation of self is unavoidable and stark. In the words of one lobbyist, office meetings provide few opportunities to "run and hide. It's you, naked and on display."

The lobbyist who fails here, fails.

## Presentation of Self: Reputation and Access

*"Is he just an advocate—my client right or wrong?—or does he put a strong emphasis on becoming a constructive contributor to the policy process?"*

No political scientist will fail to recognize the phrase "presentation of self." It comes from Richard Fenno's classic work, *Home Style: House Members in Their Districts,* which examines members' behavior as they present themselves to their constituents. Fenno begins with this description: "This book is an exploration. It is an exploration of the relationship between members of the House of Representatives and their constituents." [2]

This book about lobbyists is also an exploration, and presentation of self goes directly to its core. Of course, the "self" discussed here is not the elected official; it is the lobbyist, the person whose constituency is Congress, and what E. E. Schattschneider refers to as the "audience." [c] [3]

Fenno goes on to say: "Members of Congress go home to present themselves as a person and to win the accolade 'he's a good man' or 'she's a good woman.' . . . The ultimate response House members seek is political support. But the instrumental response they seek is *trust*." [4]

Lobbyists do not "go home to present themselves"; they go to Capitol Hill. But venue aside, the mission is similar: Like the "instrumental response" members seek, lobbyists too seek trust, whether for sage counsel or for exchange of information. That quality is no less important to them than it is to the lawmaker.

Capitol Hill is a constant swirl of entreaties, advice giving, and advice taking. Information swapping is an integral part of all of this activity. Amid the fast-paced and seemingly endless permutations that define policy options and political intrigues, the opportunities to mislead—intentionally or not—are as abundant as the temptations to do so.

David Austen-Smith and William H. Riker find that even among legislators who are debating a policy issue, complete disclosure of information is not always assured: "While agendas indeed are set under effectively pooled information, coherence—in the sense of information sharing—is not generally guaranteed." [5] In this environment, members learn quickly to identify and appreciate both the honest broker of quality information and the truly knowledgeable source.

Congressional colleagues, executive branch officials, lobbyists, and the experts whom a member learns to rely upon for good information—those she knows to be both honest and accurate—are the ones with whom she ultimately does business. This is likely to be true in any professional environment, but the exigencies of political life—constant press attention, probing questions from adversaries, pressures from interest groups, and ever-pending reelection contests—intensify the value of an established reputation for trustworthiness.

Sizing up people—figuring out how much they can be trusted and how keenly they have developed their political acumen—is a way of life among legislators and staff. The process is constant, and it is important: How an individual is perceived by policy elites affects, and is affected by, almost everything a lobbyist does, whether on Capitol Hill, in executive branch offices, or in interest group strategy sessions. An individual's presentation of self reflects his congressional IQ (CIQ)—the direct consequence of his

---

c. Schattschneider's theory was as follows: "The outcome of every conflict is determined by the extent to which the audience becomes involved in it." (*The Semisovereign People,* 2.) In our case, the audience may consist of members of the "Washington community" who have an interest in the issues at hand.

overall approach to his work, the skills he exhibits, and the sensitivities he manifests. The reputation that emerges plays a decisive role in determining who the lobbyist is among his peers and among other members of the inside-the-Beltway community. And once established, "who he is" most often is who he remains. The self he presents is not likely to vary much from issue to issue, venue to venue, or time to time.

Raymond A. Bauer, Ithiel de Sola Pool, and Lewis Anthony Dexter note that "the individuals with whom a legislator interacts in one transaction may be the same ones involved in another." [6] In the competition for legislative time, the quality of one's past professional performance emerges as a salient factor in gaining repeat access to congressional and executive offices. A former Senate counsel confirmed this point: "Sometimes we'd see people because we had to. But that was the first visit. After that you had to earn your way back in."

A New York moderate emphasized that excellence in the arts of policymaking contributed to the level of trust accorded to a lobbyist—especially when it was based on first-person experience. Reputation can make or break a lobbyist who is pursuing complex, long-term issues that require ongoing legislative alliances. The New York member put it succinctly:

> [The lobbyist] is either someone to take seriously and feel you should hear out, or he is not: Is he just an advocate—"my client right or wrong?" Or does he put a strong emphasis on becoming a constructive contributor to the policy process—a representative of bona fide interests with a legitimate point of view on legislation that is [under consideration]. . . . It's your whole body of work—your reputation.

A former staffer who served in several capacities on both sides of the Hill offered related observations:

> *Staffer:* Members will sometimes do things because they like and trust someone.
>
> *Author:* Does that mean a lobbyist or just members?
>
> *Staffer:* No, it's both. [A member] would distinguish between the client and the lobbyist. He might do something for a lobbyist even if he didn't know or care about the client.
>
> *Author:* What happened if he knew but did not like the client?
>
> *Staffer:* It depended what it was. He'd probably still help if he could.
>
> *Author:* And if it were the reverse—if he liked the client but not the lobbyist?
>
> *Staffer:* He'd probably tell them to get a new lobbyist. . . .

This is not to suggest that a positive reputation assures a favorable result every time; it certainly does not. But reputation can influence every aspect of an individual's professional performance. Beyond the opportunity to gain access—especially ongoing access—to congressional offices, it colors expectations about performance. If positive, it predisposes the people to whom a lobbyist makes his case to listen intently and to give his positions serious consideration. As one representative noted, "A lobbyist is preceded by his reputation and by that of the organization he works for." In the words of another lawmaker: "The most fundamental thing is for him to be seen as knowing his stuff. He must know what he is talking about. The more detail, the better."

Political scientist Lester Milbrath agrees but places a special emphasis on character: "My personal feeling is that a great deal of the success of any man in lobbying is dependent on the character he has got: his reputation for telling the truth and the facts as he knows them. Once you have developed a reputation, you have gone a long way toward getting unsuspicious consideration from the man you are talking to." [7]

It should be noted that reputation, as applied to lobbyists, is a somewhat obtuse term. Generally speaking, reputation connotes a widely held opinion about a person. And although opinions certainly exist in the cases of members whose work is known (or thought to be known) by colleagues, constituents, the press, and others, such may not be the case for lobbyists who work "behind the scenes" and thus may not gain a broad reputation. Nevertheless, members of Congress and their staffs do talk about lobbyists, and reputations do develop. The interviews produced significant evidence of this:

- Sure, there is a member-to-member grapevine sharing opinions about the quality of various lobbyists.
- Members do share opinions about lobbyists. Usually when members speak about a lobbyist it is to warn other members that he is not very good, maybe that he cannot be trusted.
- This sort of conversation occurred in one of the caucuses that I belonged to. . . . Members do talk about which lobbyists are good or not. You get a reputation. "This guy is not good." "I'd stay away from him."
- My staff would tell me "stay away from this guy."
- I liked my staff to see people first. They could then let me know who I should see and who was not necessary. . . . Yes, sometimes this was because they thought somebody was good. They might say "he really knows his stuff; he is worth talking to."

When a lobbyist develops a reputation, it is likely to have consequences. Among them is the degree of access to other members of Congress (other than members he has already done business with). Milbrath has it right: As much as any other trait a lobbyist may claim for himself, a reputation for trustworthy behavior is the fundamental component for establishing a working "partnership" with congressional offices. As noted, successful lobbying requires access to congressional offices; and access, if it is to matter, must be a long-term proposition; few if any legislative issues are settled in a single visit to a member's office.

Of the former members who responded to my survey, 72 percent agreed that "reputation was an important factor in deciding whether or not to meet with a lobbyist." Of these, nearly half (32 percent of the full cohort) said they strongly agreed with the statement.

A moderate Democrat from the Midwest linked reputation to professional longevity. He argued that a lobbyist who was not good would not last long in Washington: "I liked veteran lobbyists; people who have been around town a long time. They have stood the test of time. If they didn't know what they were doing, you'd hear about it. . . . They wouldn't have lasted so long." At a different point in the interview, he added: "There is always some talk about various lobbyists."

A former ranking committee member remembered his days as a freshman member of the House: "As a junior member I noticed who the more highly regarded senior members talked to. In this way I was able to learn who the respected lobbyists were."

But members do not routinely conduct a thorough background check on the lobbyists who seek their support. In fact, the interviews did not reveal much purposive activity directed toward that end. Thus, consistent with the relatively obtuse nature of its meaning, the word *reputation* as used in this book should be read with the understanding that it is often an informal construct, frequently based on the opinions of just a few people (often employees of the same congressional office). It may be the result of informal member-to-member conversations among many or just a few lawmakers at the gym or eating lunch.

Except for a very few marquee names—the lobbyist equivalents of Tiger Woods, Tom Hanks, and Oprah Winfrey—few lobbyists enjoy, or for that matter desire, celebrity status. Of the lobbyists interviewed for this book, most felt that the lower their profile, the better. An executive at one major lobbying firm went so far as to say, "Because of my position [president of a major public affairs firm], lots of people know me. Sometimes I wish I had a disguise. Believe me, I am not kidding about that; there are many times it would make my life easier." In answer to a follow-up question, he theorized: "I'm not sure why that is. Sometimes I think it just sets the bar higher; other times it might have to do with being a bit of a target."

A final point about reputation: Notoriety frequently exceeds mere recognition. One current staffer quipped, "If you have a reputation, it is usually a bad one. We never talk about the good people." He was not the only interviewee to suggest this. Where lobbyists' reputations are concerned, bad news really does travel faster than good news.

Although the perception of a given lobbyist as a trustworthy source of ideas and information, once established, is not easily altered, it is not set in stone either. Ongoing scrutiny always offers the possibility of changed perceptions. Thus each contact may be seen as a potential opportunity or risk for a lobbyist. First, he has an opportunity to succeed or fail in achieving his client's objectives (for example, to have a favored amendment supported or an objectionable provision rejected). Not surprisingly, Washington loves winners—almost as much as do prospective clients. Losers, of course, are not so highly valued.

But second, and equally important, the manner in which the lobbyist pursues a desired outcome will elevate or diminish his professional standing among members and clients. The process is unrelenting—issue to issue, office to office. Said one former member turned lobbyist: "You can win pretty; you can win ugly. When you win ugly, you lose."

A western Democrat emphasized that lobbyists are constantly subjected to the congressional microscope: "[The lobbyist] is under scrutiny, conscious or not, by members and staff. They want to know if he is likely to be a valuable ally—someone who can hold up his end of the bargain or maybe help me with my constituency or with members of Congress." The notion of the "valuable ally" may be function-dependent. That is to say, not all lobbyists do all things well. The Democrat gave as an example a lobbyist from a pharmaceutical company: "She had some pretty good ideas—she knew legislation—but she also acted like her client was God. . . . It was a real put off."

A former staffer went on at some length about what he called "the company hubris syndrome": "Working for the committee, I learned that some lobbyists really do seem to buy into 'what's good for [my company] is good for the country.' . . . These people advocated only for [their] client's position; that did not help us do our jobs. They had nothing to offer for the commonweal."

## Be a Help, not a Pain

*"Sometimes he [the lobbyist] cannot pussyfoot around; sometimes he has to ask the member to come out of her comfort zone."*

A lobbyist may have a well-earned reputation for trust. But more is needed if he is to maximize his prospects for success. If at all possible, he should be seen as offering a positive service or opportunity for the member—a person who will help the member deal with the many challenges that are likely to confront her during the legislative cycle. "The extent to which you help other people solve their problems, you can expect (within limits of course) to draw on them to help you." [8] In short, the member should see the lobbyist as an asset to her immediate legislative objectives and thus to her political career.

Spoken or unspoken, consciously or not, congressional offices are constantly weighing the potential utility of the people whom they meet and the issues with which they are confronted. One member was blunt: "What is in it for me? That is *always the test,* and don't listen to anyone who tells you different." (The emphasis was his.) Although making quid pro quo deals is rare in the corrupt sense, matching proposals to members who will benefit from pursuing them is not.

Even so, there is a difference between what a so-so lobbyist might be able to achieve and what a truly excellent lobbyist can accomplish. Not all members react the same way to lobbyists who offer them the benefit of their political counsel. Some members welcome a lobbyist who suggests, even explains, a political benefit that will accrue to them if they pursue the lobbyist's proposals. Other members abhor this practice.

A veteran Republican chief of staff thought it was "presumptuous as hell" for lobbyists to tell, even "[suggest to] us that something would work to our political advantage." He stressed: "We were smart enough to fit together the pieces. Anyone who knew [the member] knew that." He went on to lay out the "screens" his office used in deciding whether or not to accede to a lobbyist's request: "We considered legislative ideas in a practical way: Did it improve our position in committee? Did it have issue or policy value? Did it have district value? Was this someone we knew?" He did add a qualifier: "Sure, it was fine if someone noted that there was strong interest one way or the other in our district. That we appreciated."

Another member found both flattery and self-serving analyses distasteful: "Some organizations would come in telling me that their position was in the best interest of the country and that I was 'the one' who could make it happen. I did not like it when they likened themselves to the American public. Many lobbyists would do this."

Political advice aside, several members agreed with one former member of the House Democratic leadership. He was firm in the opinion that lobbyists should demonstrate an ability to "help the member solve problems." He added that part of the definition of *help* is to ask of a member only that which is possible, that which the member can do or have a reasonable prospect of doing. As noted in chapter 2, he emphasized, and reiterated throughout our conversations, "the art of the possible." Unreasonable requests or pressure to do what one cannot do makes the lobbyist an amateurish, or worse, inconsiderate irritant.

This is not to say that lobbyists should never ask a member to cast the tough vote or to take on the party leadership, in committee or on the floor. A veteran committee staffer who served in senior positions in both the House and the Senate, and who is credited with writing major legislation in the late 1990s, agreed that able lobbyists must sometimes "go in the tank" and "maybe take their clients in with them." He was adamant in this view: "The lobbyist has to represent his client. That means that sometimes he cannot pussyfoot around; sometimes he has to ask the member to come out of her comfort zone." He then added: "Because clients frequently accompany lobbyists to meetings—especially when they are constituents [of the member being visited]—the lobbyist has to make sure that the client understands what is going on—that he [the lobbyist] knows he is taking the member out of the comfort zone but thinks it is necessary in order to achieve a positive result."

The former counsel pointed to a critical link between this apparent contentious behavior and the need for a lobbyist to be respected on Capitol Hill. His thinking, which harks back to the twin matters of trust and reputation, was profound and representative of much that I learned from other interview subjects: "Your reputation is a combination of a lot of things. If they [members and staff] respect you, you can take more risks. But you have to earn your reputation; you have to be straight with them, and they have to believe that you know what you are talking about. . . . Then, you might even gain more respect by urging them to do what is uncomfortable for them."

So being a help does not necessarily equate to making things easy. Nor does "not being a pain" mean always avoiding the uncomfortable. Sometimes the easy way or the comfortable way is just not possible. But even when presenting a member with a difficult policy option, lobbyists can do much to ensure that the welcome mat remains in place. Intelligent requests supported with cogent arguments and, if applicable, good data are always in order, even if they are not necessarily pleasing to recipients.

On this point the chief of staff and the former committee counsel had decided differences about how a lobbyist should deal with problematic requests. According to the chief of staff, "Just as long as you give us an out, you're okay." In follow-up, "Just tell us you know this is difficult for us and we might not be able to help."

The former counsel favored "playing hardball": "It is not always about making them love you. It's more about making them *believe* you. If they believe you, then it's their problem if they won't do the [right thing]." [d]

## Provide Good Substantive Information

*"Members who know how to [collect information] had gravitas."*

Good information is a relative concept. Of course, it must be accurate, that is indisputable. But it must also be of value to the recipient, and not every recipient has the same informational needs. Two elements are fundamental in this context: (1) The role of information as a foundation for policy decisions, and (2) the role of information as a means of giving a member an advantage in the incessant battle for prestige and influence among her colleagues in Congress. Clearly, the two are related: The more influence a member can accrue, the more say that member can have in determining policy outcomes.

Richard Fenno understood this connection: "Most members are also interested in gaining influence within Congress and in making a contribution to good policy." [9] Even legislators who are predominantly reelection seekers or "status types" have some legislative hot buttons. Some members may have more than others, but all have at least a few.

Richard Hall adds further dimension to Fenno's link between members' interests and "contribution[s] to good policy." His insights regarding the nexus between policy interests and the amount of time, energy, and, presumably, political capital a member is willing to spend on an issue are particularly instructive. For lobbyists, they provide a useful basis for making decisions about whom to approach—especially when deciding upon the "horse" [e]—and on what arguments to make: "Members have no simple, generally applicable motivational map that they introspectively consult. Rather, members define what we refer to as goals as they make concrete behavior choices regarding particular issues. . . . Our analysis, then, must be focused on the relevance of specific issues to members' (single or several) interests." [10]

---

d. Some conjecture here: The chief of staff is paid to watch his boss's political flanks; thus he may be more attuned to looking for an out for his boss than is the counsel, who is trained to think in terms of the "right" policy option.

e. The horse is Capitol Hill–speak for the member who agrees to be the primary advocate for a lobbyist's position.

A member of his party's congressional leadership stressed the importance of in-depth knowledge as key in two regards: It was key to producing intelligent policy and key to providing the expert with influence, whether that influence was between member and member or between interest group and member. For him, understanding "ramifications" was essential. That is why he preferred speaking to individual companies or to trade associations: "I did not have much faith in the think tanks—too academic." He concluded with this observation about how important it is to select the best information sources: "Members who know how to do these things [collect information] had gravitas."

Barbara Sinclair, noting the importance of those with in-depth knowledge to Congress as an institution, provides an added dimension to the idea of gravitas: "The committee specialist who develops real substantive expertise is critical to Congress maintaining its powers in the political system." [11] Thus specialists are among the most important protectors of the congressional role in policymaking.

There is also, not surprisingly, an electoral component at work. It comports with the image of lawmakers as being risk averse. "If you feel one way and constituents another" said a six-term member currently serving in the House, "you will have to try to convince them of your position. Here, it is particularly important that you have good information in order to sell constituents and to maintain your status with them." Thus, in this member's view, good information is important not just for arguing within Congress but also for justifying one's position to constituents.

As unquenchable as is the congressional thirst for good information, the distaste for bad information is even more pronounced. Wrong information given to a legislator, even when given in good faith, does almost as much, if not as much, damage to a lobbyist's credibility as does outright lying. In either case, the lobbyist's reputation may be destroyed. Of course, there is always the possibility of an even worse scenario. "I suppose," mused a former staffer, "you could be a liar *and* incompetent; that would be worse than just being one or the other."

Providing bad information, for whatever reason, is a confidence killer. An especially colorful and relatively young congressional retiree (who insisted that our conversation take place in his favorite pub) shared this bit of congressional wisdom: "You only get one chance to embarrass a member. *A good lobbyist will never meet that quota.*" (The emphasis was his.)

This former member's observation was not unique; several of his former colleagues were just as intense (and as entertaining):[f]

f. For an interesting series of comments on this subject, see *The Ethics of Lobbying: Organized Interests, Political Power, and the Common Good* (Washington, D.C.: Woodstock Theological Center, Georgetown University Press, 2002), 3–4.

- It's like a business deal—put someone into a bad deal once and they'll never come back to you again.
- Never lead a legislator down a blind alley. That puts you on his shit list forever.
- Get a member fucked over one time. Even if you had no intention of having that happen—and you might as well lose his number—you're history.
- All you have in this town is your word. . . . The legislative process often moves very quickly; sometimes there just isn't time to check out information.

A Blue Dog Democrat remembered the time when a major communications company was "trying to misrepresent an issue. That was the last time I would have anything to do with them. For me, their reputation was shot. I didn't go out of my way to tell people about it, but neither did I go out of my way to keep it a secret."

## Pass Along Useful Political Intelligence

*"Who is against this?"*

Not all information has to do with substance. Some respondents were as concerned about the sources and intensity of potential opposition as they were about the content of the arguments. They were interested in learning from where opponents might emerge—committee leaders, other committee members, party leadership, special-interest caucuses, constituents, or organized interests—and they wanted to know if opposition would be "real" or token, scattered or well organized.

Former representative Lee Hamilton, D-Ind., provided some insight: "One of the most important and time-consuming aspects of the legislative process is conversation: the scores, even hundreds of one-on-one talks that a skillful member will have with colleagues to make the case for a particular bill, [and] to learn what arguments opponents will use to try to block it." [12]

As we have seen, there was a wide range of opinions on this matter—nothing close to the virtual unanimity on the necessity of good substantive information. But the clear consensus was that good political information is valued when offered:

- The source and the level of opposition acts across all categories: "Who is against this?" The more (in terms of quantity), and more important the opposition that is anticipated, the more time that is needed and, perhaps, the more members that are needed to be involved.

- The intensity of arguments was always important. The lobbyist should have been able to [forewarn you] about this.
- Well, just generally, I had some very good [lobbyist] friends that I would play golf with. They were very astute politically. We'd talk about matters, and they usually had some good ideas about who would be for it and who would be a problem.
- I would say, "Let me know of any political concerns about your position—who is supporting, who is opposing."
- I would always ask, "Where is the chairman on this?"
- Good lobbyists can evaluate what is going on politically . . . within their area of expertise.

Of course, there were dissenters. Some members thought lobbyists should stick to substance and leave political assessments to members and staff:

- I was a better person to sort this out.
- I did not need much political information; I wanted the issue [facts] *clearly* laid out.

One interview produced a hybrid response: "I certainly welcomed all political intelligence that they had. But I drew the line at suggesting what I should do about it. I did not shut them off; I just did not pay attention to what they had to say about that." In answer to the question, "Did you mind that?" he answered, "No, I didn't. I just listened politely and then went on to another subject."

There was another hybrid response. This one had less to do with identifying potential sources of agreement or disagreement and more to do with recognizing lobbyists as political information resources: "Lobbyists would tell you who are the effective members and the ones that could help you or give you a problem [on your issue]."

The bar for providing political information to congressional offices was set considerably below the bar for substantive information: "Unless someone really wanted to stir up trouble, I couldn't see any reason to lie about such things." Another person likened political intelligence to military intelligence: "Unless it came from someone I knew well and respected, it was not actionable intelligence as far as I was concerned—just some more information to have in the back of my mind."

## Be Forthcoming

*"Misleading a lawmaker is a lifetime disqualifier."*

This section may seem to be a repeat of the discussion on good substantive information; it is not, although the subjects are closely related. This discussion looks at the interview subjects' opinions on how proactive a lobbyist should be in divulging the bad with the good. It addresses the question: Does failure to disclose negative arguments or facts breach the ethics of the lobbyist–member exchange?

Good information, in congressional terms, presupposes all relevant information—or at least as much as the lobbyist has at his command. Michael Watkins, Mickey Edwards, and Usha Thakrar quote an unidentified government relations professional: "Washington really is a small town. . . . If you present your side of the story with any inaccuracies, with information that will not stand the test of the light of day, you may win the battle, but ultimately you will lose the war." [13]

That much is well settled. However, some of the interviews cast doubt on how likely it is that a lobbyist could even win the battle if he presented incomplete or, worse, inaccurate information to a congressional office. What is less well settled is what constitutes a complete definition of good information, and what is the lobbyist's obligation to supply the other side without prompting by a lawmaker or staff person? On these points there was a want of unanimity as to the extent of a lobbyist's obligation to disclose all that he knows to be, or suspects to be, relevant to his "ask." Interview responses on this subject ranged from a strong preference for full and voluntary disclosure of all relevant facts and arguments, to "only if I ask for it," to no expectation at all for complete disclosure—though this last view was rare.

The predominant view was reflected in this remark presented by a Republican from the East: "[Lobbyists should be] up front about what the opposition is going to say." He refined this statement to include "what they [the opposition] can say *legitimately.*" (Emphasis added.) In other words, congressional offices need to know what might lurk around the corner—what convincing arguments they might have to counter as the policy debate moves forward. This member noted that he was most impressed when a lobbyist volunteered that "this might be a problem area." He appreciated being put on notice and saw this intelligence as providing a "double flag": There would likely be opposition, and that opposition would be based on a viable set of facts and arguments.

Other observations about the need for full and forthright disclosure either spell out a direct connection between up-front disclosure and trust, or they strongly suggest such a nexus:

- It is very important that a lobbyist be able to tell the bad with the good.
- A relationship of trust is absolutely key. And this is built on [providing] good information including the good with the bad.
- Trust is everything. . . . This also means that a lobbyist must tell you *all* of the facts—the ones he likes and the ones he doesn't. *Don't ever bullshit me!*
- The good lobbyist will alert you to the other side without you ever having to ask him [to do that].

Between the members who expect full and voluntary disclosure and those who expect and accept one-sided presentations are the "only if I ask for it" members:

- I expected that [full disclosure] only when I asked for it.
- I would follow up by asking if there was anything that I should know [about] the other side of the matter.
- Volunteer [information] or not, I routinely asked for the opposition's view. And to me, it was no answer that they didn't know. . . . Even if they did not actually know, they should have thought about this.

One member claimed not to have expected such information under any circumstances: "If someone was paying his lobbyist to represent him, he certainly did not want the lobbyist to compromise his position. I could see that some lobbyists would think that that was not his job to do." But, he added: "That does not mean that I would countenance misleading information that someone gave me intentionally. That would have been way out of bounds."

Other members confirmed that they did not rely on lobbyists to provide all relevant information. A normally soft-spoken, gentlemanly Republican bellowed: "That was my job! It was up to me to assure that I was in command of all the facts I needed. I told staff to find people who would advocate from the other side. We did this all the time." [g] He further explained

g. Kay Lehman Schlozman and John T. Tierney, in *Organized Interests and American Democracy* (New York: Harper and Row, 1986, 165), made the point that members, through their power to provide or deny access, can influence the extent to which they receive balanced information: "There is nothing automatic about the representation of all possible political points of view . . . access and influence are not fully separable. Reasonable arguments can ordinarily be made on more than one side of a political issue. A policymaker who hears from only one side—or who hears much more from one side than the other—is likely to be persuaded by the arguments and information to which he is exposed. Hence, if access is unequal, it is not surprising if it were to have consequences for influence."

that he did not think he could "rely on someone to present the other side's side of things and do it well."

This member also made an important aside: He recognized that there is a "tendency in some offices to seek out sources of information based on the probability that they will receive reinforcement for the position(s) that they favor." Bill Tate, an experienced administrative assistant, remarked that all lawmakers need to work hard to avoid hearing only what they want to hear about issues that matter to them:

> You have to be selective in your choices of sources. . . . You have to be more aware of your own biases in making that selection so you are not getting only one side. That is very hard. If you agree with one position, you have to seek out the opposition and consciously seek to get the other side. I'll ask people who come in, "Why is there so much opposition to what you are saying?" If they are smart, they'll give a true answer and say, "You ought to talk to so and so." [14]

From these observations it is difficult to understand how a lobbyist can go wrong by offering all relevant information, favorable and unfavorable, to the people he is lobbying. The effort to provide all information will add value to his reputation and to the quality of his presentation. It will also eliminate the possibility of leading the member down a blind alley. Thus on both sides—the lobbyist's and the lawmaker's—good information should be understood as a practical tool. Its value may perhaps be measured by its contribution to good policymaking. If the receiving member does not want full disclosure, he has the option of saying, "You needn't bother; I'll take care of that." Odds are this will be a rare response.

## Function as an Adjunct Staffer

*"Lobbyists are now really adjuncts to the process."*

The hail-fellow-well-met lobbyist is becoming an endangered species in Washington. In fact, he may already be extinct. A person may be a hail-fellow, but he must also know his stuff; only in that way will he be "well met." [h] According to the interview subjects, a lobbyist must have a working knowledge of the issues he brings to members' attention: "the more the better." Several members placed particularly strong emphasis on a

h. A retired staffer remembered the time when a major professional association would make the rounds of congressional office buildings during the December holiday season. "They came right down the halls with forklifts full of liquor and stopped at virtually every office." The ex-staffer remembered that the forklifts were operated by building custodians.

lobbyist's ability to field questions and otherwise to "hold his own on the substance of his issue":

- Good lobbyists have subject expertise.
- Be able to answer questions. Be knowledgeable. Know your stuff.
- If I asked a question of a lobbyist on an issue that he was representing, and he could not answer. That was a real sign of weakness.
- I liked experts—people whose reputations preceded them.
- They had to be knowledgeable and honest.
- You give them a situation and they could respond, "here is my solution."

These comments may seem to conflict with the commonly held view of lobbyists as people with congressional knowledge but no extensive knowledge of issues—and to a limited degree they do. The interview subjects varied on the level of expertise they expected lobbyists to have, but all agreed to the "hold his own" standard. The lobbyist should, at a minimum, have knowledge akin to that of a well-informed layman.

Further, if a lobbyist expects to receive questions that go beyond his level of knowledge, he must ask to bring his experts along. The source of the information—lobbyist or accompanying experts—will not matter as long as the information is accurate and in a readily digestible form. (See the discussion later in this chapter in the section called "Select the Entourage.")

Charles E. Lindblom and Edward J. Woodhouse argue, "There is ample evidence that communications from interest groups often do serve an enlightenment function." [15] They credit Jeffrey Berry for the following observation:

> One reason lobbyists tend to specialize and work with particular committees and their staffs is that "in time and with regular contact, lobbyists have the opportunity to prove that their information is reliable. . . . No tactic is considered more effective by lobbyists than personally presenting their case to a member of Congress in a private meeting. [It is] an opportunity to press the case home and make him or her truly understand the virtue of the group's position. Washington representatives know that being seen as a good source of information is the entree back into office." [16]

Political scientist David Truman agrees. He argues that for many lobby groups it is the store of good information and the ability to convey it in a useful way that provides the most important, and perhaps most honorable, source of access to policymakers. As Truman observes, "Any politician, whether legislator, administrator or judge . . . is obliged to make decisions that are guided in part by relevant information that is available to him." Poor information resulting in bad policy decisions "may be reflected in a diminution of 'reputation.' "[17 i]

Truman has an especially high regard for the type and quality of information provided by industry associations. He argues that lobbyists for these organizations are able to provide "specialized information about industry conditions" and that even those who are generally suspicious of lobbyists agree that such information has legitimate value in congressional deliberations: "Those who are preoccupied with moral judgments of group politics . . . normally treat the supplying of such information as a 'legitimate group activity.' "[18] Truman notes that this kind of information alone, or in combination with good political information, may well convince a "leading legislator" to make himself accessible to particular interest groups—if only to learn what the opposition is planning to say on an issue.

Several interview subjects pointed to trade associations as sources for dependable information. The staff in one Senate office contrasted the associations' overall performance with that of some smaller organizations: "Trade group lobbyists tend to be very professional. They know the rules and toe the mark. Some smaller [organization] lobbyists are not as good; they make mistakes."

A former Senate staffer who served as both a committee counsel and as a chief of staff to a senior Republican presented an interesting theory that may explain why well-informed professionals have replaced the "good ol' boy" lobbyist. Technology-driven changes in the congressional work environment have shortened response times in many instances. What in the past may have been work for another day is now the subject of required and immediate attention. Members need answers, and often they need them quickly. There just may not be time for a lobbyist to call upon his corporate specialists. A staff ally may be pressed to respond to his boss or to another member's office: "I need to know now if you'll take this language. If you can't tell me, I'll use my own judgment or I'll talk to somebody else."

Knowledgeable lobbyists shorten turnaround times and facilitate a member's ability to work out compromises. And compromise is what legislation is all about. According to the former counsel:

> The new thing in Congress is outsourcing. That's because things happen faster now than ever before. We used to get information off of a ticker

---

i. Congressional veterans, scholars, and others who have examined decision making in Congress have long recognized the dearth of good information available to congressional offices. A 1970 report by the New York City bar argued: "In a recent survey of problems of Congressmen the one most frequently mentioned (cited by 62 percent of all members interviewed) was the complexity of decision-making and particularly the lack of information on which to make decisions. All observers of Congress agree that members need better information and improved analytical tools and methods." (James C. Kirby Jr., *Congress and the Public Trust* [New York: Atheneum, 1970].)

> or maybe from a network bulletin. Now it's instantaneous information all the time. Plus, every group has its watchdogs and its instant [contact system].[j] So now a lot of what we used to do ourselves has to be outsourced to lobbyists. This provides more demands for lobbyists. They can do more, but they need to do it quickly.

Another interview subject had this to say about providing members with documentation:

> But this [accepting an outsourced assignment] also means that you have to know how to do things. . . . You cannot be too aggressive in pursuing your own ends. These documents must be honestly prepared. The [member's] office will be interested in both sides. . . . The smart lobbyist will not overreach and must be honest and not be too one-sided in what he prepares for the office. . . . Lobbyists are now really adjuncts to the process.

The words *outsourcing* and *adjuncts* capture a point of view that explains much about the lobbyist–legislator relationship in the twenty-first century. It is often more than a simple plea-and-response proposition. Working at its best the relationship facilitates a meshing of the public interest with legitimate private interests; it assumes compromise and—if it is to work well—requires mutual trust that can be forged only with time and consistent displays of good faith on both sides.

Examined closely, the observations made by the former Senate committee counsel portray a Congress that has little choice in managing its workload other than to deputize those who "know how to do things" and are willing to compromise in "pursuing [their] own interests." One is reminded of the Brownlow Commission, established by President Franklin D. Roosevelt in the late 1930s to access the policymaking and political resources available to the president.[k] In similar fashion, the yearly workload confronting Congress may be outstripping the ability of legislators' to stay on top of their constitutionally assigned tasks. The proliferation of federal programs (with the consequent need for oversight), globalization, international dislocations, a decaying infrastructure, the graying of America, a poorly funded Social Security system, and soaring health care costs may be demanding more than an understaffed, time-starved, and expertise-short Congress can cope with on its own. Another "Brownlow Commission,"

j. He was alluding to automated systems that contact members of a group about events in Washington and then mobilize them for immediate grassroots communications to Congress.

k. The commission's report, issued in 1937, famously declared, "The President needs help." It stated, "The president's administrative equipment is far less developed than his responsibilities." The report is credited with leading to the creation of the Executive Office of the President. (From Richard W. Waterman, *The Changing American Presidency* [Cincinnati: Atomicdog, 2003], 13.)

one directed to Congress, could be expected to find that Congress needs help.

The following comments indicate the extent to which lobbyists are consulted for information and other forms of support that may not be available from congressional sources:

- The exchange of ideas and information is the currency of legislation. This means more than just between congressional offices. Sometimes it is very helpful to go to the outside, to people you've learned to trust.
- More and more writing and passing [of] legislation is dependent on getting good information. You can connect two people who are often worlds apart but who have interests and information that each can use. Together they can help you to make things happen.
- Members seek to gather information about a bill or an amendment: "I would like to know more about this." That's where lobbyists can play an important role.
- I can't get it all done with just my staff.

Of course, the idea of outsourcing to vested interests is not without concern. One former Ways and Means Committee member, now a prominent attorney, revealed his lawyer-like approach to this problem. To ensure the veracity of the arguments and information he was being asked to accept, he "played devil's advocate" to see how well lobbyists could defend their position. He explained that the exercise did more than elicit facts he needed to know; it also "gave me a great insight into the lobbyist and his client." The suggestion here was that if the lobbyist passed the test he was pretty much assured access for the matter at hand and on matters that would arise in the future. He would thus be positioned to function as an adjunct to the member's staff.

A practicing lobbyist who had had a strong relationship with his former boss in the Senate remembered how demanding the senator could be: "No way you went into him [as a staff person] unprepared. He was all over you with questions, and you had better be able to answer. Now, I always go in with our tax people."

Several respondents proved to be equally demanding. This was the case with a hard-nosed Washington lawyer who had served for more than a decade in Congress. He did not want to "waste time with generalities." He wanted expert and detailed information:

> If they expected me to run with something . . . I wanted experts. I would call a lobbyist to ask about the consequences if x or y happened. . . . I needed well-informed people who could do more than just present an argument. They had to do more than just say words; they had to know

> what they were talking about and then be able to make me understand it. [Then, with a chuckle] That part wasn't always so easy.

And, finally, a former representative, now lobbying on Capitol Hill, may have been self-serving, but several interview subjects agreed with him: "The big difference in lobbying today is that the lobbyists are more competent—better on the issues and better on legislative strategy and legislative culture. They have to be."

## Provide Legislative Subsidies

*"Subsidization . . . is very important. Talking points, legislative language, even floor statements or speech inserts can really help a member."*

It is a given that the information lobbyists supply to congressional offices must be accurate. But almost as important are the quantity and format of the information. Although outsourcing has become a common practice, it is by no means universally sought or appreciated by congressional offices. Skilled lobbyists will take the time to size up the office they are lobbying and then cut their product to suit the customer. Some offices welcome a complete, prepackaged kit with all relevant materials included: legislative language, statements to be delivered on the floor of the House or Senate, technical information, and talking points for press interviews. Others will consider all these offerings to be too much, perhaps a bit officious, and would prefer to produce their own materials. Of the survey respondents, 84 percent agreed with this statement: "I appreciated it when lobbyists provided me with support documents—amendment drafts, talking points, etc." One-third of the full cohort responded that they strongly agreed.

A senior midwestern member advised: "On some issues a member may be an expert and deeply involved in the relevant details, but that is not usually the case." He went on to say that when a member is not an expert, or when an issue is of marginal or little interest to the office, lobbyists must be certain that the materials they supply are "simple, accurate, and easily digestible by me [the member] and staff." If the bar for understanding the material is set too high, the office may disregard the matter altogether: "It just is not worth the time or effort needed to get our arms around it all." Sustained efforts by a lobbyist to interest the member by sending in reams of unsolicited materials will likely result in a backlash.

If an office does have an interest in a matter, the lobbyist's job is quite different. In these instances the lawmaker may function like James L. Payne's "program type" legislator discussed in chapter 2; there is a good chance that she will be interested in as much detail as can be provided. Both the need for good information and for adequate resources to produce and screen that information will be triggered. Thus the lobbyist, often working closely with the member's staff, will be well positioned to provide the necessary materials and adequate assurances of accuracy. According to one legislative director, "It's sort of counterintuitive. The more we knew, the more we appreciated the material. It's like we knew enough to understand the value of what we [had been given]."

Political scientists now use the term *subsidy* to describe this sort of assistance to congressional offices—and it fits nicely. Of course, lobbyists are more than happy to be subsidizers: "I know people think it's because we can get *our* points across, maybe even rig some of the information. Sure, it's good for us, but it is also pressure [on us]. One screwup and no one will believe it was unintended." A legislative assistant thought most lobbyists were too smart to abuse their opportunities to act as adjunct staff: "No one I worked with was that stupid."

With only rare exceptions interview subjects said they were comfortable with the integrity and competence of outsourced materials. In fact, none recalled an incident in which their trust resulted in embarrassment or disappointment:

- Subsidization, as you call it, is very important. Talking points, legislative language, even floor statements or speech inserts can really help a member—obviously that helps the lobbyist.
- Lobbyists can help draft legislation, can prepare you for debate, can educate you.
- I had many interests, so staff needed to be augmented with lobbyist input. I asked for many materials from them [lobbyists].
- You never have enough time or staff. A good lobbyist can augment your staff—assuming your staff has done a good job.
- You calculate your chance of success, and having good information is an important part of that. Legislation professionally prepared with good support [material is useful]. . . . A professional lobbyist can help supply some of this and increases your chance of success.
- [Lobbyists] understand that they are not being issued a blank check. . . . The information must be accurate and to the point.

The last speaker emphasized that he "would have staff look at the package. . . . They [staff] were always responsible for assuring that what got to me was right." A legislative director to a Democratic senator reinforced this point: "We screen everything. If it goes through and is bad stuff it is on my head."

A legislator known for his entrepreneurial style noted his appreciation for lobbyist-provided technical materials. He made a point of saying that he had "relied heavily on lobbyists" for these sorts of materials. "I had to." He then added: "Lobbyists are generally important because they are able to preprocess so much technical input and data. You say, 'OK, but there is no way I could explain that.' So, sometimes while sitting in my office they would write up a clear, easy-to-understand explanation that I could use in committee. . . . Things are becoming so technically oriented that this sort of help is almost a necessity."

The "blank check" comment above was not directed at integrity alone. Lobbyists must know how much outsourced staffing is too much. Written material, though potentially helpful, can be laborious to wade through. Loose-leaf binders chock full of reports, analyses, and complex datasets are not consistent with congressional work styles. One of the enduring axioms on the Hill is, "If you can't give it to me on one page, don't give it to me at all." Interview subjects confirmed that this sentiment lives on:

- Brevity regarding written materials is important.
- Don't leave too much reading—it absorbs too much time.
- Always leave behind the one-pager.

With the need for increased outsourcing, it is not surprising that several respondents spontaneously linked subsidies to the revolving door. A chief of staff to a senator emphasized that those who have swung through the door understand "what has to be done and *how* it needs to be done." He linked skill in preparing helpful subsidies to eventual lobbying success: "It did two things for [the lobbyists]; it convinced us to become involved and helped us to help them." He then added a comment that pulled together notions of utility, professionalism, and reputation: "Anything that makes it easier to do makes it more likely that you will do it. But it is more than that—it is a sign that the lobbyist knows his stuff—especially if the work is well done. It affects his credibility with us and the office's confidence in him. All of that is important."

Par for the congressional course, there were dissenters. Several members noted their displeasure with excessive input from lobbyists; they considered it to be a trespass on their prerogatives as members. One legislator considered the "whole [subsidy] business" to be "intrusive and presumptuous." In a variation on that theme, another legislator revealed that he did not "like having lobbyists visit me . . . with strong preconceived ideas about what my position should be on a given issue. I once threw a lobbyist out of my office for this."

## Tactical Best Practices

Although few formal rules exist for lobbyists, some things almost always make a meeting go better and can enhance a lobbyist's reputation among the offices with which he does business. Conversely, there are things that are almost universally noticed and frowned upon. This section and the next look at these behaviors. I make no claim that what is offered here constitutes an exhaustive review of qualifying behaviors. The matters discussed are those that two or more interview subjects identified without prompting and were endorsed by subsequent interviewees when prompted for a response (but not for a specific point of view).

### Build Credibility Through Networks

*"There are policy wonks for every issue. . . . It's good to get to know them; they carry weight with some offices."*

Not all lobbying is focused on members of Congress, legislative staff, or other public officials. There is often a "policy subsystem," or "issue network," that is deeply interested in a legislative issue, especially the more visible and more "important" of these. Subsystems are informal groups of people who have a stake in the legislation at hand. The stake may be purely intellectual, bred of a policy conviction, or the result of a material interest. These systems are difficult to characterize because they have no official status, no membership criteria, and most often do not meet as a body. In the truest sense, one cannot join an issue network. They are more of a conceptual construct than a tangible entity; they are not really groups.

In past decades they were frequently known as "iron triangles": triangles because they were composed of three sets of operators—legislators and staff, executive personnel, and lobbyists with a stake in the subject matter of the legislation—and "iron" because outsiders were not welcome to participate in their deliberations. What gave the iron its impregnable quality were the shared interests and policy views of those who represented each corner of the triangle. Although differences about details may have existed, there were few arguments about fundamental policy prescriptions.

Today the iron triangle is a relatively rare legislative creature—gone the way of "King Caucus" and the committee fiefdoms that were controlled by senior, sometimes doddering, chairs. Rules requiring transparency of deliberative processes and the rise of aggressive public interest groups have done much to soften the iron. The triangles are now more porous; their work is heavily influenced by open, reasonably diverse subsystems. Roger

Davidson and Walter Oleszek define these as "fluid issue networks, in which diverse participants and groups influence decision making . . . within and among policy domains." [19] James Thurber describes them as "decentralized power structures with close informal communications among their participants." He goes into further detail: "Participants are primarily representatives of interest groups, members and staff of congressional committees and subcommittees, bureau and agency personnel in the executive branch, and other policy specialists from universities, state and local government, and the media. . . . Functional specialists, or people with expertise and technical competence in an issue or program dominate the subsystem." [20]

In short, issue networks, or subsystems, make up a who's who of stakeholders for particular policy domains. The participants come and go as issues rise to the top of the congressional agenda and, with or without definitive resolution, sink out of sight to be replaced by a different issue or series of issues.

In chapter 2, a Republican from the East Coast, speaking in the third person about his criteria for evaluating lobbyists' positions, alluded to the importance of one's standing among "members" of the relevant issue network: "A proposal must . . . redound to his [the legislator's] credit and help to enhance his reputation in Congress. Also, it should enhance his reputation in the broader community of experts in the field."

To this member's way of thinking there is an important link between a lawmaker's professional reputation among policy elites and her opportunities for legislative effectiveness. The same may be said for lobbyists; here the link may be of still greater importance. Acceptance among policy elites gives a lobbyist the credibility necessary to be taken seriously by the legislators he seeks to influence—a sort of Good Housekeeping seal of approval.

This observation is in line with Schattschneider's expansion of the scope of conflict theory about resolving political debates. Schattschneider argued, "To understand any conflict it is necessary therefore to keep constantly in mind the relation between the combatants and the audience because the audience is likely to determine the outcome. . . . This is the basic pattern of all politics." [21]

A midwesterner attributed his awareness of issue networks to a "natural selection process" that frequently brought "me in touch with the lobbyists and other interested parties" who focused on his areas of legislative responsibility: "You see a lot of some lobbyists and other people because of what they do and what you do. This is a sort of natural selection process that results from committee assignments and expertise, as well as from people's interests."

So issue networks may serve two functions for lobbyists: They may help the lobbyist establish an aura of substantive credibility. A lobbyist, formerly a legislative director, admitted, "I like to rub elbows with these people. Just being seen at conferences or presentations helps get past the glad-handing image. They know that I am serious about [these issues]."

A senior Senate staffer discussed the second function. His comments were a bit disjointed, but the thrust is clear: "I ask people that I know really know the subject area. If they agree with a lobbyist's position, that is a big help [to the lobbyist]. . . . Smart people will know that there are policy wonks for every issue. . . . It's good to get to know them; they carry weight with some offices." In other words, smart lobbyists will make an effort to persuade "the audience."

## Select the Entourage

*"Keep It Simple, Stupid."*

What may at first seem to be an impressive visiting team can rapidly degenerate into an incoherent and unfocused minimob if a meeting is not properly ordered. Providing members with good information in a well-organized manner becomes more difficult in direct proportion to the number of people attending a meeting. (Remember, from chapter 1, that Pete Stark was obviously annoyed by the number of people Stuart Eizenstat brought with him to their meeting.) A team, if well ordered, need not encumber senior executives or technical experts; rather, it assures them that their information will be heard and have the best chance of being understood in proper context. But the challenge in doing this is suggested by the words "if well ordered." Too much rehearsing can have a chilling effect on presentations; it can also cast doubt on the quality of information being conveyed. Although only a small number of respondents unprompted (8 percent) identified "too much choreography" as a problem, many agreed that some presentations seemed to be overrehearsed.

The challenge is to maintain an orderly flow from one participant to the next while avoiding the appearance of rote presentations. A spontaneous conversation has undeniable appeal to legislative people. It accomplishes a number of objectives. According to interview subjects:

- I could get to know the person and feel comfortable if he just talked to me.
- "Spontaneous" is another way of saying "being open." I think it added to the credibility of the presentation.

- If you felt that you were having a conversation . . . you were more relaxed. . . . It was easier to ask questions at any point; I didn't feel that I had to let him finish his point first.

In a business in which credibility is *the* prized attribute, the ability to put the listener at ease and, at the same time, instill confidence that what she is hearing is right, cannot be underestimated. A lobbyist who knows what his objectives are, is in command of his arguments, and has reasonable facility with the relevant facts is best able to engage in such a conversation. As one interview subject said, "Just talk to me. I always felt, 'just talk to me.' . . . Do not present. . . . No scripts."

Members of Congress expect that lobbyists have expertise on congressional procedures and work habits. They also expect, at a minimum, that lobbyists will have a conversational knowledge of the client's case: "If I ask a basic question, I don't expect them to act like they have a thumb in their ear." But lack of personal expertise—especially if the topic is complex—is easily forgiven if the lobbyist thinks to bring a bona fide authority to the meeting. One respondent remembered with pride: "I met with four Nobel laureates on [that issue]. They convinced me, and so I was the first one in our party to recognize and deal with the problem."

A lobbyist, highly regarded in Washington circles, noted that "Part of being an effective lobbyist is to select your entourage wisely, with an eye toward their ability to deal with the congressional environment." Although this approach makes sense, it is easier said than done, and overcoaching is the all too frequent result: "It was clear they had this poor guy muzzled. . . . What good was it to us if they wouldn't let the expert be an expert?" This former committee staffer then made a profound observation on this subject: "All this [overrehearsal] does is to make us certain there is something they don't want us to know."

A former House committee counsel attributed some of the overcoaching to a "litigator's mentality." "Sometimes the lawyers got involved. They thought they were going to trial. . . . All it ever did was to piss us off." Another counsel, this one from the Senate side of the Hill, expressed a similar sentiment: "If you are not going to let your expert speak freely, then don't bring him at all. We'll psych that out in a nanosecond."

Of course, there are other risks that come with bringing in an expert. One of those is an overzealous witness. A former committee counsel-turned-lobbyist remembered a toxicologist he brought in to meet with congressional staff. The meeting was in preparation for a regulatory oversight hearing: "He would not shut up. He gave away the farm, the farmhouse, the tractor, the kids—*everything!* . . . When we got into the taxi, he asked how he had done. I said, 'Great! Just great!' As far as I know, he has never been to Washington since."

A veteran lobbyist understood the need for bringing in experts—including company executives who certainly qualify as experts in their company's business.[1] But he was not without trepidation; many executives and specialists are uncomfortable speaking with public officials, especially well-known public officials. It is not what they normally do for a living. Said this lobbyist: "No doubt they can add to [the meeting], but not if there are too many of them. . . . I want to control what goes on—certainly for our part of the meeting. Every time you bring someone else along, you run the risk of losing control. My rule is *one* other person. No more!"

Some wisdom from the gridiron: Football coaches, charged with getting eleven players to execute precise assignments at precise times, are well advised to adhere to the familiar KISS principle—"Keep It Simple, Stupid." This is not to suggest that members of Congress (or football players) are unintelligent or that they are incapable of grasping new and complex concepts. But lawmakers attempting to write legislation that affects a client's industry may have only a rudimentary knowledge of the issues that need to be addressed. Further, members are subject to information overload and are concerned about being diverted from what should be their primary legislative focus. For them, the simplest, least arcane descriptions and explanations are the most effective.

In these circumstances it is not surprising that members will eventually lose interest and focus; so KISS seems a reasonable strategy. Most interview subjects who addressed this issue agreed with the lobbyist quoted above—only one person other than the lobbyist: "Quantity does not count; give us quality and clarity."

Perhaps the best advice for lobbyists contemplating the team approach was offered by the former chief of staff, also quoted above: "If you think you need to bring in a few people, check with staff on that. It is going to be different by member and probably issue by issue. . . . There is such a thing as overkill and that can clutter the meeting. It might be impressive clutter, but it is still clutter."

A former member from the Midwest agreed:

> Too many people at a meeting is not good—too much going on. If you are going to do this, then your lobbyist should start off by laying out who is going to speak and what part of the issue they are going to cover. Frankly, though, it usually is not helpful to have a lot of people. Most people in Congress are not expert enough on these matters to absorb everything [that's said]. It's generally a waste, even annoying.

---

1. One former member confided that he especially liked meeting company executives: "I liked when a lobbyist brought in a top executive—good for fundraising and general contact building. . . . I liked to meet the heavyweights."

Another former member added this consideration: "The more people, the more time." And, as we have said, time is one of the most valuable resources a member has. It is not given away lightly.

## Arrange a Premeeting

*"It is always a good idea to meet with staff before you see the member."*

Some members strongly prefer that lobbyists meet with their staff prior to a face-to-face meeting between lobbyist and member. In fact, many insist on it. (See chapter 2 for discussions of staff functions.) Of the survey respondents, 84 percent agreed with this statement: "I preferred lobbyists to conduct as much business as possible with staff." One-third of the respondents said they strongly agreed with the statement.[m]

- I always wanted them to meet with staff first.
- Unless I knew the group well, I rarely saw someone that had not seen the staff first.
- Staff could meet with them first and then decide if I should see them.

The staff meeting, or "premeeting," serves a variety of functions for both parties. Staff frequently uses the opportunity as a screen to determine if a session with the boss would be productive. It also serves as a scouting opportunity that allows staff to size up members of a group and to gain an understanding of their issue. Further, it helps staff prepare the lobbyist by letting him know what sorts of things the member will be interested in learning about, thus ensuring the best possible answers to the legislator's questions.

- The goal was to make the meeting [with the legislator] worthwhile and as informative as possible.
- It is an important tool for planning the upcoming meeting so that everyone gets the most out of it.

The premeeting may resolve the issue at hand and render a time-consuming session with the legislator unnecessary: "Sometimes that is all they [the lobbyists] needed; though some of them still wanted their fifteen minutes with [the boss]—sort of like a battle ribbon to show off to the client."

---

m. The wording of the question here is not as precise as it might have been, and thus the responses may not be identical to what I would have received had I examined specifically for preferences regarding premeetings. With that said, and given the interview content, I am confident that the responses to the question as asked are very similar to what would have been produced had the question been more specifically directed.

Lobbyists realize similar benefits in premeetings. A lobbyist who now ranks as one of the best known and most highly regarded in Washington emphasized that a premeeting with staff is "very useful . . . for intelligence gathering":

> It is always a good idea to meet with staff before you see the member. I do not pretend that I am there to convince them of my position or to ask their sign off on what I am going to ask from the member. I am straightforward; I tell them that I am there because I want to know what their boss will expect from me and how he likes to deal with these meetings. Nothing subtle about it.

In answer to a follow-up question, this lobbyist explained: "Certainly if they want to get further into the issue I am prepared to do that. . . . But I would resist any effort to talk me out of having a meeting with their member. . . . That doesn't happen very much, but it does happen." [n]

The lobbyist laid out a number of informational items that he commonly gleans from sessions with staff. What follows does not reflect an effort on his part to be exhaustive; his thoughts were more by way of examples and are not presented here as exact quotations:

- What sorts of arguments does she like to hear about?
- What kinds of information does she expect? Does she like to learn what other members are thinking? How about a briefing on where various interest groups are on the issue? Does she expect to hear something about how our position might affect her district?
- How much detail does she like? Is she into technical data? Is she a so-called generalist?
- Does she like visual aids? Maybe an $8^1/_2$ x 11 piece of paper that she can have in front of her? Perhaps some charts?
- What kinds of legislative things does she like to do and what kinds of things does she not like to do—submit report language, put together coalitions, offer amendments in committee?

The speaker also confirmed that these "scouting sessions" could be used to "piece together the kinds of questions that we might expect to get."

A senior Republican was gruff in acknowledging the value he derived from lobbyist–staff premeetings: "No surprises. I didn't want to be surprised. Staff was expected to head that off. [Premeetings] gave them a chance to do that."

A high-ranking Republican picked up on the "no surprises" theme. He cautioned: "Don't blindside a member or permit him to be blindsided." In

n. Given the status of this lobbyist and his firm, he is not likely to encounter such requests by staffers.

subsequent conversation he reiterated the importance of being given prior notice about the subject of the meeting. He also favored receiving a "heads-up" on what the lobbyist would be asking him to do. The thrust of his position was defensive in nature. He was most concerned with avoiding surprises that would lead to embarrassment.

This view was in sync with advice offered by a former Democratic subcommittee chair: "If you have any doubts about what [we are expecting], let my staff know about them before you come in. Let them know what you think I should hear before we meet. That way we're both covered."

Some members require a briefing sheet laying out the purpose of the meeting and an overview of the material that will be covered. Other members may not ask for such a briefing sheet but welcome "some information [in whatever form] about what they [the lobbyist and client] plan to talk about." A former chief of staff said his office "usually asked for a letter requesting the meeting and stating its purpose. If we needed more information, we'd follow up with them."

In short, the premeeting serves the interests of both members and lobbyists. It provides important intelligence for both parties, leads to a more efficient meeting, and serves to head off unpleasant surprises—from the member's perspective perhaps the most important benefit of all.

## Build Rapport

*"I did not mind getting-to-know-you office visits. 'I'm not here to ask you for anything—just would like to introduce myself.' "*

Building rapport with a congressional office is a sometimes subtle, frequently challenging, process. If done well, it helps condition the playing field by putting the legislator at ease with the lobbyist's presence, even if only for the short term. Members cannot—and do not want—to become best friends with every lobbyist they meet; they have neither the time nor the inclination to do this. A former administrative assistant remembered that one of the lawmakers he worked for "used to go around muttering, 'I got too God damn many friends.' " His frustration, or maybe it was anger, was a consequence of having friends who expected too much of him—too much time, too many deals (that is, expectations for legislative deals), and too many favors. According to the administrative assistant, it was a "classic damned if you do, damned if you don't." In the lawmaking business, "you are damned if you have too many friends and you're damned if you don't have enough."

Rapport might be described as friendship light, the result of socializing light. It does not anticipate an enduring friendship, the sort built over a period of years. Rather, it can be established through a simple getting-to-know-you exchange of pleasantries that may occur before or even during an office meeting. One former congressional leader favored the "before" strategy: "The good lobbyist will take the time to get to know you before he needs you. That way you would at least have some idea who he is before he shows up wanting you to do something." A former colleague agreed: "I did not mind getting-to-know-you office visits. 'I'm not here to ask you for anything—just would like to introduce myself and tell you something about my company [or client].' "

Other members seemed not to care whether the comfort-building exercise occurred before or during the initial meeting. The former leader believed "You could do that just as easily with a little small talk before launching into your business."

A Democrat from the Southwest pointed to pictures of his grandsons, both in baseball uniforms: "Some people would come, see the picture and say, 'Hmmm, they look like pitchers. Are they righties or lefties?' I knew what they were doing and went along with it every time. It was pleasant conversation and it did break the ice. Not so much because it was about my grandchildren but because it was about baseball. Nothing wrong with that." [o]

Another senior member virtually wrote the "Legislator's Guide to Rapport Building" while we chatted in his office. The chapter headings:

- Write a note congratulating him on a speech.
- Meet him at a reception and have a pleasant chat. Don't do any business.
- Invite him out to see one of your [or the client's] facilities and to meet some employees.
- [At the meeting] notice the pictures in his office; ask about them.
- Ease into the meeting. Begin with some small talk.

Although more efficient, let's-get-down-to-business members might cringe at this waste of valuable time, and probably debunk it as old-fashioned schmoozing, this member saw great value in learning something about the person who was about to engage him in a matter of important business.[p]

Another member recalled how important it was for lobbyists to signal that they shared his point of view on policy matters. Obviously, this could not be the case for every lobbyist who met with him; but, circumstances

o. This session produced one of the lighter moments during the interview process. The former member recalled that a lobbyist had once seen the same picture and asked if it was his grandson. Bad move! He [the congressman] said, "Nope, that's my son."

p. Before we concluded our interview session, I shared the Ben Franklin–Manasseh Cutler story with this member. His response was predictable and emphatic. "That's it! That's exactly what I'm talking about!"

permitting, this sort of signaling could be helpful in creating a congenial bargaining forum: "I was generally lobbied by those who 'shared my convictions.' It was not so much that I had actually indicated support for their proposal; rather, it was more a question of shared philosophy of governance. This helped build the rapport. It also worked toward building confidence in each other."

A rapport builder would argue that there is nothing inefficient about this exercise. If members are going to be lobbied by someone, and if there is a reasonable chance that they will be convinced of the merits of that person's arguments, they should have a good sense of who that person is. Better to invest a little upfront time than to learn after commitments have been made that you really do not get on with, or trust, your new legislative ally. From the efficient member's perspective, rapport between lobbyist and lawmaker should have little to do with decision making. The "ask" and supporting arguments either make good policy sense or they do not. Comfort zones should have nothing to do with the matter.

## Listen and Learn

*"You can't negotiate if you don't hear what he's saying."*

A veteran lawmaker pounced on my opening question to him, "What makes for an effective lobbyist?" His answer: "Be a good listener." He leaned forward in his chair: "You don't learn anything when you're talking." A border state Democrat could not have agreed more: "First, be a listener, and then you can be a teller."

Lobbyists, the good ones, know that they are pleaders. Sure, they may also be supporters or confidants, enjoy an impeccable reputation for honor and for providing good information, and in some cases have better name recognition among Washington elites than the member of Congress they are speaking to. But at the end of the day they cannot accomplish anything without the consent and cooperation of legislators. Getting what they want requires more than making their case; they must also know and understand the target member's case. That requires listening.

Another Democrat went further: "You [the lobbyist] need to add to your information base—what is going on on the Hill? How does this member feel about this issue? Where does he fit in? How much time does he have? Who else might be interested? . . . Be prepared to change your argument or strategy based on what you learn." In other words, learn and then be prepared to use what you learn.

By being tuned in one hears more than "yes," "no," or "maybe." The attentive listener picks up inflections, pauses, hesitations, bursts of excitement, and even hints of annoyance. Words do not always speak for themselves. A marquee lobbyist advised: "What you see and hear is more important than what you say. Always!" This was something more than a bromide for him; it was a rational approach to legislative give-and-take:

> You can control what you say, if you want to say it at all. But you cannot control what the other person is saying or how he is saying it. And that matters. If you miss it the first time, it may be gone; you can ask him to repeat the words, but he may not say it the same way [the next time]. And the way he [said it] may have been the most important thing to know.

A lobbyist, also a former staffer, summed it up: "Focus! Total focus! That's how you get the most out of each meeting."

## Negotiate and Compromise

*"I will be asked to compromise. Will you be willing to work with me on that?"*

Compromise is fundamental to representative democracy. Without it, our Constitution could not have been written, signed, and ratified. Without compromise, there would be no Bill of Rights, no Fourteenth Amendment abolishing slavery, no student loan program, no Medicare program, no modifications to our tax code, and—well, you get the idea. The art of making law is the art of compromise.

During the interviews much was made of this point; interview subjects, many of them unprompted, identified willingness to negotiate and compromise as an essential trait for lobbyists. Here, state of mind is what matters most. Members do not like to be straitjacketed. Who does? But politicians more than most people find comfort in recognizing and maintaining their options. If for no other reason, a little room affords them more opportunities to accommodate more interests. Thus lawmakers look for and welcome signs of flexibility from lobbyists. A willing negotiator is seen as a realist, someone who, according to a member now representing an eastern district, "is not going to bust my chops."

A northeastern Republican was both realistic and direct in providing advice to lobbyists: "Everyone needs to get something. Remember compromise and the need to be prepared to do that." His words matched advice offered by a former colleague: "The best lobbyists try to solve your problem for you—maybe come up with a good compromise or an artful duck. They may suggest language that has wiggle room."

Other former legislators agreed:

- Lobbyists have to know how to compromise. For one thing, that is the only way they will be able to build and hold together legislative coalitions.
- Bad lobbyists cannot empathize with the congressman. These are people who think that a member who disagrees with him is stupid or corrupt. They could not understand why they should even think about compromising. They could not understand that to disagree with them was not necessarily being closed minded. They closed off any chance of negotiating a deal. . . . Stupid!

One form of legislative compromise has to do with venue almost as much as it does with the precise language that is used. Many lobbyists spend a fair amount of time negotiating committee report language.[q] This vehicle is sometimes used to buy off an interest group lobbyist by allowing him an opportunity to spin the language of the bill itself. Of course, committee staff usually keep a close eye on the process and do not let the spinning spin out of control. But sometimes this is the best the lobbyist will be able to do—find a compromise that he cannot afford to walk away from.

Lobbyists will do better with some compromises than with others. That is expected. What is not expected, and is rarely countenanced, is the lobbyist who says, "It's all or nothing." He had better get used to nothing.

## Mind Your Manners and Treat the Staff Well

*"Sometimes staff would freeze out an arrogant, self-important lobbyist who was trying to blow by them. They knew that would be fine with me."*

It may seem strange that common decency and awareness of another's sensitivities should matter to hard-driving politicians who work at the highest levels of government, but they do. Congressional offices are not immune to such mundane-seeming matters as politeness and expressions of appreciation. As one midwestern Democrat put it, "We're people too." Several interview subjects noted that members are aware of and do care about the "amenities." Almost every former member who responded to the survey agreed that they were told about "lobbyists who did not observe common courtesies with my staff." This was the only question to which there was this degree of unanimity.

---

q. Most bills reported to the House or Senate floor are accompanied by a committee report. The report does many things; one of those is to use nonlegislative language—sometimes restricting—to explain the intent of various provisions in the bill. Although not as powerful as the actual legislative language, reports can influence the thinking of judges and executive branch officials as they seek to interpret and implement the new law.

One could argue that this response is to be expected; what member (or former member) of Congress would want to appear not to be interested in such a matter. Fair enough. But the magnitude of the response was corroborated by the tone of the interviews. Rude lobbyists were identified and in some instances dropped from the list of welcome advocates:

- It was surprising that some lobbyists had such lousy manners. . . . They were just plain rude.
- Sometimes staff would freeze out an arrogant, self-important lobbyist who was trying to blow by them. They knew that would be fine with me.
- I didn't get too many complaints [from staff] on this. My chief of staff and I talked about the subject fairly often. He knew that I wanted to know how staff was treated.
- Maybe one or two now and then [were rude], but for the most part they [lobbyists] seemed to be a pretty decent group.
- Believe me, I think the lobbyists treated staff a hell of a lot better than some of my colleagues. . . . Some of them turned over staff a couple of times a year. Or at least it seemed like it.

Although it is not necessary or expected after every office visit, a thank you note or appreciative phone message is usually noticed and always welcome. This is especially true for staff people, who are generally more likely to see or hear the message and are pleased to know that they are being accorded as much deference as has been given their boss. "It was really more for the staff. I would learn if someone had been rude to them or if they had observed common courtesies—saying 'thank you' to my scheduler for setting up the appointment. My secretary was careful to bring in thank you notes." (Presumably, these were thank yous for meeting with the lobbyist.)

One lobbyist claims to have made these communications a "habit" because "staff does not like be treated like second fiddles": "There is value beyond just being polite. A thank you [to the right staff person] helps to implant your name and remind them of your meeting and what you were talking about. This is especially important if you have just met someone for the first time. To be honest, sometimes it is as much a 'hey, remember me' note as a thank you note."

This lobbyist continued, expanding on the theme that deference to staff is just plain good business: "The smart lobbyist invests constantly. He is investing in people. The kid right out of college, the L.A. [legislative assistant] will someday be a legislative director or maybe even a committee staff person. They'll remember you, especially if you came on arrogant or dismissive [of them]." Then, after a brief pause and with a slight smile, he added: "Shit, one of those kids I lobbied almost twenty years ago is now a member. . . . You ever see how many members were once staff? A lot!"

## *Ask* for the Meeting

*"I did not like it when they pushed too hard to meet with me."*

This discussion is closely related to the previous one. Members usually review and give final approval for their schedules. But the work of getting the meeting request to the member, perhaps accompanied by appropriate notations, and finding the time and place is staff work. That is to say, there is usually a considerable amount of back-and-forth between lobbyist and staff before a meeting is put on the calendar.

Sometimes the outcome of a meeting is sealed by what happens during this lobbyist–staff interface: "I did not like it if people were too pushy about meeting with me, especially if they did not have a good reputation." This Republican admitted that he sometimes "had to see someone like this" but that he usually went into such meetings "with my guard up."

Another member recalled that "every now and then my staff would comment on how nice somebody was or on how obnoxious they were," when seeking a meeting with him. "Sure it makes a difference when you finally sit down."

A staffer observed: "Some of these people are self-important asses. It's not so much that they do not want to meet with us [staff]; sometimes I can understand that. But it's the way they go about it—a kind of 'my business is too important' attitude." Later in the conversation this staff person did make a point of noting that "Most lobbyists are not that way. They are pretty decent—either because that's just the way they are or because they have learned what flies around here and what doesn't."

Many congressional offices distinguish between regular, or known, commodities and first-time visitors. A chief of staff, speaking of the latter, set out his office procedure: "We usually require a letter—it could be a fax—requesting the meeting and laying out its purpose. It helps if they tell us who is going to be there." When asked, "If you know the lobbyist but not the client, does that matter?" he responded, "Sure, it can [matter]—especially if we have confidence in the lobbyist." Then he added, "If it was a new issue . . . I usually liked them to meet with staff first."

A former chief of staff offered this advice: "When asking for an appointment, the lobbyist should be up front about his reason. He should make his subject and his position clear so we are not surprised when he gets here. It helps us prepare him [the staffer's boss] for the meeting."

No matter the mechanism used, congressional offices seek to protect their principals from surprise and from occasional unpleasant encounters. Even if the visitor does not intend to be contentious, an unprepared legislator is often an unhappy legislator. Perhaps it was for this reason that a former Ways and Means Committee member, by his own estimate, "saw only about 15 percent of those who wanted to meet with me; and those were only on issues I thought to be important." He concluded with this advice: "Do not try to see the member on every issue—make it an important issue."

## Get to the Point

*"They come in only when they need to and leave as fast as they can. That is smart."* [r]

Once inside the member's office, lobbyists will find any of several professional personalities waiting for them. At the two opposite poles are the let's-get-down-to-business hyperefficient members and the let's-get-warmed-up rapport builders.

A midwesterner who served in Congress for nearly three decades was clearly the efficient type. He spoke in the present tense: "You have to come in wanting me to do something; otherwise you should not be taking up time. So get to it. Tell me what it is. What are you asking me to do?"

Several interviewees subscribed to this approach. A recent retiree suggested a link between the need for brevity and the utility of having command of one's arguments. He insisted, "You have to get it right. There is no substitute for knowing your facts and where they fit into your argument." This point has been discussed in the context of demonstrations of issue competence, but here it has a slightly broader application. The former member saw a correlation between proficiency in answering questions and the expeditious flow of the meeting. This, in turn, added to the perception of the lobbyist as efficient and professional in his demeanor:

> When a lobbyist fumbled for an answer, you felt embarrassed for him, but you were also angry at the same time. "Poor guy, what's he doing in here if he doesn't know that he can't answer that question." For me it was a distraction. I lost interest and the focus of the meeting was thrown off. . . . If you can't answer, then acknowledge that quickly and say you will get that answer and get it to me as fast as you can. That way you do not look like a fool and you maintain the continuity of the meeting.

r. There is another context in which time is an important consideration for lobbyists: the amount of time it takes a member of Congress to accomplish an objective. This will be discussed in the next chapter.

Two Democratic veterans of several terms each emphasized the premium they placed on brevity:

- I liked lobbyists who were aware of my time demands. I would never shut anyone off, but I could get pretty darn fidgety if they droned on. I didn't try to hide it, but usually that didn't matter. They just kept talking.
- Members' time in D.C. is now scarce. Most [members] do not live in town much, so that makes it even more important to be efficient with your office time. . . . People who can make their point quickly are appreciated now more than ever.

A Republican made a particularly direct tie between brevity and the idea of the savvy lobbyist: "Brevity is important. It shows that you understand what I need. You know that you are not the only meeting of the day [for me]." A former Democratic colleague came close to being emotional: "Time! Time! Time! Time! The good ones [lobbyists] know that. They come in only when they need to and leave as fast as they can. That is smart."

Some additional observations:[s]

- When meeting with members, be brief and spontaneous.[t]
- A good lobbyist must be willing to do that [meet with staff]. Saves member's time.
- One-half hour is way too long; ten minutes is about right. Some lobbyists go on and just never pick up on the fact that we want them to be quick. I would remember this and send them to staff in the future.
- Do not take too much of a member's time and know your subject—that makes things move faster. This is important if you want to get a return visit.
- Be aware of the member's time; don't just hang on. When you are done, end the meeting. It's easier to get the next appointment if you are in and out.
- You must be able to hit the member's hot button. His time is scarce and his attention to any single issue is limited.
- Don't prattle on. Be brief.
- I hated the big multimedia presentation—just get to the point.

---

s. Many of these make clear the importance that members attach to brevity and ancillary matters, which, of themselves, provide important insights into members' thinking about their relationships with lobbyists.
t. A handful of members and staff noted their displeasure with having to endure obviously rehearsed presentations and prescripted answers. A former committee counsel, himself a lawyer, complained that "[one meeting] had the stench of being both overlawyered and underingenuous."

The importance of the final observation—"just get to the point"—may be masked by its simplicity. Remember the response to the question in chapter 2: "What distinguishes the super-lobbyists from other lobbyists?" The answer: "Most of them know how to present a case. Take Boggs—he is well informed and quick. He is especially good at frontloading his arguments; this is an important timesaver." "These people also school their clients to be quick."

"Frontloading" was viewed as an important asset for lobbyists. Although only one interview subject—the one quoted just above—used the exact word, others said similar things in slightly different ways:

- A meeting can be pleasant but also very businesslike. State your purpose so that I know what we will be talking about. This was important because even though staff might brief me before the meeting, it was always helpful [to know] how the lobbyist saw the meeting.
- I think one thing that separates us from corporate people is that they just love presentations. We hate them. We just don't have the time for slide-showarama.

But not all members were consumed by a desire to save office time. Some seemed to enjoy the company of favored lobbyists—those who had become friends as well as professional associates or who offered the prospect of a few minutes of diversion or, even better, some reelection-related goody:

- Time was not too much of a factor—*especially if I liked the person.* [The emphasis is the speaker's.]
- I did have a few [lobbyist friends] that came by the office to hang around once in a while; you could say it was more like a circle of friends, primarily from the district, that I would spend time with.
- If they were constituents, I really didn't care what their company or position was; they always got plenty of time and generally got it when they wanted it.

A former staffer remembered that "[staff] time was another matter. . . . I could usually fit someone in; that was seldom a problem. What was irritating though was that some people felt that because I wasn't the congressman I had unlimited time to give them. I was pretty busy too."

This staffer was among several who complained that they, like their bosses, were "always pressed for time." None of the staffers argued that time management was as much of a challenge for them as it was for their principals, but most felt that their schedules were hectic and that they noticed and appreciated people who understood this: "Everyone answers to someone, but up here crisis mode is the rule, not the exception; if the boss wants it done he *wants it done now!* He doesn't want to hear that I am tied up talking to some lobbyist."

The messages that emerged on the importance of time were consistent and direct: There is not enough of it; and that makes it valuable. Of the survey respondents, 92 percent agreed that brevity was important to them, though slightly less than half said that it was very important.

## Pay Attention to Timing

*"They were on executive time; we were on Congress time."*

Three former members and one former staff person complained that lobbyists, "even some experienced people," would come to see them either too early or too late in the legislative process. Of the two miscalculations, the former seemed the less harmful: "Too early might annoy a member, but there is always the chance of making things right [with him]; arriving too late usually means that the deal is done and you are not part of it. The time for any hope of [remedial action] has passed."

What respondents judged to be too early or too late was a relative matter. On the first count, two factors were mentioned: the nature of the lobbyist's request (Is he merely looking for a vote or a sign of support for his position, or is he looking for some hands-on legislative participation?) and the member's current interest in the matter. In the view of one legislator, "Yes, you could be too early." He explained that he seldom had the "luxury" of looking very far ahead: "On most issues my focus was on the present—not much more than a few weeks in advance. . . . Of course, there were some things we were especially interested in. If I was taking the lead, then we would be getting ideas months before a bill was introduced. So it depended."

Other members spoke about the opposite end of the spectrum—lobbyists who were too late in making their requests: "Some lobbyists would come in right before a [floor] vote. They should have seen me when it was in committee." This member explained that by the time the bill got to the floor he had probably already "committed."

When a lobbyist wants hands-on action from a legislator, the general view of legislators and, especially, staff, was "the earlier the better; within reason, of course." A senior majority member of a legislating committee spoke about his committee chair's work style: "The chair does negotiate provisions early on. If you want to get something in or changed, you have to get in early. . . . The chair is then able to defend those provisions whether he likes them or not—they are now part of his deal."

Another member gave a similar example: "Participating in early drafting sessions can be very important. Some legislation can be very technical. Getting into the chair's mark can have real advantages. It puts your spin on the matter. It can put the burden on other members to get your provision out of the bill."

In these instances a lobbyist frequently must begin work long before a draft bill surfaces. He will need this time to prepare his chief congressional allies. Richard Hall explains the importance of this early involvement:

> By playing a major role in the drafting process, a member helps define the markup agenda.[u] . . . Often a bill entrepreneur will consult with the members he thinks will be especially interested or might be important for building a coalition. . . . Involvement in behind-the-scenes negotiations can be an alternative and less-risky means of affecting some particular provision than offering amendments during subsequent markup. Getting what you want in the chairman's mark is really important. . . . If you get it in the original bill . . . it stays there unless someone decides to make a fight out of it.[22]

A former ranking minority member offered the quintessential statement of the obvious: "This all takes time." Nonetheless, his emphasis was well placed; members frequently appreciate the opportunity to work "behind the scenes where the profile and risk levels are relatively low." This means "getting up to speed on the issue and working with other offices." Hall again: "Committee staff members suggest that this [working behind the scenes in early drafting sessions] often is the case on major legislation, which sometimes requires several days of staff meetings, during which objections may be aired and a particular provision renegotiated." [23]

Because members of Congress are generally risk averse, they welcome opportunities to test the waters before going public with an idea. If they are able to float proposals, effect compromises, or negotiate points out of the range of prying eyes and ears, they are likely to take greater risks than when they are compelled to legislate in a public forum. This does not mean that anything goes, but it does mean that if lobbyists make reasonable requests, and time them well, their chances for success are maximized. The lobbyist will have adequate opportunity to convince legislators that his views are worth considering and that he and his client will be effective allies.

Hall's observations were confirmed by several interview subjects; the process takes time, and the wise lobbyist will give himself and his client plenty of time to allow for unforeseen opportunities or problems.

---

u. Markup is the committee or subcommittee process of amending and generally rewriting bills before they are reported to the full House or Senate chamber.

One opportunity that is often fraught with problems is working with the executive branch. A southern Republican, speaking about Congress generally, made a special point of discussing both the potential benefits and problems inherent in recruiting support from the administration:

> We [Congress] would work with other institutions and various interests in structuring hearings. When committee leadership was the same party as the administration, then they would sometimes collude on the timing and content of hearings. . . . Even in instances when the minority party in Congress and the White House [was] in the same hands, they would strategize with each other. This included attempting to affect timing, witness lists, and agreeing to areas of questioning.

The speaker then focused on what he saw as a "constant irritant" in working with the executive branch: "their lack of sensitivity to . . . our timing problems." A former counsel, remembering similar problems, concluded, "They were on executive time; we were on Congress time. . . . If I never hear the words 'sign off' again, that would be too soon." [v]

Perhaps this explains why many lobbyists are slow to enlist executive branch support. Rogan Kersh found that "lobbyists spent much more time targeting legislators than they spent targeting officials from the executive branch. . . . Even the two lobbyists in my sample who had an agency or executive-branch background dedicated more working hours to legislative activities." [24] Kersh offers the "greater permeability of the legislative branch" as the reason for this. But given the incongruence between "executive time" and "Congress time," it is reasonable to assume that time and timing are factors in lobbyists' decisions not to await input from the executive branch. Of course, this situation changes if members demand such an alliance.

It is perhaps both unavoidable and unfortunate that bureaucratic processes often take so much time, and hurried and harried lawmakers must often squeeze their legislative projects through what John Kingdon refers to as "policy windows": "Policy windows, the opportunities for action on given initiatives, present themselves and stay open for only short periods. If the participants [in the policy process] cannot or do not take advantage of these opportunities, they must bide their time until the next opportunity comes along." [25]

With policy windows constantly opening and slamming shut, it is easy to understand the importance congressional offices place on timing. There is clearly such a thing as the right idea at the wrong time.

---

v. By "sign off," the counsel meant "clearance," the process of gaining approval for policy positions, testimony, and other policy inputs that is common to all administrations. It can require several signatures and take considerable time.

Members also have their own policy windows. A former House Energy and Commerce member explained the importance of knowing where in the legislative universe a member is situated at any given time: "Look, you have to know what is on his agenda; that's very important—how much time he has to do something." In other words, when the member had a full agenda he did not appreciate pressure to pursue yet another objective: "If I really knew the guy well, I might suggest someone else on the committee. But that was the best I would do."

## Know Congressional Procedure

*"We don't necessarily need them drawing a roadmap."*

Lobbyists need not be parliamentarians, but they should be familiar with the basics of congressional procedures. Not knowing that the House has a Rules Committee, what a "hold" is, what it means for a bill to be put on the suspension calendar, or what basic rules govern conference committees can make one look like the amateur's amateur. As one interview subject said, "We don't necessarily need them [lobbyists] drawing a roadmap for us, but we'd like to see that they at least have some idea what we are talking about when we are discussing procedural matters."

This was another issue in which the revolving door was frequently mentioned: A committee staffer thought about his first year with the committee: "Some of the former staff people were pretty impressive leading me through procedural strategies. It was like a fraternity, I felt they were mentoring me. They were!"

## Follow Up on Everything

*"[Following up] can help credibility for both member and lobbyist."*

A common request made during congressional hearings is, "May I supply that for the record?" This is a witness's way of saying, "I do not have that information now, but I will get that to you as soon as possible." In-office meetings do not have the official standing of a hearing, but the stakes may be even higher for the lobbyist who promises to follow up afterward by supplying information or by doing some other chore agreed upon during the session:

- It's really rather simple. If you say you're going to do it, then do it.
- Following up is important. It not only shows that you are well organized; it shows the other side that you are reliable. This can help credibility for both member and lobbyist.

A lobbyist explained how he makes follow up work for him. "I try always to say that I will send or bring something up. That way I get a second meeting [usually with staff] to see how the first went and to make my key points again."

A former member was especially attuned to who did and who did not follow up: "I always had a staff person there to take notes. He was instructed to make special note of what the people agreed to do after the meeting and then to keep track of it. I almost never reminded them if they did not come through. We just made a note for future reference."

A surprising number of follow-up matters have nothing to do with legislation. Many are directly related to doing personal favors: "I'll get you that name." "We'll be happy to call your constituent." "We'll make a copy of those pictures and send them to you." The nature of the follow-up item aside, reliability is what is at issue: If you say you are going to do something, then do it.

## Tactical Missteps

Meetings with lawmakers are professional encounters. Threats, grimaces, and demeaning remarks about one's adversaries are out of place. Such behavior does nothing to enhance the professional standing of the offenders. What follows are insights into behavior that qualifies as a turn-off in most congressional offices. The interview subjects did not dwell on these matters, but their views, brief as they are, are worth remembering.

### Badmouthing

*"You can certainly disagree with them, but don't use incendiary language."*

A former member from a southwestern state was particularly hard on "badmouthers." He was clear about the kinds of messages he welcomed and the kinds he found "out of place": "I did not like badmouthing other lobbyists or organizations. You could say, 'I do not think they are right and here is why,' but I expected people to be respectful—to maintain a professional demeanor. And I certainly did not like it if someone took after another member. That was out of place."

Another southwesterner expressed much the same view: "You should give the other side of the issue, and you can certainly disagree with them, but don't use incendiary language. Most [members] do not like that. Let me decide if I think they make sense or not." In essence, this member was arguing for a dispassionate presentation of the opposition's case. The member could then decide what he felt he should do—follow up with the opposition to learn more, disregard their position, or consider accepting some or all of their arguments.

Of the survey respondents, 84 percent agreed that "I became upset when a lobbyist badmouthed their opposition." However, only one-third of respondents said they felt strongly about the matter.

## Threatening

*"His [company] chairman said he was very disappointed in my decision and would have to revisit some of his company's past decisions."*

Another taboo is the threat. In unminced words a former Senate chief of staff said, "Don't do it!" Several former members confirmed that some lobbyists or their clients had attempted to intimidate them. "Some people made clear that they would be withholding or even redirecting campaign money. Others suggested some other form of retribution if I did not give them support or vote their way."

A former House member was "shocked" by this sort of behavior. He could not believe that "such a basic rule [not threatening] could ever be violated. But it was!"

Other comments:

- Some would threaten, "We will get you."
- Some lobbyists did try to threaten members. I never got that, but I know that others did.
- There were a few veiled threats. But a few weren't so subtle; some were quite blatant.

In an incident that could serve as a poster case of what can happen when clients are not adequately controlled, a former Democratic member seethed: "His [company] chairman said he was very disappointed in my decision and would have to revisit some of his company's past decisions. It was clear what he meant—their PAC contributions to me."

The former member recalled that the mortified lobbyist "was trying to whisper his apologies as he was going out the door." Of course, the damage had been done; even if the member was inclined to accept the apology, the lobbyist, who worked only for the one company, could not hope to be disassociated from his pompous, ill-tempered CEO.

## Kissing and Telling

*"Legislators always want the ability to exercise an 'out'."*

The advantage of working behind the scenes is that it provides confidentiality in an ever-changing environment. Business conducted in venues outside the public eye is, as a former Budget Committee member said, "*our* business." (The emphasis was his.) Confiding in others what you have discussed, certainly what you have agreed upon, with another office can be dangerous work. A legislative director gave what he viewed as "the rule": "Always get a sign off." In other words, ask the person with whom you have met if you are free to share the content of your meeting or any agreements that may have resulted from the meeting.

Overkill? Maybe. But it is smart overkill.

Legislators and their staffs function in a fluid environment; what is certain today may be in flux tomorrow. As circumstances change, so may opinions and consequent decisions. A phone call from the leader, a meeting with a major constituent, an entreaty from the White House—these are but a few examples of occurrences that may reorder political imperatives for the lawmaker. To the extent that these events occur after she has met with a lobbyist, their prior agreement, as far as she is concerned, may be rendered inoperative: "Legislators always want the ability to exercise an 'out' if one is made necessary by factors such as the emergence of pressure from the leadership or if one provision is being packaged with another. . . . All such possibilities have to be anticipated." [26]

A lobbyist who had once been burned for telling a congressional office that another office was "okay on the issue" made this point: "There are just too many things that can change. A staff person can be covering his butt by denying that he told you something that his boss later overruled. . . . These people [members and staff] are not always above lying either."

Lying is one possibility, but confusion is the more likely culprit. Citing the volume of activity "that came through my office every day," and his "busy schedule of meetings," one lawmaker confessed to "occasional confusion or misunderstandings. . . . I am sure it could have been my fault. . . . I may not have made myself clear, or I may not have understood what they were asking. That's why I always had staff with me at these meetings." But staff can mishear or misinterpret too.

It is not always necessary for lobbyists and congressional offices to disagree on what was said at a meeting for there to be an alleged breach of confidentiality. The same former member cited above noted the difficulty in discerning what was "confidential" and what was not. "I certainly do not think that most lobbyists I dealt with would intentionally violate a confidence. Look, it is a very public business we are in, and I can understand why people would just assume that they could use what I had said when they met with other people." In further conversation this ex-lawmaker noted that "sometimes it was obvious" that he had been speaking confidentially. In those instances, "You would expect somebody to know that. . . . The experienced lobbyists did . . . at least as far as I ever knew."

This matter came up in only six interviews; nonetheless, the "always get a sign off" rule makes good sense in the context of those discussions.

## Flashing Your Money

*"I don't care about your friggin' house on the Eastern Shore!"*

Flashing company money or one's personal wealth is obnoxious wherever it is done. But on Capitol Hill it is downright stupid. Staff people in Congress generally work for very little money, and by today's standards even members are not especially well paid.[w] They know that almost every lobbyist, certainly those in the private sector, earn more money and have considerably more worldly possessions than they do. It is not necessary to remind them of this—yet people do "all of the time."

"I don't care about your friggin' house on the Eastern Shore!" Several staffers repeated variations on this impassioned observation by a career congressional chief of staff. Another much younger staffer even questioned expense-account meals: "They come in here pleading poverty for their client, or wanting never to have to pay a tax, and then they say, 'Let's go to lunch at the Capital Grille next week.' Huh?" [x]

A much-sought-after lobbyist understands these sensitivities and acts accordingly: "Sometimes a client wants to get a limo to go to the Hill. I say, 'No, let's just cab it.' The last thing I need is for someone I know up there to see me disembarking from the Queen Mary."

---

w. Members of the House and the Senate earn a bit over $165,000. Staffers with professional responsibilities—legislative people and senior administrators—generally earn between $40,000 and $158,000. As a rule Senate staffers earn a bit more than do House staffers for the same or similar work, and committee people earn more than people who serve on the staffs of individual members.

x. The Capital Grille is a pricey Washington insider's restaurant. Of course, now that restrictions have been placed on lobbyist-purchased meals, this sort of invitation is no longer appropriate.

## Taking Allies for Granted

*"They had never come in to see me. They just assumed I would be with them. But when they needed help, they came screaming in."*

A ranking minority member of a major House committee cautioned against taking "your friends for granted. . . . The pharmaceutical people did that to me once; they had never come in to see me [on the issue]. They just assumed I would be with them. But when they needed help, they came screaming in. I asked why I hadn't seen them before and then closed the meeting."

A House chief of staff had a more positive spin; he recalled a story about a legendary baseball player: "He said he used to complain about autograph seekers. 'I couldn't even have lunch with my wife without someone sticking some paper and a pen in my face. But after I retired—was out a few years—people stopped recognizing me. That's when I wished people still wanted my autograph.' "

The staffer went on: "We are like that on the Hill. We complain 'too many lobbyists,' but when they don't come in, we get angry. You can never take your ally for granted; you have to show them the respect of at least trying to get into see them. Let them say, 'It's a waste of time, I am already with you.' "

## Behaving Obsequiously

*"Resist shining the apple."*

Members of Congress are by no means averse to flattery. In fact, they tend to seek it; but that is most often at public gatherings where constituents' ears can hear it all. In private, however, sycophants are not well appreciated: "A lobbyist from a utility always found a way to compliment me—on a speech, on a bill I had put in, on the way I conducted a hearing. It was overdone by half."

An appropriate compliment—not a gushing testimonial—is fine, but the few members who discussed the matter during our conversations were unanimous: "Resist shinning the apple." A staff person added this thought: "It got a little thick in there. Did they think we didn't understand what was going on?"

A former member remarked, with a twinkle in his eye: "You don't have to tell a politician he's good; he already knows it."

## Conclusion

All of the preparation, all of the positioning, will come to naught if the lobbyist does not perform well in the legislator's office. No matter how skillful he has been up to that point, his chances of success will be diminished if he is not persuasive, informative, credible, and agreeable in a face-to-face meeting.

Early in the interview process a former member, maybe the brightest of all those I was privileged to interview, made the following observation about politics generally (though he did note its particular application to the lobbying profession): "It is not about what you want; it is about what the other person needs. It's like a marriage; if you think about your spouse before you think about yourself, your relationship will just get better."

So what does the "other person" need? The answer is important in more ways than might be readily apparent. Certainly, members seek to press every advantage they have, and access to quality information from a variety of sources is one of those advantages. It is clearly something that they need and value; its practical application to writing law is unquestioned. Lobbyists who supply important information are more than lobbyists; they are valued resources. They are instrumental in moving a legislator's reputation forward, both for her expertise and trustworthiness.

That is the positive, or offensive, side of the needs–advantages agenda. On the defensive side, lawmakers are deeply concerned about protecting against the vulnerabilities inherent in their profession—public scrutiny, a constant stream of political rivals waiting for them to stumble, and, in this context, a virtual obsession with their reelection prospects. These are their words:

- If a lobbyist can match his interests with [those of] the public interest . . . if he convinces you of that, then you feel that you will be able to [defend your position]. You won't be vulnerable to charges of favoritism or of being influenced by campaign money.
- It is not always easy to know who is a genuine friend and who is just very clever at trying to use you.

One does not have to accept the thesis that members of Congress are motivated primarily by their fears to accept the idea that insurance against risk is much on their minds as they contemplate policy decisions and the public actions they take in support of those decisions. Recall Douglas Arnold: "Legislators need to be concerned with both the positions they take and the effects they produce . . . [and] they need to consider both the known policy preferences of attentive publics and the potential policy preferences of inattentive publics." [27] This is where veteran lobbyists can rise to the top of extracongressional resources available to cautious members.

This chapter is not intended to be a simple itemization of lobbyists' tactics—some positive, some not. Rather, the itemized points should be understood as presenting components of an integrated whole. The whole is the perception of the lobbyist as a dependable, safe-bet asset for the member and for the policymaking process.

Such lobbyists will not embarrass a member or present her with inane requests. They will not push her to take positions that she cannot possibly accede to—not without committing herself to an early and involuntary retirement from Congress. In conducting their business, they will provide her with assurances against unwarranted risk—unspoken, of course. In so doing, they will free her to move forward in pursuit of her own legislative and career agendas.

## Notes

1. John R. Wright, *Interest Groups and Congress: Lobbying, Contributions, and Influence* (New York: Longman, 2002), 109; E. E. Schattschneider, *The Semisovereign People: A Realist's View of Democracy in America* (Fort Worth, Texas: Holt, Rinehart, and Winston, 1983).
2. Richard F. Fenno Jr., *Home Style: House Members in Their Districts* (Glenview, Ill.: Scott, Foresman, 1978), xi.
3. Schattschneider, *The Semisovereign People,* 2.
4. Fenno, *Home Style,* 55–56.
5. David Austen-Smith and William H. Riker, "Asymmetric Information and the Coherence of Legislation," *American Political Science Review* 81 (September 1987): 897–918.
6. Raymond A. Bauer, Ithiel de Sola Pool, and Lewis Anthony Dexter, *American Business and Public Policy* (New York: Atherton Press, 1963), 407.
7. Lester W. Milbrath, *The Washington Lobbyists* (Chicago: Rand McNally, 1963).
8. Michael Watkins, Mickey Edwards, and Usha Thakrar, *Winning the Influence Game: What Every Business Leader Should Know About Government* (New York: Wiley, 2001).
9. Richard F. Fenno Jr., *Congressmen in Committees* (Boston: Little Brown, 1973), 1.
10. Richard Hall, *Participation in Congress* (New Haven: Yale University Press, 1996), 77.
11. Barbara Sinclair, "An Effective Congress and Effective Members: What Does It Take?" *PS: Political Science and Politics* (September 1996): 438.
12. Lee Hamilton, "What I Wish Political Scientists Would Teach About Congress," *PS: Political Science and Politics* (December 2000): 760.
13. Watkins, Edwards, and Thakrar, *Winning the Influence Game,* 94.
14. Quoted in Ronald Kessler, *Inside Congress* (New York: Pocket Books, 1997), 81.
15. Charles E. Lindblom and Edward J. Woodhouse, *The Policy-Making Process,* 3d ed. (Upper Saddle River, N.J.: Prentice Hall, 1993), 83.
16. Ibid. The quote is from Jeffrey Berry, *The Interest Group Society* (Boston: Little, Brown, 1983).

17. David B. Truman, *The Governmental Process,* rev. ed. (New York: Knopf, 1971), 333.
18. Ibid., 334.
19. Roger H. Davidson and Walter J. Oleszek, *Congress and Its Members,* 11th ed. (Washington, D.C.: CQ Press, 2007), 362.
20. James A. Thurber, "Dynamics of Policy Subsystems in American Politics," in *Interest Group Politics,* 3d ed., ed. Allan J. Cigler and Burdett A. Loomis (Washington, D.C.: CQ Press, 1991), 325.
21. Schattschneider, *The Semisovereign People,* 2.
22. Hall, *Participation in Congress,* 41.
23. Ibid.
24. Rogan Kersh, "Corporate Lobbyists as Political Actors," in *Interest Group Politics,* 6th ed., ed. Allan J. Cigler and Burdett A. Loomis (Washington, D.C.: CQ Press, 2002), 233.
25. John W. Kingdon, *Agendas, Alternatives, and Public Policies,* 2d ed. (New York: Longman, 1995).
26. Bruce C. Wolpe and Bertram J. Levine, *Lobbying Congress: How the System Works,* 2d ed. (Washington, D.C: CQ Press, 1996), 15.
27. R. Douglas Arnold, *The Logic of Congressional Action* (New Haven: Yale University Press, 1990), 82.

# 6 The Lobbyist's Ask

For lobbyists, the "ask" is the prime mover. It frames the legislative mission and sets all that must follow in motion. Its importance cannot be overstated. Some asks are simple; they request a lawmaker to perform an act that she can do unilaterally with little or no special preparation (for example, casting a yea or a nay vote). Others are more complex. In those cases lobbyists ask members of Congress to take on a proactive role in support of a policy position by interacting with other members, sometimes for an extended period. Writing bills, drafting and shepherding amendments, and participating in strategy planning and agenda development are of this ilk. At a minimum these activities require a significant commitment of time and expose the member to the possibility of incurring IOUs from congressional colleagues.

Yet it is not all cost and no gain for the legislator. Many legislative offices are continually in the market for new projects; they see them as an important part of their responsibility in fulfilling the public trust and at the same time as a way of furthering their own career interests. For these "policy types," the ask may present as much of an opportunity as it does a potential cost. In the best cases it provides the raw stuff of policy innovations and strategic initiatives.

A New England Democrat explained in some detail how he incorporated interest group lobbyists into "ad hoc brain trusts" designed to yield such constructive results: "Members can put people from outside of the Congress—interest group lobbyists, academics, think tank experts—and other environments together in different combinations. The point is that members are in a position to hear and learn a lot from a variety of sources; they can then act as matchmakers or brokers in putting experts and people of common interest together. Information about legislation and ideas for policy can thus be developed."

Other members, though less proactive in soliciting ideas, agreed that interest groups frequently are sources of legislative proposals. One former member estimated that as much as 80 percent of his policy initiatives came from requests by interest groups: "About half of these were from the district and about half from groups outside [the district]."

Several responses from interview subjects reinforced the prominent role that interest group requests play in the development of members' legislative agendas:

- Ideas came in from all over. Certainly, sometimes lobbyists would generate an idea for a proposal.
- Generation of ideas for legislation came from my staff and often from interest group lobbyists. One source did not predominate.
- How much did I rely on lobbyists for ideas? I would say about 20–25 percent.
- On the reauthorizations, about 50 percent of changes came from interest groups. We had plenty to do; I wasn't looking for more ideas. But many were good; so it was a full-time job just managing them.
- Members are not all the same. Some generate ideas from staff, some from the news, and some from associations and the like. Some members have a sort of kitchen cabinet. Actually, most members do some of all of this.
- Unless someone expressed an interest, we were unlikely to take on something new. . . . It [Ideas] could be [from] lots of people or organizations—sometimes committee staff who got it from an interest group or a think tank or maybe someone in an agency.

In acceding to the more complex requests, especially those that require alliances with and approvals by several other members—often the case for such projects—legislators frequently take on the role of de facto coalition leader. The very acts of entreating colleagues, negotiating mutually agreeable legislative terms, and settling upon strategies and tactics require that members forge alliances, make deals, and assume commitments.

Although it may be true that the president is the nation's lobbyist in chief, members of Congress can be effective generals when they engage in legislative combat. They are uniquely situated to do this work. As a Democrat from New England said, "Members do not need an appointment to speak with their colleagues." They clearly have unparalleled access advantages. White House operatives, for all of their prestige, must make appointments with legislators in order to present their wares in person. They cannot sidle up to a colleague on the floor, sit down next to her in the cloakroom, or casually stop by her table in one of the congressional lunchrooms—not without an invitation from a member. Nor are most lobbyists able to approach a colleague in the House or Senate gym, a tactic that many interview subjects found to be bad form anyway.

So members have the tools and frequently the incentives to convert favor to advantage. But the conversion is not likely to reach fruition if the process does not begin with intelligent selection of the lobbying objective. Remember the former chief of staff quoted in chapter 4? "A member of Congress is bombarded daily with dozens of good ideas." Good for whom? Action requests are nothing exceptional in Congress; the test for the congressional office is to select wisely from among them—wisely, as defined by the quality of the project as reflected in the ask and the competence of the ally.

## Forms of the Ask: Enlisting Support from Other Members of Congress

In chapter 5 a legislator instructed an imaginary visitor: "You have to come in wanting me to do something; otherwise you should not be taking up time. So get to it. Tell me what it is. What are you asking me to do?"

The context for this quote was a discussion about the importance of brevity during office meetings. The focus was on "get to it." Here the focus is shifted; it is now placed on "Tell me what it is" and "What are you asking me to do?" In short, the focus here is on the exact form of the action request, the nature of the tactic that the lobbyist is asking the legislator to employ—for example, "Please call the chair" and "Kindly offer this amendment." The variety of these requests is limited only by the ingenuity and sophistication of the asker, that is, the lobbyist. The options are virtually limitless for lobbyists who are legislative pros and who are able to construct innovative, yet practical, approaches to pursuing their clients' objectives. The balance of this chapter looks at several examples of the ask. Some of these are simple and direct: "Vote this way." Some request more complex and finely nuanced responses: "Could you work with us in getting labor on board?"

Because much meaningful legislative activity occurs outside the public's view and never becomes part of an official record, action requests are frequently what Richard Hall refers to as "informal" behavior.[1] Such behavior is informal in that no official record is made of the request; nor is a record made of the ensuing actions. I expand on Hall's term to emphasize the nexus between these informal acts and their consequences for legislative policy development. Thus "informal" behavior becomes unrecorded legislative behavior (ULB).

It is worth emphasizing that neither members nor lobbyists resort to ULBs solely, or even primarily, because these vehicles allow them to avoid public scrutiny. This is no more the case for lobbyists and legislators than it is for business people negotiating a contract, architects drawing up building plans, or families mapping out their next summer vacation. People do not issue press releases laying out their latest conversations on these or most other matters. And, although members of Congress are public figures doing the public's business, we would no more expect that every conversation and every strategic move to which they are a party should be vetted through the media. Most often, ULBs are ULBs because that is the way people do business—nothing sinister about it.

Some lobbyists and some members, of course, may be happy to hide their actions from the general public, especially their constituents. But this is more a by-product than an intentionally sought result. The intent is seldom to cover over nefarious activity.

In fact, privacy allows legislators the latitude they need to serve the public. Asking a member to intervene with a colleague is best done informally. If the member agrees, the subsequent communication between colleagues—the asker and the askee—is also best done discreetly. It is also possible that lobbyists and members might avoid making an important ask for fear of public humiliation if they were rejected. Again, no sinister intent would be present. The first of the action requests that we will discuss makes the case perfectly.

## Asking Members to Intervene with Other Members

*"Congressman, would you call Representative Smith to see if she would meet with us?"*

The discussion here is relevant to virtually all of the remaining parts of this chapter. Almost everything that members do to affect policy outcomes, including pursuing lobbyists' objectives, requires them to interact with other members of Congress. Thus they are frequently asked by lobbyists to use their good offices with other members.

These requests occur in a variety of circumstances and for a full range of reasons: "Could you ask her to vote against this?" "Would you mind seeing if she would cosponsor the bill?" "If you could convince her to speak for the amendment, that would be great." "We have never worked with her; would you mind asking her to meet with us?" According to one legislator, these are common, run-of-the-mill requests.

During the interviews I asked a former member, "Isn't asking other members to do favors for you, especially if they are really for the benefit of a lobbyist, the most expensive thing you can do? After all, you are giving out an IOU?" The answer was immediate and unequivocal: "Not at all. This is what we do." In response to a follow-up question, however, there was some equivocation: "Oh, sure! If it was something that would be asking a lot of [the other member], then that would be different." The idea of "asking a lot" almost always translates into putting one's political capital at risk.

Another former member was of like mind: "Members commonly go to other members to ask for favors. There is usually great reciprocity among members—that is the expectation. The key to getting most things done is personal relationships. . . . Politics is human relations. That's how we campaign and that's how we do our work in Congress."

But acting routinely is not the same as being on autopilot. When lobbyists make these requests, they must be familiar with the positions favored by the member they are seeking to mobilize. She is not about to lobby her colleagues for a position she believes to be wrong; nor is she likely to importune other members if she believes the request would be abhorrent to them. The suggestion of such an ill-conceived mission would likely alienate the member and make the lobbyist look the fool. So when a lobbyist is mobilizing one member to entreat another member, the burden for the lobbyist is doubled; he must have a good read on both members he seeks to influence (or to have influenced).

A veteran northeasterner who had served as the ranking minority member on a full committee for several sessions, and who enjoyed a well-earned reputation as a nonpartisan lawmaker, made a distinction in how he would respond to lobbyists' requests to intervene with other members. He employed two criteria when deciding on "marginal matters." First, the request could not be "inconsistent" with the member's own thinking. Second, he was more likely to agree to the request if he was favorably inclined toward the lobbyist or the client.[a] In these instances he would send out "flash faxes" or "Dear Colleague" letters. On matters he deemed to be more important, he "would lobby other members—'I need your vote.' But I would pretty much [stay within] my own group." [b]

A former subcommittee chair provided insight into how the importance that members attach to an issue might affect how they approach their colleagues when lobbying them on behalf of an interest group: "Some

---

a. There was a strong hint that campaign contributions might affect the extent to which the member was favorably inclined to the lobbyist or the client.

b. In a sense this statement reflects John Kingdon's finding (in *Congressmen's Voting Decisions* [Ann Arbor: University of Michigan Press, 1989, 76]) that "in a full 86 percent of the cases [in his study] in which fellow congressmen were consulted . . . informants were largely of the same opinion as the decision-maker, and in nearly half of these cases, there was no disagreement . . . at all." In the Kingdon study it was the member about to cast a vote who was importuning a colleague for advice.

people prefer one-on-one conversations with other members for the things they think are important. Written communications usually go through staff and are for lower priority matters. . . . Verbal is more confidential, more flexible, more personal, and usually more informative."

Several interview subjects emphasized the importance of ideology when encouraging members to lobby other members. This should be no surprise to political actors; ideology has long been recognized as a key component in legislative decision making. John Jackson and John Kingdon list ideology first among the variables that affect members' votes: "Actual legislative voting is driven by a complex mix of factors—ideology, the motivation to select 'good' public policies, a desire for reelection, party loyalty, career advancement, the pursuit of power within the legislature, and probably several others. Most of the time, various considerations that legislators weigh point in the same direction." [2]

The interviews reinforce this view; lobbyists who ask members to do what they (the members) could not do in good conscience are deemed to have crossed the line. Two former northeastern members were very clear on this point:

- You cannot be asked to do something that is not in your district's interest, or to do something that is against your overall philosophy.
- Most members on most issues are guided by their own views and philosophy. If you ask for anything that goes against that, it could be a real problem.

A former legislative director for a mid-Atlantic Democrat was perhaps the most instructive. He became animated in issuing this warning, "Don't come in here and tell us to go against what we stand for; the G. D. business is stressful enough without that horse shit."

## Asking Colleagues for Votes

*"Representative Jones is sitting on the fence on this one. If you could give him a call that might nudge him our way."*

Asking for the order is the quintessential form of ULB. Nothing significant will result unless the votes can be rounded up. Legislative proposals may serve as expressions of interest, statements of political philosophy, and notification of intent, but they have no final effect. Law does. And to make law one must have the votes—in committee and on the floor. So sponsors and supporters of amendments and bills must attract and deliver a majority of their colleagues.

But votes are a matter of a highly visible record, arguably the most visible and easily accessed record that a member of Congress can establish. Voting is not something that a member takes lightly. A Democrat from the far Midwest was passionate when characterizing the extent to which he valued his vote: "The vote is a sacred act. . . . For me it was almost like a religious act; it was value laden. It is an indelible mark, a statement of your inner being. . . . I always felt that it was intrusive [for me] to ask a member to vote one way or another." In his view "the lobbyist should say, 'here is my case and here is my argument,' and then let me decide what I would do."

A Blue Dog Democrat agreed: "It is each member's definitive substantive and political statement regarding a particular issue that is before the House. You might be able to explain it later if you have to, but it can never be erased."

These comments suggest that most members would consider lobbying other members for legislative votes to be among the most difficult, most potentially expensive requests (in terms of political capital outlay) that one lawmaker can ask of another. But the interview responses do not bear this out. One member who represents an East Coast district gave what he saw as the reason: "We are expected to ask other members for votes. If we don't, we're not doing our job. . . . I certainly don't see how we could be."

Without question members are in the best position to lobby their colleagues. To the extent that logrolling occurs within Congress, members can trade in a common currency. Members, not lobbyists—not even the lobbyist in chief—control this currency. And, as already noted, members have access to members. Margaret Thompson observes that "the persons with the greatest potential for securing access [to other members] were those already within the system, that is, the members of Congress themselves. Thus clienteles that found elected advocates already in place . . . generally had a tremendous edge over those that were without this base." [3]

John Kingdon reinforces the importance of member-to-member lobbying: "Apparently, the two actors most in the minds of congressmen as they decide [how to vote] are congressmen and constituencies, with interest groups and the administration coming next." [4]

A former chief of staff and legislative assistant (at different times in his career) explained that "the member-to-member contact could be fairly intense. Staffs will prepare hunting sheets. These are members that they target on the floor or anywhere else to get them to vote or do something else to help the [requesting] member's position." The ex-staffer attributed some of these efforts to lobbyists: "On some occasions members' staffs may work with—maybe even at the direction of—an interest group in putting these lists together."

It is no surprise that clienteles must be constantly attentive to the preferences of their legislative allies; they cannot afford to put at risk potentially "exhaustible and unstable" [5] access by asking for what is too difficult for the member to do.

Two members provided further insights into the variables that a member might weigh when deciding whether to ask a colleague for a vote:

- Of course, it would be more difficult to do this if you had to ask a member you did not get along with that well or who might not normally want to do what you are asking. In fact, you probably would not ask such a member unless you were really pressed.
- Members tend to talk to friends and people who vote like them, regardless of party, though they tend to stay within their own party.

A former member who had been a chief of staff before being elected to Congress recalled that when he needed the votes of members with whom he frequently disagreed, "[He] would try to find a third party." He thought this was not an unusual practice. "You try to work around that by having a colleague with a better relationship with the member you want to get on board [to speak to him]."

So asking for the vote may be an accepted part of the congressional culture—an act that is done mostly among friends, fellow party members and, generally, well-trusted colleagues. In these circumstances it is relatively inexpensive to do. But when the mission entails lobbying a colleague who is most often not of like mind, costs can add up. A lobbyist who served for a short time as a congressional staffer was firmly of the opinion that "It is not so much who you are asking; it is who you are asking him to ask." Translated: Lobbyists must anticipate the cost to the member even before the member makes this calculation herself. This is the sort of foresight that distinguishes veteran lobbyists from their less-experienced colleagues.

## Rounding Up Cosponsors[c]

*"Our trade association people are saying that leadership wants to see some bipartisan support on this bill. We think Representatives Smith and Jones would go on the bill if you were to ask them."*

When a bill is introduced, the name of the sponsor (the author) appears near the top of the front page followed by a list of the cosponsors. Supportive lobbyists frequently share in the task of lining up cosponsors, and,

---

c. A cosponsorship is a form of coalition building. I discuss it separately here because the responses from interview subjects on this matter were paradoxical, inconsistent, and nuanced. They reveal some interesting insights into the legislative process and legislator–lobbyist relationships.

perhaps more important, enlisting congressional offices to recruit colleagues for cosponsorship. According to one former staffer, interest group activity accounted for "about half of the requests to cosponsor." He added that "it was common for interest groups to be involved in virtually all aspects" of cosponsoring, from making direct requests for members to sign on to asking known supporters to approach other members. The reverse was also true: Members would ask lobbyists to solicit cosponsors.

At first glance this might seem to be an important assignment. Cosponsorship is thought to be a signaling device that sends a message to other members and to interest group leaders—conservative, liberal, pro-this, anti-that—suggesting that they might want to support (or oppose) a bill. It provides information about the supportive coalition in Congress; the more senior and prestigious the listing, the more powerful the signal is deemed to be. It is also said to be a reelection-related device; lawmakers can claim credit for cosponsorships and indicate to their constituents positions they have taken.

Daniel Kessler and Keith Krehbiel agree that cosponsorship is most likely intended as an internal signaling device among legislators; however, they are less convinced that it is also used as an adjunct to electioneering: "On balance, the combination of findings, interpretations, anecdotes, and additional data analysis favors an intralegislative signaling view of the dynamics of cosponsorship rather than the view of cosponsorship as electorally targeted position taking." [6]

Even on the use of cosponsorships as internal signaling, the interviews produced less than overwhelming results. Some subjects saw the recruiting process as "routine stuff" and relegated the function to staff (or to lobbyists): "Sending a Dear Colleague letter [asking her to cosponsor] was routine. If we wanted to put more effort into it, we had our staff call around." One former staffer remembered, "That was usually our job. We got out the Dear Colleagues and kept track of who agreed to go on."

Other members' views ranged from the relatively indifferent to the outright cynical:

- This was done in person or through a fax blast. The more cosponsors you have, the better off you are.
- If you are not the chair of the committee the bill will be going to, you will have a harder time convincing other members that this is important.
- Seeking cosponsorship was especially easy if you could assure that the bill wasn't going anywhere.

In subsequent interviews several former members and staffers acknowledged that cosponsorship campaigns might sometimes be as much for show as for legitimate political purposes—perhaps another example of lobbyists and legislators colluding to make each other look good to client organizations without actually furthering a legislative objective. According to Rick K. Wilson and Cheryl D. Young there is good reason for cavalier attitudes and cynicism: "At the margin cosponsorship makes a difference, but its impact is very slight. The number of cosponsors has no impact on the likelihood that legislation gains final passage." [7]

As with most political matters personal relationships are important when considering whom to approach for cosponsorship: "If you have not been able to support a member in the past, you are not likely to go to him to ask for a vote or to cosponsor . . . not unless you can justify the request in terms of the other [member's] interests." Several respondents hammered at this same point: "What is easy to ask of one person might be virtually impossible to ask of another."

Congressional attitudes about agreeing to these requests were as uneven as were the views on soliciting cosponsors:

- We'd take great care in deciding which bills to cosponsor.
- We'd go on lots of different stuff—as long as it wasn't bad for the district. Maybe we could help some group that had helped us.
- I would tell them, if you want me to go on this bill, then you'd have to show me that you could get cosponsors. And [some] from the other side.
- They'd come to me with something they wanted me to do. I would tell them if they could get the chairman to go with me and if they would line up some of [the right] cosponsors, then I might do it. Otherwise, they'd have to find someone else.

In all, cosponsorship—agreeing to do it and recruiting others to go on the bill—could best be characterized as a "let's get on to the next question" subject for the lawmakers. Wilson and Young have it just about right: Cosponsorship is of "marginal value" in moving legislation forward and is thus of limited interest to members.

## Influencing Committee Agendas

*"Congressman, we think the committee is being a bit hasty here. Could you call the chair to see if he would put off hearings for a few months?"*

Perhaps the most important, and maybe most sophisticated, contest among political actors is the politics of agenda control. E. E. Schattschneider offered this classic observation: "The definition of the alternatives is the supreme instrument of power; the antagonists can rarely agree on what the issues are because power is involved in the definition. He who determines what politics is about runs the country, because the definition of the alternatives is the choice of conflicts, and the choice of conflicts allocates power." [8]

Schattschneider's point explains why the ability to affect agendas and schedules is one of the most valuable strategies that a lobbyist can employ in his client's interest. But it also explains why it is among the most difficult to accomplish: Agenda control is integral to the "allocation of power." Legislators know this. For committee chairs it is a prime source of power, one that they will not readily abandon or in any way compromise. In fact, according to Barbara Sinclair, the rank-and-file expect chairs to wield this power with great energy: "Agenda setting involves singling out, focusing attention on, and attempting to build pressure toward action on a problem, issue, or policy proposal, and members expect their leaders to employ their institutional powers and their media access to that end." [9]

Although some long-in-the-tooth lobbyists, many of them former members, may have access to chairs and are comfortable discussing such matters with them, most lobbyists do not have these kinds of credentials. For them the best course, perhaps the only course, is to work through a well-regarded, usually senior, committee member of the chair's party. But even this is no cinch. A former member with more than two decades of experience in Congress cautioned: "Yes, a member might try to help out a supporter by seeing if a chair could delay a bill. But this, I imagine, was pretty rare; I didn't see much of it. . . . Someone must be in charge and that's the chairman." Other former members agreed:

- I always felt that scheduling was something we let the chairman do.
- That is for the chair to do.
- Going to the chair on these matters was not hard to do. But getting a good result wasn't so easy.

Thomas Dye, referring to the "chairmen of the most powerful standing committees," argues that these committees "virtually become 'fiefdoms' over which [the chairs] exercise great power, often independently and occasionally even in conflict with their . . . party leaders." [10] Whether the chair exercises total control over his "fiefdom" or enjoys a somewhat less commanding position, rank-and-file members must convince him of the merits of the measure they are seeking to advance.

A midwestern Republican believes that ultimately "lobbying chairs on agenda matters is members' work. . . . Members will seek to serve an interest group by affecting the committee agenda." In other words, agenda lobbying should be done through committee members. But, even if a member agrees to approach the chair on a lobbyist's behalf, success is by no means guaranteed.

It is also true that the hegemony of committee chair and party leadership has by no means been uniform from committee to committee and from era to era. Even in the absence of rules changes there have been and continue to be significant inconsistencies. Some committee leaders are by nature or design collegial in their leadership style. One former subcommittee chair noted that he would try to meet with his subcommittee colleagues "once or so each session to find out what was on their minds." If there was sufficient interest in an emerging policy matter, "then we might at least see if we could do a hearing."

In the capital cost-gain discussion in chapter 4, a former subcommittee chair conceded that even if he did not agree with sponsors of a bill he might schedule a hearing "as a result of pressure from members who want to appease an interest group." Whether it was to appease constituents, interest groups, or simply to assert their "rights" (my term) as members of Congress and the committees on which they served, junior members in the mid-1960s began to seek to impress "collegial" work styles upon not-so-willing party leaders and committee chairs. By the early 1970s, reports Burdett Loomis, "backbench members of both parties wanted more responsibilities and greater impact on the legislative process. . . . Between 1971 and 1975, the House acted to reduce the authority of full-committee chairs." In doing so, they clearly reduced their hegemonic control over calendars and agendas [11]

In the aftermath of the "Republican revolution" of 1994, when the GOP took control of both chambers of Congress, the pendulum seemed to swing back; party leadership was accorded new and greater powers. Specially empanelled and empowered task forces were sometimes permitted to bypass committee leaders. Add to this the degradation of seniority as a factor in determining committee chair positions, and it would seem that the importance of committee work in Congress would have been seriously diminished.

But not so fast. Two years after Rep. Newt Gingrich, R-Ga., took the gavel in hand as Speaker of the House in 1995, Sinclair pointed to an immutable truth about how Congress must conduct its business if it is to continue as the nation's primary lawgiver: "The power of Congress, especially that of the House, in the political system depends on its specialized, expert committees. The issues and problems with which the federal government deals are too numerous, diverse, and complex for any one person to master. For a relatively small body such as Congress to hold its own vis-à-vis the executive branch and outside interests, it must divide labor and rely on its members' expertise and their area of specialization."[12]

The essence of Sinclair's observation has never been challenged for any extended period: All—or almost all—roads to the committee docket run through the chair. A former committee counsel emphasized this point in the context of efforts to affect committee agendas: "Lobbyists and members do lobby on agendas, but this is sophisticated lobbying—it means you have to deal with the chair or with leadership, or with both. It also means that you may be interfering with the party's or the chair's priorities."

Another counsel gave the clear consensus of opinion among the interviewees: "It's best left to experienced people who know just where and how far to go."

## Providing Questions for Hearings and Influencing Witnesses

*"The committee has not called our major trade association to testify. That is a mistake. Could you see if the chair would invite them?"*

It is common practice for interest groups to supply members of congressional committees with questions to ask at hearings. Interest groups also attempt to get "their" witnesses on the docket. The purpose is to build a hearing record that the group believes will support their cause. Sometimes, particularly in the case of an administration witness, a testifying organization will suggest questions that it would like to answer in a public forum. This is prime operating territory for lobbyists who are savvy enough not to overplay their hand.

Most former members acknowledged that they are willing to ask lobbyist-provided questions. One claimed not to have been particularly discriminating about the source of the questions as long as they were good ones: "It did not usually matter if the group had been supportive of me or not. They frequently had better questions than I or my staff came up with." He then emphasized that quality questions were especially important to him. He personally reviewed each prepared question before he went into a hearing. This level of scrutiny may have been due in part to his position as a subcommittee chair. It also may have been a function of learned behavior; he was a well-regarded attorney before coming to Congress.

Another former member virtually said "ditto." He agreed "to ask a line of questions at a hearing if they were useful. . . . I would say that it could be a favor to a member to staff him out with some good questions. Sometimes they were better than the ones my own staff had prepared."

A long-time ranking minority member was more restrained; he suggested that he would agree to use the questions "only with great care."

"I had to be convinced. If I was, then I would use it. . . . Some of the groups came up with some excellent stuff. That was good for both of us."

This approach, receptive but discriminating, was the common denominator for most congressional offices:

- Only the interested members ask questions. Lobbyists do plant questions, but not very often. Still, members will only ask questions that they are comfortable with. Asking someone's questions may happen more often at high-profile hearings that are not really especially important in terms of policy output. Certainly, more people try to get their questions in at high-profile hearings.
- Asking questions at a hearing is not always that easy because you are before God and everybody else. [Chuckle] Well, I am not sure that God is exactly like *everybody else*. It isn't hard to figure out where questions come from. Sometimes you have to work them around a bit to make them a bit less obvious and a bit more legitimate in terms of what your goal is and what the committee is looking for. A question that is a blatant plant can make you look like you are in someone's pocket.
- It has to pass the "red face" test. Is this something that he [his boss] would really ask?

Other members saw asking lobbyists' questions as a "fairly easy way" to please supporters. A northeastern Democrat conceded that he had done "a fair amount of using lobbyists' questions," but he emphasized that he "could never guarantee a satisfactory answer" from the witness or that he "would leap to [the lobbyist's] defense if the answer came back *wrong*":

> Members have to stroke people all of the time. This is an easy way to do it without really committing to a policy position. . . .
>
> Asking a question or two at a hearing might be one way to [please a supporter]. This is not really [unethical] behavior; asking a question doesn't even assure what answer you're going to get. In fact, sometimes the answer might hurt the group that wanted you to ask it. That can be all the more reason not to go with them on their policy direction. Anyway, if you ask the question that gives the group something that matters to them, they think that you've done them a favor.

Members still guard their reputation among their colleagues, even when doing a relatively innocuous favor without committing to a position. Using the same metaphor employed by a previously quoted interview subject, a retired Armed Services Committee member concluded that the "last thing an aggressive questioner wants is to do something that can make you look like you are in someone's pocket."

## Hands-on Legislating

The political science equivalent of the child's question "Where do babies come from?" is "Where does legislation come from?" The sources of public policies are diverse and numerous, with major legislation usually tracing its lineage to more than one source. Many things trigger activity in Congress.[d] Among them are cataclysmic events; presidential initiatives; media coverage; pressures from business lobbyists; efforts by public interest groups to correct economic or social injustices; and reports from governments, think tanks, and academia. Our interest here will be centered on the generic role of lobbyists in the legislative process, bearing in mind that their efforts are often collaborative and multisourced.

### Drafting Legislative Provisions

*"We have drawn up a set of specs. We would appreciate it if you would look at them and maybe draft an amendment for the upcoming markup session."*

If there is a prototypical lobbyists' action request, it is for a legislator to author a bill or to propose an amendment. Sometimes this is a fairly routine matter—a bill can contain a minor change to an existing law, or an amendment can be a recommended phrase or two to be inserted into a bill working its way through subcommittee. These provisions are usually drafted quickly; many require little or no new research to support them. In the best of worlds these provisions address an obvious oversight in the original document and thus are excellent candidates for expedited action. But that is not always the case.

Some legislation addresses multifaceted problems requiring equally complex solutions. A well-known governor, once accused of favoring large and expensive government projects, observed, "You do not solve complicated problems with simple solutions." For these matters legislative remedies can be technical, highly nuanced, and broad in their policy scope. Months, even years, of preparation may be required to put together the right proposal. When it emerges, it is usually the product of several authors—some in Congress, many not—who have relied on input from a multitude of experts and other interested parties.

The research, planning, and especially the drafting stages of legislation are classic forms of ULBs. Here, in countless unrecorded meetings, phone

d. For an insightful presentation on the origins of public policy, see John Kingdon's classic *Agendas, Alternatives, and Public Policies,* 2d ed. (Boston: Addison-Wesley, 1995).

conversations, exchanges of draft proposals, and encounters between congressional offices and lobbyists (and their clients), policy begins to emerge in its most embryonic forms. Not until all of this effort culminates in a bill that is introduced in the House or the Senate is there an official action that one can learn about from a public record. What information there is, assuming there is any at all, is the product of gossip, leaks, or skillfully floated "trial balloons."

In chapter 5 a former Senate committee counsel observed that "things happen faster now than ever before. . . . So now a lot of what we used to do ourselves has to be outsourced to lobbyists. This provides more demands for lobbyists. They can do more, but they need to do it quickly." A recently retired member from the West Coast complained that "more was being asked of all governing officials and, in some cases, we had to do it with fewer resources." He later added: "Of course, we would take help from where we could get it. I did. . . . But they [lobbyists] had to be reliable . . . many were every bit as [good] as my staff."

Thus the way to early participation and influence in the legislative process is opened to skillful lobbyists, who can supplement existing congressional resources by providing ideas for new or modified policies, developing support materials, and crafting legislative specifications, if not the actual bill language. All of this, of course, is subject to the approval of the chair and other interested congressional offices.

In chapter 2, former members spoke about what one of them called "pre-introduction negotiations in legislation." The subject is relevant here as it gives a sense of who is or is not to be lobbied on a given issue. If a member has no interest, or if the chair is running a closed shop, access points for lobbyists are limited:

- This [pre-introduction negotiating] was mostly done on the big issues: I told the [state] agencies to review provisions and draft changes. Also, the [state] Chamber of Commerce was involved. Then I would sit down with the chairman and see what could be done. This was sometimes done for private interests too, but not as often.[e]
- We would put together what we wanted; then the committee would sit with the chair and go through everyone's interests. Often we could not agree on a bill. Democracy is about the extremes at both ends and then melding something in the middle.
- Often this [preliminary work] is done in the form of having a meeting with the chair and having him approve or disapprove what it is that you want to put into the bill.

---

e. Clearly, this former member did not consider the Chamber of Commerce to be a "private interest."

- It depends on how the chair was working. Sometimes the chair would not seek input from other members; sometimes he would solicit opinions, suggestions, and positions. I think it probably had to do with how much he wanted to get something done—how much he wanted some policy or other. If he didn't care so much, he'd open it up.

The discussion in chapter 2 makes clear that members of Congress are themselves "not much involved in early drafting sessions. . . . This work is mostly done by staff." But this does not mean that members are totally divorced from the process. According to one active legislator, whose preference it was to perform a supervisory function, "The [staff] would check in," presumably for approval, and/or direction. "I was the leader of the team, but they did the actual meeting and drafting." Pursuant to this scenario lobbyists would err if they focused solely on staff, as the member intends to actively exercise her supervisory authority.

A former Senate counsel (who had reported directly to a committee chair)—after noting that "my senator never personally participated in early stages of bill preparation. . . . It was strictly a staff function."—went on to discuss the genesis of legislative concepts: "They can come from almost anywhere, and do. My job was to select what I thought were the best of these and bring them to the chair's attention." Then, after meeting with the chair—presumably to gain her approval—he would contact the legislative directors of committee members' offices (only offices of the chair's party). They would meet to discuss the bill. From that point forward, he would have meetings with members' staffs as a group or individually to review text and to consider additional ideas. Consistent with Hall's finding, "in fewer than 25 percent of the observations did a member play a role at any point in the information discussions or negotiations." [13] He observed that most members did not actively participate at this stage of the process.[f]

The counsel did not dwell on the chair's role or the role of any other member. But the between-the-lines message seemed to be that at least the chair was kept regularly informed of the bill's progress.[g]

---

f. My interviews for this part of the study focused on the act of drafting—that is, writing legislative language. Although most former members did not recall being personally involved in this specific function, many discussed activities that suggested early awareness of and input into the content of bills that would come before their committees. Some members participated in informal, though not necessarily off-hand, conversations with chairs and other colleagues about what ought and ought not to be included in the chair's mark. Others, while not involved in drafting, had some say about legislative strategies: "We would put together coalitions by designing bills including provisions that other people can be for." (Note the reference to another form of informal behavior, assembling legislative coalitions.)

As in the instance of committee report language, former members may have little recall of the early bill preparation stage, either because they did so little of the work themselves or because their involvement was so natural and informal—for example, a hallway conversation with the chair. It is not surprising then that few former members recall investing their scarce time in this activity.

g. This was a House committee counsel speaking. A Senate counsel likely would have shown a bit more policy discretion.

## Drafting Language for Committee Reports

*"We are going down the tubes on this bill. Would you work with us to get up some report language that might soften a couple of points?"*

As explained in Congressional Quarterly's *Guide to Congress,* "House rules and Senate custom require that a written report accompany each bill to the floor." The written report serves a number of functions. Among other things, it "describes the purpose and scope of the bill, explains committee amendments, [and] indicates proposed changes in existing law. [14] The committees that draft appropriations, tax, and public works bills, for example, frequently place precise instructions to the act's ultimate administrators in the report rather than in the act itself. According to an East Coast Republican, "These are the committees in which the report determines who gets what, where, and when." Moreover, the report will guide the executive agency charged with implementing regulations for the new law, and the report's exact language may provide an important basis for crucial judicial decisions in subsequent litigation concerning the subject of the act. Thus it is no wonder that lobbyists focus on the content of the report as much as that of the actual bill, if not more so.

This lobbying activity, and members' responses to it, received a wide range of comments from interviewees—everything from blank stares to "it's very important." If there was any one view approaching a consensus, it was that report language is most often a closely held function reserved for committee chairs, with only occasional input from ranking minority members. Rank-and-file members can "ask for language," but the chair (often through committee counsel) must approve a provision before it can be inserted into the report.

- The chair and ranking member generally control [report language]. The chair is the "captain." This is generally a staff function. A member will go to the chair or his staff to negotiate the language. Interest groups often are key here.
- Usually you will need the chair and often the ranking minority member. Good lobbyists will keep both of them in the loop.
- Report language is the chair's prerogative.

In the opinion of one former subcommittee chair, "getting report language" can exact a substantial political cost: "It can be very hard to get done if the chair has to sign off, or if the language really does put a spin on a new law." In these circumstances, "You would only do this for a lobby group if you were really convinced that you could trust them." Such caution is required because "most times it would be obvious who put which provisions in a report." From the point of view of this former member, lobbying the chair for report language was more akin to recorded formal activity than mere off-the-record informal activity.

The practical effect of report language is far from settled. When legislative language is general or vague—which is often the case—many authorities consider the report to be an indispensable tool for deciphering congressional intent. Both courts and executive agencies are likely to rely on a report as a basis for justifying their decisions. A retired Blue Dog Democrat (and one-time powerful subcommittee chair) agreed, noting that lobbyists play a "major role" in supplying and arguing for specific language: "If the language was vague, then we would try to get staff to fix it up [in the committee report] and, maybe, get it more to our liking. Lobbying groups often got involved in asking for that. In the Senate they sometimes could go right to staff. I don't know—in the House I suppose most [staff] would check with [their] member."

One former Senate employee turned lobbyist was convinced that report language is both important and, potentially, costly to obtain:

> This is very important. How much so depends on a few factors. Much legislation is complex and sometimes it's ambiguous. Members frequently can't agree on language, details, or even whether or not to include a provision at all. So report language can be key. That happens all the time. It really can be important in determining how a bill is interpreted by the agencies and judges.
>
> It can be [inexpensive] if you think few people will be aware or care about it, or, [because] the language may . . . be technical and simply clear up an ambiguity that does not have strongly contested policy implications. Also, sometimes no one figures out what you are doing. But it can also be [expensive]. Other people may know and care and it may require getting a number of people, sometimes the executive branch to support you.

Another lobbyist, a former Senate staffer, was unequivocal about the importance of committee reports and other forms of legislative history: "Some bills have been turned on their heads through the use of legislative history." Perhaps it is for this reason that several authorities, most notably Supreme Court justice Antonin Scalia, have serious reservations about relying too heavily, if at all, on report language: "Committee reports are not authoritative because the full house presumably knows and agrees with them but rather because the full house wants them to be. . . . It may or may not be true that the house entertains such a desire. . . . But if it is true, it is unconstitutional."[15]

Scalia's thesis was supported by an East Coast Democrat: "It's a way to fudge a position and it might be useful if there is a divided committee, and a member wants to put a spin on a position. . . . Some lobbyists were very shrewd in drafting [this material]. We liked the smallest possible spin, and they appreciated that and gave us that."

Another former Senate committee staff person offered a mixed opinion about the utility of committee report language: "Outside of Appropriations it may not mean very much. It has become diluted and so has become mostly irrelevant." Later in the interview, he admitted to the possibility of a long-term benefit:

> Even though report language may not have an immediate positive effect, it still may be used to support future legislation: "You were instructed to do this, but you never did. Now we need legislative language." Also, report language may be used to give the agency support to do something that it wants to do. So, in the right circumstances, it can help a member or a lobbyist if they are far-sighted and clever enough.

According to one law-firm-based lobbyist (and former representative), "It can mitigate a loss." A fellow trade association lobbyist who had also swung through the revolving door agreed: "You can retrieve a little bit by tweaking the report language. I've done a lot of that."

In addition to accomplishing a policy objective for their clients, lobbyists work at assuring the organizations they represent that their "man in Washington" is earning his keep: "Frequently lobbyists' purpose has little to do with influencing public officials or otherwise 'representing their clients' interests, but rather with creating favorable impressions of clients." A one-time chief of staff for a West Coast lawmaker said, "More than once we got something in a report that meant nothing, but it gave the lobbyist who had helped us out something to take home. . . . Of course, [a lobbyist] wouldn't want to do too much of that. [Overdoing it] would make you look weak, like a beggar."

Two former members confirmed that report language could be supplied as much for show and face saving as for any substantive value it may have carried:

- We felt that it was a way of giving them something without really giving them anything. . . . This is done all the time. It's easily done. It makes people happy, but I'm not sure that it matters very much. It may not have much, or any, policy effect. What it is, though, is a concrete way of showing something given to an interest group. It gives them a basis to talk to an agency.
- It was a small piece of salvage that a member could show to a constituent–lobbyist or to an interest group lobbyist and claim that he

> had gotten something done for them. The lobbyist could then go to his dues-paying members and demonstrate how effective he had been on the Hill. It was a win-win-win. Everybody got something.

There can also be collusion between a member and the executive branch. A well-experienced staff person revealed that his boss would find out what report language an agency needed to administer a bill "so that it would be helpful to these people," and he would then insert the language in the report. The staffer remembered: "One lobbyist took it upon himself to go back and forth between us and the agency to see if we could agree to language that the chair could accept. To be honest, I don't even remember how it turned out, but I do know that I was impressed with that guy; he really knew what he was doing and was giving his client their money's worth."

A slightly different dimension was supplied by a former member of the Republican House leadership: "Often, a member will prebargain report language instead of pushing for legislative language he knows he will not get or at least might not get."

In this scenario a member may be looking for a relatively quick and cheap means for pleasing a lobbyist or his client—he can claim credit for a partial victory. More honorably, upon sensing impending defeat of a favored position, a member of Congress may not want to establish a negative record for the provision by suffering a defeat in committee. Instead, she might opt for an "incremental" approach—for example, settling for report language now with the hope of legislative language in the future.

Whether one subscribes to Scalia's dismissive view or to one more favorable to the legitimacy and importance of interpretative language in committee reports, it is clear from the interviews that negotiating and constructing such language is frequently left to staff—especially to committee staff. Although this is sometimes true of legislative language, the interview subjects—mostly former staffers in this instance—were unequivocal in their opinion that there is typically less back and forth among staffers and members regarding report language than there was for legislative language.

This may explain why some former members responded with a blank stare when they were asked to comment on this form of unrecorded legislative activity. When serving in Congress, they had to be aware of committee reports, but some apparently did not spend much time actually working on them. For these members, their staffs—working with committee counsels—took care of that business and merely reported the results to their bosses, offering them only the opportunity for a veto. It is reasonable that these former members would have little or no recall of doing this work. It was after all unrecorded (never voted upon) and usually hammered out during closed meetings with few participants present.

## Competing for Earmarks

*"The university really needs this funding if they are going to build the new labs."*

Earmarks are legislative provisions that are inserted directly into appropriations bills for the purpose of funding specific projects. Often these projects are public works or research based. Because they circumvent normal congressional procedures, no hearings are conducted, and no other public deliberation takes place prior to adoption. These stealth-like add-ons are the prime vehicles for delivering pork to congressional districts. One interview subject did, however, qualify this assertion: "Pork," he argued, "is an earmark for the *other member's* district."

The practice of special funding has been around for decades, maybe even centuries, but it did not emerge as a routine tactic until the 1970s. By the time of the 2006 congressional elections, congressional watchdogs had begun to set their sights on earmarks as being deficit drivers as well as of dubious legality. The Republican leadership had been making extensive use of earmarks to fund pet projects for their members since the late 1990s. By controlling who got what, they were able to exact enhanced loyalty from their partisans. A former Republican chair of an authorizing subcommittee claimed that Rep. Tom DeLay, the former GOP majority leader, would use earmarks as a way to "keep people in line."

Majority members were not the only ones to board the gravy train. Some scholars have argued that by making earmarks broadly available to minority party members the majority was able to pursue a "blame avoidance" strategy: "By giving the minority some pork, the majority inoculates itself against charges of wasteful spending." [16] A former appropriations subcommittee chair agreed: "There is a reasonable amount of comity in the process. The ranking minority member gets an almost equal allocation [of earmark funds]." The allocation process is then filtered down to the rank-and-file, who also receive allocations.

As politically profitable as earmarks have proved to be for members of Congress and for local politicians, they have been an even bigger boon for many lobbyists. Some practitioners take special pride in having mastered the arcane ins and outs of lobbying for earmarks. This mastery is important, as each lobbyist is involved in a zero-sum game in which his request is matched against the importuning of other lobbyists—a sort of "our issue versus yours" contest. If a lobbyist emerges as the winner, his award is subtracted from the pool of funding available to the awarding source.

What results is a laddered process in which lobbyists lobby against each other for the support of their primary congressional champion, who is usually the client's member of the House or Senate. The champion then lobbies either a committee chair or perhaps a delegation chair; who then lobbies a member of the Appropriations Committee; who may need to lobby an appropriations subcommittee chair and perhaps even the full-committee chair.

Contrary to popular opinion, few "bridges to nowhere" emerge successfully from this winnowing process. Members' reputations are often an important factor in their decisions to move forward or to sit on a constituent's request. Appropriations subcommittee chairs are considered to be among the more powerful members of Congress. They are also likely to be among the most durable, their reelection virtually ensured: "What you do not want to do is to alienate them by asking for something that would only embarrass them." That means that members must provide adequate support for their recommended earmarks, a requirement that filters back to the original requesters who must have begun the process by making smart requests and providing excellent information.

A West Coast member pointed to some of the other special characteristics of earmark lobbying. For purposes of brevity I present his points in the form of bullets:

- Most members would prefer that the lobbyist approach staff first. This may be even more important for earmarks than it is for other forms of legislation because members usually ask their staff people to present all of the requests to them at the same (or approximately same) time, thus facilitating the business of "making the cuts."
- Because the pleaders are in a more direct competition with other programs, it is especially important to provide strong arguments in support of their request: "Here are our priorities." (Prioritization was especially important for communities or large organizations, for example, universities and hospitals, which might be seeking funding for more than one project.)
- For the same reason, precise and reasonable dollar requests are especially important: "Know the limits. . . . Don't ask for the world."
- For earmarks, perhaps more than for any other form of ask, lobbyists are expected to understand the system: "We would expect them to know what needed to be done and so give us the kind of information that would be helpful."
- Would-be recipients were not routinely kept up to date on the status of their requests: "I would tell them that I had sent a letter to the chair, maybe even show it to them. But that was it. After that I told them there would be no more information until a decision was made. Of course, if they got it, I would call them immediately."

There are no doubt several variations on this process that are active at any given time. But what is constant is that lobbyists who are lobbying for an earmark are held to a high standard, perhaps precisely because the process is so irregular and the competition for dollars is so intense. Although the work of allocating and awarding is not generally visible, the result is visible—at least for those willing to do the detail work of reading through appropriations bills line by line. And that is precisely what watchdogs do. If there is such a thing as a bridge to nowhere that makes it through the process, the watchdogs will find it. The resulting publicity, while seldom politically fatal, will give the perpetrators a few uncomfortable moments.

## Lobbyists and the Executive Branch

Most legislative lobbyists avoid dealing with the executive branch, especially with career service executives, like the proverbial plague. There may be several reasons for this, but chief among them is the difficulty in reaching them. The bureaucracy is huge, and lines of communication and decision-making authority are not always clear. Further, bureaucrats do not have a culture of being lobbied; in fact, some resent it vigorously. For these reasons, and there are certainly others, lobbyists sometimes seek to employ legislative personnel as interveners. This usually happens in one of two contexts: attempts to affect regulatory matters or attempts to influence executive branch views on legislative policy. Although all recent administrations have virtually forbidden career service–congressional communications unless cleared beforehand, some congressional staff indicated that they continue backdoor contacts with career personnel for "technical" input.

### Interceding on Regulatory Matters

*"Representative Smith, we are not asking you to tell the agency how they should come out on this. . . . Could you please let them know that you are aware that they are well overdue in publishing this regulation?"*

Congress has constitutionally-derived authority to make laws establishing broad regulatory policy. And it has not been bashful about using this authority—certainly not in recent decades. Cornelius M. Kerwin reports that during the 1970s "by one count, 130 laws establishing new programs of social regulation were enacted." [17] Federal agencies are charged by Congress—sometimes with very specific direction, sometimes with little or no instruction—to implement laws in an evenhanded manner. In theory at least, these regulators should enforce the law as written, without intentionally favoring or disfavoring anyone.

Although this idea is good in theory, the very act of deciding what can and cannot be done among competitors and consumers is inherently prejudicial. Even in the case of a regulation that is obviously necessary to protect public health and safety, and that is completely consistent with the authority granted to the implementing agency by Congress, complaints of "unfair!" or "overregulation!" are likely to result. In practice it is nearly impossible to create a regulation that does not favor one interest over another. But that fact alone does not make it unfair.

Congress maintains oversight authority for this process; it "remains free to intervene in ongoing rulemakings and to review completed rules using a variety of devices. . . . Some of these devices allow members to perform services to individual constituents." [18] This responsibility (and opportunity), combined with its control of agency budgets, gives Congress extraordinary leverage over regulatory processes. The door to political pressure from the Hill remains open, claims of neutrality (both substantive and political) notwithstanding. Thus it is not surprising that interest group lobbyists spend much time trying to get legislators to take advantage of that open door.

The most public form of congressional intervention is the oversight hearing.[h] It is the formal mechanism by which legislators examine the manner in which regulatory agencies implement the laws Congress has written. But these sessions often prove disappointing. And they frequently turn out to be anything but unbiased investigations. Christopher Foreman, a student of the oversight process, points to some of the biases that contaminate supposedly objective investigation: "Players with strong 'proregulation' views retain a powerful incentive to berate the opposition publicly, thus galvanizing public and congressional opinion favorable to their cause." [19]

The very process of investigation can have significant political ramifications. "Oversight is not merely a process of professional, disinterested monitoring," Foreman observes. "Rather, scrutiny is a *weapon* used by persons and groups with all sorts of personal, institutional, and political agendas." [20] There is another political motivation for conducting oversight hearings, this one generated by internecine turf wars. In a study published in 1995 Jeffrey Talbert, Bryan Jones, and Frank Baumgartner found that "often, the justification for oversight is to claim future jurisdictional control

---

h. The Senate and the House each have a committee that does almost nothing but conduct oversight. Additionally, several legislating committees have their own oversight committees, and some legislating subcommittees conduct oversight hearings, with a focus on agencies whose programs fall directly within their jurisdiction.

from a rival committee which may have a vested interest in the maintenance of the status quo." [21]

In lay terms this means that congressional committees may use oversight hearings in an effort to clarify, expand, or even usurp legislative authority over a federal program that does not reside squarely within its jurisdiction. A classic example of such conflict is health policy. In 1993 the Republican members of the Joint Committee on the Organization of Congress offered this ominous observation: "The present structure of the committee system is the largest impediment to the effective functioning of the Congress. . . . Our expectation is that, absent jurisdictional reform, the prospect of a coherent Federal policy in health care is problematic." [22]

Thus the decision to hold such hearings is itself fraught with strong political overtones; so too are the decisions about the specific issues to be investigated and the witnesses who will be called before the committee. Lobbyists for both private-sector and public interest groups are inextricably intertwined with these proceedings. Indeed, they cannot afford not to be; the high visibility often attendant to these hearings may affect an industry's interests as much as any piece of legislation.

A former committee staff person recalled pressure brought to bear on his chairman by public interest group lobbyists when a decision was being made whether to go forward with a set of oversight hearings: "The [public interest group] wanted us to take hold of that issue. [Name of committee chair] had no interest in it, and they wanted us to claim it." Industry lobbyists did not offer outright opposition: "We never heard that we should not do the hearing. Their main interest was in who got called [to testify] if we did it. They wanted us to select certain experts to testify." The inference was that these "experts" would testify in a manner favorable to the industry. (In the end the chair opted to forgo a hearing.)

In a follow-up telephone interview, the staffer said that he did not reject out of hand suggestions for witnesses. Rather, he would sometimes recommend to his chair that one or more of these people be called, "but only if we thought that they were legitimate and could help us to understand what was going on at [the agency]."

A second former committee staffer recalled that "[name of company] tried to get everyone they could think of to call us to back off the hearing. They even got hold of some state legislators. But the best I can remember is that no one [from the committee] ever did, but we heard about what they [the company] were up to. The more they tried to pressure us, the more the chairman dug in. . . . He really resented their tactics."

Again there are unspoken messages here. It is generally understood that the decision about whether to conduct a hearing, and on what subject, is the chair's to make. Other members are reluctant to challenge these decisions. They may ask to have the schedule altered or to invite witnesses who are opposed to the chair's views, but they will rarely offer anything more than token opposition to the threshold decision of whether or not to hold the hearing. From the chair's perspective, attempting to up the ante by asking her committee colleagues to lobby against the hearings infringes upon one of her most important prerogatives as chair: Any outside interference is an unacceptable challenge to her authority.

Hearings are by no means the only route for influencing regulatory policy. Interested parties frequently attempt to stimulate more direct forms of intervention by legislators, especially those members who have some claim to legislative jurisdiction over the relevant agency. Several members discussed the extent to which they attempted to influence regulatory outcomes. Note that some members evidence extreme caution, while others were more aggressive:

- Encouraging a result was easy to do, but getting a result was not. [I] used the classic front-page test: If you could envision it presented in its worst light on the front page of your local paper and you would be OK with that, then you could do it. But very carefully.
- We would certainly let agency heads know if we thought that they were going in the wrong direction. Sure, sometimes we would tell them that what they were doing would be too tough on some businesses.
- Sending letters or comments to agency people is fairly common for chairs and more senior members. But we were always careful about doing it. . . . It was not uncommon to bring an agency person into the office to weigh in during the regulation-writing process. "We authorize your budget" [was always implicit]. Agency people do respond to that message. Nor was it uncommon to send a letter. Generally the member would want to protect himself by having the exchange on the record, but members certainly do make phone calls on these matters.[i]
- Members will become involved in trying to influence broad regulatory results in the executive branch. Members will look at their own politics. They might speak out in support. Normally, for a member from an eastern state to encourage enforcement of environmental conservation standards against a midwestern utility company is easy. "It would be no skin off my back." [j]
- A member would be foolish to try to convince agency people to do something that was totally unsupportable.

---

i. This member noted that "Some of the Congress–agency exchange takes place in informal settings—at receptions and the like. It is virtually impossible to limit exchange to formal settings."

j. This member did mention that campaign contributions from the utilities in question could affect a member's decision about whether to "go on" a letter to the regulators urging such enforcement.

But some offices claimed to have denied all requests to intervene with regulators. "I would not do this; this is a no-no. I would tell people, 'Look, this is a regulatory issue. I can't help.' "

A former subcommittee chair provided a tutorial on what lobbyists and members should be thinking about when they are addressing an executive agency official on a regulatory matter:

> We would call officials at the agencies or take advantage of other opportunities to communicate with them, including sending them a letter. Even after the S&L [savings and loan] scandal, members still communicate with regulators.[k] This [should] never be done unofficially if there is a formal proceeding already in process, but absent this, members can carefully communicate with regulators asking them to focus on an issue, to reconsider a position, to pay attention to a matter.

This former chair's observation points up the critical nature of the ask. Asking a lawmaker to intervene during a proceeding is rightfully characterized as inappropriate and possibly even illegal. Any experienced member should reject this request out of hand; a pointed rebuke to the lobbyist would not be out of the question.

A request that a legislator insist upon a regulatory outcome solely because it favors a particular industry or company would be equally inappropriate. On the other hand, suggesting that someone focus on an issue, reconsider a position, or pay attention to a matter is subtler and seemingly less offensive. A former committee counsel recalled a favorite technique of his passive-aggressive mother-in-law: "She will never say that I am driving too fast. She will just say something like, 'This is a wonderful car. You can't even feel how fast you're going.' Message received." Neither the member nor the mother-in-law had expressly advocated for an outcome. Thus neither was interfering.

One other form of intervention is worth mentioning: asking regulators to meet with a lobbyist or his client. Regardless of the reason for the intervention or the venue in which it is requested, respondents agreed: "There are partisan considerations here. If it is your party in the executive branch, or if it is the other party, [it] makes a difference. But either way, you don't want to come on too strong—certainly not with the career service people." One interview subject called this the post–S&L mentality.

---

k. During the 1980s and into the 1990s hundreds of savings and loan associations became insolvent. Because deposits at these institutions were federally insured, the failures cost U.S. taxpayers billions of dollars. (Most estimates run between $150 and $180 billion.) Many scholars, journalists, and policymakers attribute the failure to lax regulation, very possibly as a result of pressures from prominent senators, who, in turn, were responding to the entreaties of major campaign contributors.

## Influencing Legislative Policy in the Executive Branch[l]

*"I have heard that the agency could support this congressman. If you were to meet with him that could make the difference."*

Perhaps no part of the federal legislative process is more susceptible to the influence of ULBs than is the business conducted in office meetings, staff-to-staff negotiations, telephone calls, and chance conversations that account for much of the give-and-take between Congress and the executive branch over policy matters. These interactions develop the initial content and chart the course for legislative provisions that may be many months, perhaps even years, from being melded into a formal bill.

All of the interview subjects with whom I discussed the subject confirmed the importance of these exchanges. They also confirmed that although lobbyists are seldom invited to these meetings their input is welcome, sometimes even solicited. Nongovernment lobbyists do not account for all of the items considered in these venues—not by a long shot—but on some matters they may account for a fair share of them. A retired member who had done some newspaper work before coming to Washington sounded very much the reporter: "Wherever in Washington there are negotiations, there are lobbyists trying to get the inside scoop on what is happening behind those doors and then get their positions onto the [participants'] agenda."

A member of President Bill Clinton's administration was generally complimentary of the role played by private-sector lobbyists in support of the people participating in these meetings: "They frequently helped to staff us out: The good ones were willing to take our lead on just how far we wanted to go. Some also knew the right buzzwords for the agency people. . . . I found some of them were better able to give us what we needed than my own people." [m]

Appealing to agency people is one of those low-profile ULBs that can make a difference far out of proportion to the expectations of policy novices. Many career service people are veterans of dozens of policy

---

l. There can be several interpretations for "policy" here. Some issues are part of the president's agenda and without question qualify as administration policy. Other matters are less important to the administration but are nonetheless subject to a thumbs-up or a thumbs-down by White House or executive department staff—including department secretaries.

m. By agency people, she was referring to members of the career civil service as opposed to political appointees. Political appointees serve at the pleasure of the president; they are part of his administration and help to set and implement his policies. Employees of the career civil service hold jobs that are "beyond reach [of the president]"—in other words, they cannot be fired without good cause, though they can be reassigned to other posts. In theory at least, career service executives are nonpartisan.

struggles in Washington. They know their facts, their issues, and their share of people in high places. Administration officials just wish that they knew their place. For political appointees, the "place" of career bureaucrats does not include them talking to members of Congress or congressional staff, not unless they are accompanied by a political appointee. This process—unauthorized communication with the Hill—is sometimes called the end run. Since as far back as President Richard Nixon, administrations have been trying to eliminate the practice. Fat chance!

James Q. Wilson provides a provocative example of backroom information exchanges that occur between congressional offices and career service personnel. The example provides evidence that administration officials have good reason to worry; these exchanges may bear heavily on congressional–executive policy struggles:

> Formally, all bureaus cleared the budgetary and legislative proposals with the White House; informally, Congress had no difficulty learning which bureau chiefs differed with the president on these matters. Formally, all agencies within the executive branch were subordinate to the president; informally, Congress, by virtue of its authority to authorize, appropriate, and investigate, had little difficulty in influencing at least the more visible activities and in shaping the more operational goals of these agencies.[23]

"Informal" is the key concept here. Just as they do in intracongressional policy negotiations, legislators and their staff regularly seek to influence administration policy through private conversations with executive branch officials, including members of the career service. A committee staffer confided, "I was on the phone with them [members of the career service] all the time. I often didn't even tell my boss about [these conversations]."

The informal back-and-forth between the Hill and the bureaucracy poses a conundrum for private-sector lobbyists. Because much legislation that affects their clients also affects agency personnel (through modifications in program mandates and legislatively determined budgets), the interests of career civil servants and lobbyists often intersect—sometimes in sync, sometimes in opposition. Jousting between the White House and Congress for control of executive agencies often occurs in periods of divided government, when the White House is in the hands of one party and at least one house of Congress is in the hands of the other party. Under these conditions divided loyalties can and do form within the bureaucracy, with some career service people siding with their executive supervisors and others covertly siding with members of Congress—thus, the importance of Wilson's observation.

These divisions, and the backroom communication channels that they spawn, make for treacherous going for any but the most sure-footed lobbyists. The challenge to them is made all the more difficult because it is not just *what* they say; it is also to *whom* they say it that can be a potential deal breaker. "The only option you have," advised a staffer-turned-member-turned lobbyist, "is to stick close to your best [most knowledgeable] congressional allies. They may not know anything either, but they are more likely to [know something] than you are; and they are certainly in a better position to find something out."

Treacherous territory or not, the career service is an organic repository of information on most issues that lobbyists try to influence. Lobbyists may find that they have prematurely written off an extremely valuable resource if they do not at least try to access this repository. Although career service personnel may have their own biases based on their belief systems, professional background, and even career interests, they are also the institutional memory for most federal programs. If a lobbyist seeks to amend an existing law, as is often the case, there is a reasonable chance that someone buried in the bowels of the executive branch will have been involved in the development of the original legislation, the law that the lobbyist now hopes to amend. There is also a possibility that current congressional staff will have worked with that person in the past, or will be consulting with that person now, or both.

A recently retired career service executive laid out the challenge and potential upside in working with career service executives: "Many of the people I worked with had close ties to Congress. Most of them did not want to be lobbied [by private-sector lobbyists]. . . . But I have to say that they provided much of the background information that the committees relied on. If a lobbyist could get them to listen, and if they could agree, it could be very helpful to them [the lobbyists]."

Here is where there is a possible disconnect. The consensus among the interview subjects was that when lawmakers attempt to influence administration policy "members [as opposed to staff] must be the ones to speak to an executive branch official, i.e., political appointees." One former lawmaker went a step further, thinking this task is best left to committee leadership: "In our committee it was usually the chairman that spoke to executive officials. He had the broadest view of things."

The interview subjects noted the extent to which partisanship played a role in their decision to approach the executive branch. They divided communications with the executive into two very broad categories: exchanges that produced policy outputs and those that were solely informational. On policy matters the party in the White House mattered quite a bit: "Oh, yes, we'd do this [lobby the executive] but only if it was [our party]."

On more objective technical matters the criteria were different, and partisanship became less relevant: "We had to work with the department regardless of party, especially when it came to technical expertise." The assumption here is that technical expertise resided predominantly with members of the career service.

But a simple two-compartment split may not capture the full range of possibilities here. There may be, as is often the case in legislative politics, a subtle in-between area that relatively few players know to explore. Sometimes an opinion offered by an expert—in our case, a member of the career service—can affect how legislators view their policy options:

> *Question:* If we do what is being suggested here, isn't there a good chance that a reduced cost of services to the elderly will result?
>
> *Answer:* Well, I really could not say for sure. But you may want to take a look at what has happened in Minnesota; they put in place something like what you are thinking about.

In this scenario the career service person knows darn well what the inquisitors will learn when they look at the recommended program. No policy recommendation has been offered, but a gentle nudge in the right direction may serve just as effectively.

The problem for private-sector lobbyists is gaining access to these officials. Notwithstanding Anthony Nownes's finding that lobbyists meet "personally with executive agency personnel . . . very often," it is frequently difficult to arrange a meeting with members of the career service.[24] As we have mentioned, many career people do not care to be lobbied; some see it as a less than entirely ethical practice. The chaperone requirement—that career people must be accompanied by political personnel when meeting with congressional types—is another reason. One careerist put it this way: "I understand it, but it is still humiliating." Finally, there is the matter of confidentiality. Most career service employees are reluctant to jeopardize their positions by depending upon private-sector lobbyists to maintain their cover.[n]

A recently retired member who had served as a staffer for nearly two decades before being elected to Congress, said, "I would put these people [career service executives] together with a lobbyist in order to flush out what I needed [to know]; but this was only for lobbyists that I could trust. . . .

---

n. An interesting dynamic plays out here. A long-time congressional staffer who has served since the early 1990s (with a short interlude) shared this view: "Most of the career people were not comfortable with me. They knew my members supported the administration. . . . Over time I was able to gain their confidence by never blowing their cover. It was more than honor; it was very practical. They were a tremendous source of information, and I did not want to lose that . . . too valuable."

They knew the consequences if they told the administration." This is another example in which the revolving door made a significant difference to the lawmaker: "I would do this with lobbyists that I knew well—mostly ex-staff people I had known." He explained that the former staffers knew "the best questions to ask" and understood and respected the importance of maintaining these confidences."

## The Peripherals

"Peripheral" in this discussion does not mean unimportant. It is simply the case that some asks are more obtuse than others, in the sense that the requested action may be less direct or less certain in its effects than the more specific requests suggested earlier. Certainly, some peripherals have the potential to yield strong and positive results, but for the most part they are tangential to the processes needed to achieve outcomes.

### Building Coalitions and Stoking Media Interest

*"We know that several groups could get on this bill. If you were to call them, we would then follow up with them."*

Forming coalitions has become more than a part of legislative politics—for many, it *is* legislative politics. Certainly this is true for the politics that surround major issues; it is also the case for some smaller issues. Lobbyists and legislative offices that have the status, energy, finesse, and contact base needed to knit together coalitions are the ones that succeed in moving their legislative agendas forward.

There is no universally accepted starting point for this process—not according to study respondents. Each issue requires its own melding of interests and mobilization of resources. With this said, the process can and often does begin during the earliest stages of legislative development, before legislative counsel has produced a first draft.

The Blue Dog who estimated that "as much as 80 percent of the ideas for legislation come from interest groups" argued that the sources of legislative ideas are themselves frequently coalitions, often in the form of trade associations or public interest groups. Because trade associations are collections of companies with common interests, a base of support automatically accompanies introduction of their bill. This is even more the case when initiatives emanate from large, multi-industry peak business associations or ad hoc associations.[o] According to the Blue Dog, "They have lots of resources and know how to put together legislation we can work with."

Another Blue Dog argued, "You put together coalitions by designing bills [that include] provisions that other people can be for." Thus committee chairs need to know what is of interest to their colleagues before they put together their mark. A former staff person described the early stages of the process: "The chair solicits ideas and requests from members. It's usually bipartisan at this point. Members may stake out their issue." Other interview subjects generally agreed with this description, though not all of them thought the process was usually bipartisan, even at the early stages: "It really depends on the chairman. Some are less partisan than others."

A former lawmaker explained that "anticipation is really what much of the coalition building is about—having a sense of what will fly with what groups. That way you have a pretty good [strategic] blueprint before you even start." Chairs and entrepreneurs must ask the fundamental question: "What do other members need to be attracted to the bill." That thinking guides, but does not necessarily control, decisions about what provisions are inserted into the original drafts: "Lobbyists can help us identify the various interests that may weigh in." The strategy is to get political allies "on the hook" by showing them that there is "something in it" for them.

Members do not always rely on their own instincts or those of their staff people to figure this out. Some offices poll their friends, including interest group allies, to see what provisions they would like to have put in a bill or, conversely, what provisions they would not be able to live with. Seen this way, the work of forming coalitions is virtually built into the lawmaking process. Committee chairs must satisfy a majority—or coalition—of their members in order to report a bill from committee. While the definition of "satisfying" might include some Lyndon Johnson–type arm twisting, it most often connotes a more voluntary meeting of the minds.

Remember the discussion about timing in chapter 2? "The chair does negotiate provisions early on." If you want to get something in or changed you have to get in early. Getting something in can also include committee report language that has been negotiated with the chair and other members. A former member of his party's leadership spoke about the process

---

o. Peak associations are organizations that comprise companies from a variety of industries. According to Kay Lehman Schlozman and John T. Tierney, in *Organized Interests and American Democracy* (New York: Harper and Row, 1986), 40, they "articulate the business perspective on broad policy issues." The Business Roundtable, National Chamber of Commerce, National Federation of Independent Businesses, and National Association of Manufacturers are highly regarded peak associations. Ad hoc organizations are temporary alliances that lobby for a specific interest—usually a bill or part of a bill—that affects a number of different companies or interests. In theory, the group disbands once the issue has been resolved.

of trading report language for bill support: "Chairs will trade report language for support for the bill. Members often try to put in language for a constituent or some other interest group. He [the chair] may not want to put a provision in the actual text because it will disturb his coalition, but he might give some report language." A southeastern Democrat made a similar observation: "Sometimes in putting together a coalition, a sponsor will agree to [accept] some report language in advance."

The message in all of this is that coalition building starts by constructing a product that will prove marketable to a particular community (or communities) of members and outside interests. If enough legislators can be satisfied early on—this may mean accepting some of their provisions—and as a consequence locked into a deal with the chair, she (the chair) will have successfully initiated the process of putting together a supportive coalition. On some issues the support of subcommittee members, even if it is only members of the chair's party, will be enough to carry the bill to passage.

This is by no means a passive process. Legislative entrepreneurs do not usually wait for potential allies to come out of the woodwork. A northern Republican and former subcommittee chair recalled that she "not infrequently" made groups aware of her legislative interests. Often, these were groups with whom she had worked well in the past or whom she had been able to help on a prior matter. For these groups the issue at hand may have been no more than a second-level priority, but their desire to support her, perhaps as an investment for future legislative interests, was enough to spur them to action. This is a classic example of a savvy legislator knowing how to use her leverage—unstated, subtle, and effective. And in her mind it was an example of "smart lobbyists knowing how to advise their clients. Surprisingly, some of these clients found it hard to grasp the concept of investment. If they saw no immediate benefit, they were reluctant to get involved."

A trade association lobbyist, a long-time Senate staffer and a successful lobbyist for several years, said that "on a few occasions" he had been asked by congressional offices to contact some of his clients to get them involved in a lobbying effort. The congressional offices asked that the client "take a position and become active" on a pending issue. "Members go to lobbyists [whom] they are close to in order to get them to mobilize [clients] for or against a position. It's part of the process, and the lobbyists I worked with liked it because it really did make them part of the process. . . . And obviously they picked up a marker."

In John Bibby's *Congress Off the Record,* an unidentified member discusses a slightly different use of outside interests: "You work your colleagues if you get a bill you're really interested in in terms of setting up your own whip organization basically. The other thing—the thing I find myself arguing with an interest group—is to get them turned on to go to work on some other member. . . . I urged them to go focus on what I thought ought to be the appropriate target. . . . They can be an ally." [25]

The rationale for complying with these offbeat requests was explained by a Florida Republican: "It is possible to get some groups that are even a little out of field to lobby an issue. This is the way a lobbyist can do a favor for a member." What this Floridian was talking about was the act of expanding a supportive coalition by enlisting organizations that have only a limited stake in an issue. The quid pro quo is a projected increase in the enlisted company's store of political capital with an important legislator.[p]

Another Republican, a self-professed legislative entrepreneur (and a highly skilled one at that), extended the scope of our conversation about coalition building to include efforts to mold public opinion. She said that she often moved her coalition-building efforts beyond Congress. In the brief dialogue that follows, she explains how she would "take an issue public":

> *Member:* Take an issue to the media; leak a potential story to an editor or producer, and make [it] sexy. The media is an important tool for members who want to gain support for an issue.
>
> *Author:* Do members often initiate contact with the press?
>
> *Member:* Absolutely! I certainly did. Sometimes we would do it; other times we would advise an interest group that it should be done and give them some ideas about how to get it done.
>
> *Author:* Does that include telling them who to talk to?
>
> *Member:* Sure.

Coalition building, whether done pursuant to a strategic game plan or done instinctively, is to entrepreneurial lobbyists and lawmakers what speechmaking is to political candidates; it is both an expected and a highly revealing process. Without it there is little hope for success. From chatting up an idea in the cloakroom, to writing provisions designed to attract colleagues, to searching for cosponsors, to contacting interest groups and newspaper reporters, the coalition-building process is incessant. The skill with which it is conducted says much about its architects.

The Florida Republican quoted in chapter 4 produced the most convincing observation of all—one that both fits and transcends the immediate subject of coalition building:

> Overall, the best thing a member or a lobbyist can do is to be persistent—to stay on top of what they want every step of the way. This includes

---

p. There is the potential for some lobbying sleight of hand here. Some lobbyists are not above trading off one client's interests in order to benefit another client or a particular member of Congress.

monitoring press coverage and ginning up press interest when that is required. The goal is to put the opposition on the defensive. Good legislators and good lobbyists are dogged. That's the easy part; the hard part is to do this without being a pain in the butt.

## Asking for Advice and Information

*"We have been thinking about asking the chair if she would sponsor this. What would you advise?"*

The ask does not always contain a request for legislative activity per se—for example, "Please speak to Senator Smith." Even veteran lobbyists occasionally need more information than they have at their disposal, or they may need advice and direction from true insiders—the members of Congress. Payne's "policy types" are likely to be well suited to these functions. If there are players in the congressional policy milieu who are savvy and wired, it is they. Everyday they hear, or are in a position to hear, the "latest" facts, rumors, suggestions, and decisions—the full gamut—from colleagues, administration officials, and other lobbyists. They learn about which bills are on the chair's priority list, what members are interested in which bills, what priorities leadership has established, what interest groups are interested, and who are likely to be the most active members on any given issue.

Such advice is not limited to the premier lobbyists. One member made a point of saying that he would "give advice to anyone who came in to see me. I didn't care what their position was." This comment was similar to one offered by a former colleague: "Most members will try to be evenhanded in whom they see and the quality of advice that they offer." A staff person recalled that his boss, a prominent committee chair, gave gratuitous advice to the pharmaceutical industry "when it was getting the [daylights] kicked out of it" by the chair's party leadership. He told them that "they should go to the White House to cut a deal. He said that Clinton would deal."

Asks for information focused primarily on the intentions of members' for scheduling ("Will the bill be taken up this year?"); positions ("Will she support us?"); possible amendments ("Will he offer an amendment to reduce this?"); procedural maneuvers ("Is he going to put a hold[q] on it?"),

q. A hold permits a senator to stop floor action on a bill for an undetermined amount of time. (The general rule of thumb was about three legislative days. Leadership would seldom let them go much longer.) Holds may be seen as a signal that the senator is considering a filibuster, though, often they have been used simply to buy time to learn more about a bill or to inform colleagues about possible problems in the measure. Historically holds could be placed without disclosing the name of the senator who had placed the hold, but the 2007 reforms now require public disclosure of holds and the senators placing them.

among many other such matters. Some information straddles the lines between fact, well-educated opinion, or best guess. In any of these circumstances, lobbyists are given the best thinking of legislative pros—thinking that they can then compare with what they are learning from other sources.

The interview subjects produced several examples of the kinds of advice that were sought and given. Many responses morphed into general discussions about strategic concerns and legislative basics, some of which could just as well have been directed to junior members of Congress as to lobbyists:

- This is who you should talk to on the committee.
- Don't do it! It will upset a lot of members.
- This is not the right time to push.
- I'd try to help them to prepare a bill so that it would go to a certain committee.
- Here's how to be sure that this bill does not get referred to two committees.
- These are the key players.
- I can assure you that running ads in his district will not get you anywhere that you want to be.
- This is how you want to lobby this issue.
- Your proposal needs to be broader, more generic. It's too obvious, too specific to your company.
- You should try to get [name of member] to cosponsor.
- [To a trade association lobbyist] You should use your grassroots network, and here is who you should concentrate on.

Lobbyists and members also participate in advice-giving (and receiving) forums that are more public than the standard in-office visit: "I was often invited to speak to groups and give speeches in which I gave political advice about what they should be looking to get done. This could be more important than people might ordinarily think. It was a way of getting to dozens of company representatives as individuals and as members of a powerful association."

## Additional Action Requests

Members and staff identified several more action requests. Some of these qualify as insider tactics, and others are just plain rare. All provide insights into the subtlety, sophistication, and complexity that frequently characterize lobbyist–member relationships—especially when those relationships are between experienced and savvy parties.

## Voting Late

When legislators know little about a subject and have not sensed much interest among their constituents, they may opt to take a cue from a colleague's vote. In other words, they will simply vote the way a colleague they have learned to trust and respect has voted. According to a New York Republican, "Some members carry as many as 50–60 votes."

One way to discourage this practice is for members who carry votes to cast their vote as late as possible. Generally these members take pride in serving as a guide to other members, but there are times when they would prefer a lower profile and for one reason or another do not want to carry votes with them:

> Sometimes I just could not help a group that had been supportive of me. That is, I could not give them a vote or do anything that really supported their goal. But, if I had no very strong interest in the matter, I could tell them that I would try to "take no one with me." So I would vote late, after all of the other votes were cast. On close votes that sort of thing could be appreciated.

## Withholding Proactive Support

Most interest group requests are positive or proactive in nature—for example, "Please do this." On occasion, however, lobbyists will seek forbearance from a member in lieu of a positive action. This may occur when a lawmaker who is usually allied with an interest group is locked into a position—perhaps because of party pressure or an agreement with another member—and therefore cannot or will not change a previously established position. If the member agrees to do nothing more to aid the progress of a bill, notwithstanding her prior commitment to vote for it, she will perform (by omission) one of the most common ULBs.

Although no chartable record is created when a member withholds informal activity in support of a measure, the member may be doing a significant favor for an interest group: "I would tell them, 'Look, I can't vote against this, but I won't do anything to push for it.' [r] You could also do this

---

r. In extended conversation this member was blunt about the fact that this was the sort of ULB that was done to respond to people or organizations that had been financial supporters of the member.

[for] other members." A former colleague saw this as a common behavior: "I think we all did this from time to time—if we could."

## Lobbying for a Rule

In the House virtually all bills that are reported from committees must be granted a rule before they may be considered on the House floor. Although rules can do many things, in some instances even rewrite the bill, they generally designate which amendments, if any, will be in order and how much time will be given to debate. An open rule permits an unlimited number of amendments; a closed rule prohibits any amendments. A modified closed rule limits the number of amendments. Thus the effect on policy outcomes and the ability for legislators to become involved in position taking can be significantly affected by rules.

A former subcommittee chair said he remembered lobbying the Rules Committee on many occasions. He noted that as a chair it was one of his more important responsibilities: "It came with the job." Another former majority member, not a chair, also recalled lobbying for rules, but he cautioned, "This isn't something you would do every day. Just when you thought it really counted. . . . I would only do this if it were *my* issue. I would never do it just because a lobbyist asked me to. . . . To me, when you lobby Rules [the Rules Committee], you are lobbying leadership."

## Addressing the Party Caucus

Each party meets in caucus to discuss its strategies and positions. Barbara Sinclair characterizes the caucus as "the place where a great deal of freewheeling debate . . . takes place." [26] A former member of his party's leadership argued that the caucus was "an opportunity to convince your colleagues about the merits or dangers of positions and strategies." He related this knowledge to lobbyists' action requests: "I don't think many lobbyists even thought of the caucus as part of the system. This seemed to be something that ex-members would think of and maybe suggest to you as a place to pick up support."

Another member who had served in the majority in the House saw the caucus as mostly a leadership-controlled forum: "The Speaker dominates the party caucus." He further confided that leadership will "attempt to use the caucus as a vehicle in an effort to bind colleagues to a party position."

Another member, a former ranking minority member, gave a partial listing of the sorts of observations that he and other members would hear and might think useful:

- There is too much labor opposition.
- Too many affected members are in marginal districts. This isn't the time.
- We need to change the language of the bill.
- Don't take it up. There isn't time and the Senate won't pass it anyway. It's a waste of time.

Not all of the interview subjects were fans of the party caucuses. One had an especially low opinion: "Lots of talk and, yeah, sometimes we'd come out of it with something. But mainly it did not usually change much. A 'Dear Colleague' could get you just as much and waste a lot less time."

At the more personal level, one interviewee cautioned that addressing the caucus is "serious business." It is an opportunity to influence colleagues; it is also an opportunity for colleagues to evaluate the member: Is he articulate or is he bumbling? Is he realistic or naïve? Is he worth listening to or is he wasting everyone's time? It is also an occasion to please leadership or to put oneself at odds with the party's hierarchy. As for lobbyists' input, "If you are going to be hauling someone's load, you had better know what the hell you are talking about."

## Developing Legislative Strategies

Shrewd strategists are to legislators what an effective general is to an army. They can mastermind a campaign from its beginning to its conclusion. Members—sometimes in meetings, perhaps even in caucuses, and often during informal conversation—are constantly seeking and giving advice about the best way to maneuver a bill through Congress and onto the president's desk. How should it be worded? Who should introduce it? When should it be introduced? Who should speak to whom? What should the rule be? Can we attract support from the other side?

All members do this, but a few distinguish themselves for their strategic thinking. The same can be said for a handful of lobbyists:

- He was as shrewd as anybody up here. He knew procedure, and he understood people. His sense of timing was impeccable.
- She had worked for leadership, and boy could you tell! She understands the hows and the whens.

None of the members perceived a strong downside for lobbyists who attempted some kibitzing on such matters, "Unless, of course, you look like an idiot. And, believe me, there are some idiots." Most ex-members, however, did agree with a former colleague who "preferred to let us [people in Congress] do that."

## Conclusion

Lobbyists are free to ask members and staff for just about anything they think is necessary to move their agenda forward. They may not get what they ask for, but they can certainly try their best. Of course, for nervous clients who are paying their lobbyists handsome fees or salaries, trying may not be good enough. Clients are shelling out for success, not for effort alone.

What then increases lobbyists' chances for having their asks yield positive results? The answer is disarmingly simple: The right matchup—of purpose, member, and circumstance. By circumstance, I am speaking of how each of the capital gain-loss factors considered in chapter 4 will bear upon the targeted member at that particular juncture and for that particular purpose. (Other factors are involved, but there is neither the time nor the space to consider them here.)

What is important to understand is the context; an ask can be evaluated only in the context in which it is offered. Before one even begins to think about cost-gain variables, some basics must be established: The targeted member should be in a position to execute the lobbyist's request. This usually means that she is a member of the relevant committee and in most cases a member of the majority party (though majority party status may mean less in the Senate than in the House, and it can vary from committee to committee). She should also have sufficient gravitas to ensure that her arguments will be heard and taken seriously. When all of these elements are in place, one can then think about which of the cost-gain variables will bear most heavily upon the request.

Few experienced lobbyists will actually take out pen and paper and do the math, but the process does take place in some form or another. For experienced lobbyists it may be done more by instinct than by conscious thought. One can make an argument, however, that even veterans should take the time to formalize the task—at least for other than routine matters. Why? Because funny things happen on the way to the committee room.

It may not be possible for a lobbyist to anticipate every impediment that may come into play as an issue unfolds, but scrupulous preparation in constructing the ask in the context in which it is being made will go a long way toward protecting against the unforeseen—the bane of lobbyists' and members' professional lives.

Even if the timing is right, the participants carefully selected, and the arguments skillfully presented, victory for lobbyists can be elusive. The definitional questions aside (what is a win and what is a loss?), there is much that determines the fate of legislative activity that is beyond the control of outside players. Remember, lobbyists may have influence, but they do not have power.[s]

I began this chapter by saying that the importance of the ask cannot be overstated—that it is the prime mover for lobbyists. But the ask is more than that; it is also the *prime indicator*—that which speaks most directly to a lobbyist's understanding of congressional systems and politics: "Smart lobbyists ask us to do smart things. Others who aren't so smart—well, you get the point."

## Notes

1. Richard L. Hall, *Participation in Congress* (New Haven: Yale University Press, 1996), 27–28.
2. John E. Jackson and John W. Kingdon, "Ideology, Interest Group Scores, and Legislative Votes," *American Journal of Politics* 36 (August 1992): 816.
3. Margaret Thompson, *The Spider Web* (Ithaca: Cornell University Press, 1986), 154.
4. John Kingdon, *Congressmen's Voting Decisions* (Ann Arbor: University of Michigan Press, 1989), 17.
5. Thompson, *The Spider Web,* 153.
6. Daniel Kessler and Keith Krehbiel, "Dynamics of Cosponsorship," *American Political Science Review* 90 (September 1996): 565.
7. Rick K. Wilson and Cheryl D. Young, "Cosponsorship in the U.S. Congress," 22 *Legislative Studies Quarterly* (February 1997): 40–41.
8. E. E. Schattschneider, *The Semisovereign People: A Realist's View of Democracy in America* (Fort Worth, Texas: Harcourt Brace Jovanovich, 1988), 66.
9. Barbara Sinclair, *Legislators, Leaders, and Lawmaking: The U.S. House of Representatives in the Postreform Era* (Baltimore: Johns Hopkins University Press, 1995), 260.
10. Thomas Dye, *Top Down Policymaking* (New York: Chatham House, 2001), 130.
11. Burdett A. Loomis, *The Contemporary Congress* (New York: St. Martin's, 1996), 79.
12. Barbara Sinclair, *Unorthodox Lawmaking: New Legislative Processes in the U.S. Congress,* 3d ed. (Washington, D.C.: CQ Press, 2007), 277.
13. Hall, *Participation in Congress,* 141.
14. *Guide to Congress,* 6th ed. (Washington, D.C.: CQ Press, 2007).
15. Antonin Scalia, *A Matter of Interpretation: Federal Courts and the Law* (Princeton: Princeton University Press, 1997), 35.
16. Steven J. Balla, Eric D. Lawrence, Forrest Maltzman, and Lee Sigelman, "Partisanship, Blame Avoidance, and the Distribution of Legislative Pork," *American Journal of Political Science* 46 (July 2002): 524.

---

s. In Jeffrey H. Birnbaum's book *The Lobbyists* (New York: Times Books, 1992), cited in chapter 1, several top-flight congressional lobbyists are followed throughout the budget and tax battles of the 101st Congress (1989–1991). These lobbyists are highly skilled, well-paid veterans of the Washington legislative wars. Their work is for the most part excellent. But, despite their professionalism, none of them achieves an outright victory when the legislation finally passes. In some cases the lobbyist flat out loses.

17. Cornelius M. Kerwin, *Rulemaking: How Government Agencies Write Law and Make Policy,* 3d ed. (Washington, D.C.: CQ Press, 2003), 13.
18. Ibid., 33–34.
19. Christopher H. Foreman Jr., *Signals from the Hill: Congressional Oversight and the Challenge of Social Regulation* (New Haven: Yale University Press, 1988), 21–22.
20. Ibid., 35.
21. Jeffrey C. Talbert, Bryan D. Jones, and Frank R. Baumgartner, "Nonlegislative Hearings and Policy Change in Congress," *American Journal of Political Science* 39 (1995): 383–406.
22. C. Lawrence Evans, "Committees and Health Jurisdictions in Congress," in *Intensive Care: How Congress Shapes Health Policy,* ed. Thomas E. Mann and Norman J. Ornstein (Washington, D.C.: American Enterprise Institute and Brookings Institution, 1995), 25.
23. James Q. Wilson, *Bureaucracy* (Basic Books, 1989), 259.
24. Anthony J. Nownes, *Total Lobbying: What Lobbyists Want (and How They Try to Get It)* (New York: Cambridge University Press, 2006), 18.
25. John Bibby, *Congress Off the Record* (Washington, D.C.: American Enterprise Institute, 1983), 35.
26. Barbara Sinclair, *Majority Leadership in the House* (Baltimore: Johns Hopkins University Press, 1983), 96–97.

# 7 Designing and Executing a Lobbying Campaign

In this chapter I present a basic guide for devising a lobbying campaign. I also include some further observations about lobbying style. Some of the latter reflect views held by virtually all of the interview subjects; others are not as broadly accepted. I make no pretense here of providing a template that will cover every possible component of a campaign or that will anticipate every pitfall a lobbyist might encounter. Doing so would be impractical, presumptuous, and voluminous. Rather, I draw upon the responses from the interview subjects, supplemented by research by scholarly authorities, to focus on the core requirements for launching and implementing a lobbying campaign.

## The Core Elements of a Campaign

Lobbying is not an event. It is a process—a living process at that. In every lobbying campaign the precise components and the methods of implementation that are employed will be as different as the practitioners who create and execute them. What works for one mix of lobbyists, clients, issues, and venues will be impractical for others. What makes sense today will be out the window tomorrow. Allies may cut and run; even worse, they may become turncoats.

Although it may be overly pessimistic to warn that what can go wrong will go wrong, prudent practice demands that lobbyists explore a variety of strategies and anticipate possible setbacks before they implement a plan. In fact, given the unpredictability of the process, having a Plan B may not be enough; a lobbyist should consider going deeper into the alphabet. And even then unforeseen events will require further regrouping, rethinking, and redeployment of assets.

Lobbyists should take a lesson from retailers, who will tell anyone willing to listen that the three essentials for a retail business are location, location, and location. For lobbyists, one need only change the word "location" to "preparation." With these thoughts in mind, we begin our discussion by looking at the preliminary activities that lay the groundwork for a successful lobbying campaign.

## Prepositioning

Experienced professionals do not wait until their issue is front and center before they begin to position themselves to serve prospective clients. True, not until a client is signed up and an issue identified can a lobbyist gauge the exact resources he will need for a particular project. But offsetting this dilemma is the fact that many lobbyists have an area or two of specialization. Thus they have already narrowed the potential universe of committees, members, and interest groups that they will need to connect with when serving their clients. Establishing rapport with these people is one important means of prepositioning themselves to do business.

### Making Early Introductions

Several legislators agreed with the gentleman from Oklahoma,[a] who warned, "You have to get to know people *before* you need them." A lobbyist made this observation: "At the beginning of every term I make the rounds of freshman members and other offices that I have not seen much of recently. That way, if I come in [later], it is not some total stranger walking in the door."

A former congressional counsel added a similar sentiment. He noted the importance to lobbyists of "sensitizing [legislators and staff] to issues that [he] sees coming down the pike." He made clear that "going into a lot of detail" ought not to be part of the sensitizing process. Rather, "It is just a sort of heads up." Like the getting-to-know-you sessions, these visits set the stage for the time when the lobbyist comes in to address an issue in depth and perhaps to make his ask. The counsel concluded, "I have never known it [an early introduction] to hurt. . . . It can only be helpful."

---

a. In formal debate members of Congress will not refer to other members by name; they will use such terms as "the gentlewoman from Kentucky" or "the honorable gentleman from Delaware." The root of this custom is concern for civility. In theory, it reduces the likelihood of ad hominem attacks that would make deliberative examination of policy positions more difficult.

Early introductions also serve to provide lobbyists with a first impression of the people they will be doing business with and allow them to check for first-impression vibes—positive or negative. A corporate lobbyist remembered meeting Rep. Jim Florio, D-N.J., for the first time:

> I met Jim Florio the first day he was in Congress—at his swearing-in reception in his office. I had heard that he would be trouble and had not even planned to stop in, but I passed his office and thought, "What the heck." We hit it off and wound up having a constructive relationship. . . . He always listened. He was a hard worker and a straight shooter. . . . We disagreed a lot but always got on well.

On paper this friendship would not have seemed likely. But the early introduction provided an opportunity for the lobbyist to receive and read the vibes that led to a "constructive relationship."

Early introductions also include getting to know staffers. A member's staff is better positioned than any other resource to provide first-person insights into the legislators they serve. There is another benefit: One of the most frequently overlooked truths about lobbying is that it is almost always easier to be candid—challenging, if need be—with staff than it is with members of Congress. This statement holds true even more in the Senate than in the House. Further, in the Senate, convincing staff may be all that a lobbyist needs to do.

In either chamber, however, ignoring or otherwise getting on the wrong side of staff can be downright dangerous. Remember, when the lobbyist leaves the member's office the staffer stays behind. The following comment by a former committee counsel was made in the context of discussing staff–lobbyist disagreements: "In the long run, staff always wins." It may be a consider-the-source observation, but it is worth thinking about.

## Understanding the Utility of "Belonging"

Extracongressional contacts provide venues ripe with prepositioning opportunities of a different sort. Issue networks (discussed in chapter 5) are such venues. Recall that these loose confederations consist of government officials, think tank and university scholars, public interest group and industry executives, and others who are immersed in a specific policy domain. Associating with these people enables lobbyists to acquire a certain intellectual patina. At a minimum it enables them to get to know and share ideas with an eclectic mix of people who may have the ear of policy elites.

Trade association memberships also offer positioning opportunities, though these are generally more targeted, industry-specific venues. These associations facilitate opportunities for information sharing and contact building by holding frequent meetings, setting up off-location conferences, and joining together in coordinated lobbying campaigns waged under the association's flag. In addition, associations enable members to locate potential allies on issues that do not qualify for full association action.

Associations also provide their membership with direct lobbying services. A lobbyist for a large pharmaceutical company confided, "On some issues, even though we feel we are right, we know that [our argument] will not play well with the public. Then we'll let the associations take the lead; they don't have a public [image] to protect."

The vast majority of interviewees who commented on the subject had high praise for the quality of representation provided by these organizations: "I liked trade association lobbyists. They were all professionals. That's why they were hired. Even some company lobbyists can be inexperienced in the way [Washington] works. The association people I dealt with knew what they were doing—[they included] lots of former government people."

One reason for the overall level of competence is that business association lobbyists are akin to the lobbyists' lobbyist. Most companies that belong to these organizations have their own lobbyists on payroll. And even companies that are too small to have an in-house government relations specialist are usually managed by intelligent, no-nonsense people. Thus association lobbyists play to a sophisticated audience that is unlikely to tolerate anything less than excellent performance.

Association membership offers a special opportunity for newcomers. It permits them to "go to school" to learn from experienced lobbyists and thus jump-start their own lobbying efforts. The expertise demonstrated by association lobbyists tends to trickle down to novices. Those who are smart enough to watch, listen, and learn—and especially those who bother to pick the brains of association staff—will improve their chances of participating successfully in collective lobbying campaigns and managing their own government-relations needs when the association is working on matters of broader industry or business interests.

## Defining the Ultimate Objective

When an urgent call comes in from a client—perhaps sounding panicky late on a Friday afternoon—a typical lobbyist's first response is, "What do I need to know about this matter?" The question seems simple enough, but the sought-after information is not always easily unearthed. Further complicating things, clients have a tendency to tell their lobbyist only what they want him to hear. In some cases this may be fine, but it can leave the lobbyist in the dark and vulnerable to embarrassing revelations, thus contriving a virtual invitation for disaster. These omissions may be the result of an innocent oversight by executives who do not understand congressional systems well enough to anticipate the kind of information needed to further their cause. But they can be the result of something less benign: intentional withholding of information that the client is unwilling to disclose for fear that it will reflect poorly on his company or cause. Successful lobbyists, like hard-nosed litigators, learn to bore in and explore beyond their client's surface presentations. As one independent lobbyist observed, "It is amazing how fast their white hats become gray."

Once a lobbyist is convinced that he knows all there is to know, he can begin to work with his client to fashion a request or a remedy: Does his client need an exemption for his class of product from specific regulatory requirements? Does he need to convince the executive branch to use its authority to place the company's product in a different class? Should the university seek a grant to construct a new health sciences building?

Whatever the result of this brainstorming process, once it is completed the lobbyist and the client should have agreed upon exactly what their ultimate goal is. Only then can they construct a big-picture strategy that should include various interim goals. (We will return to the subject of interim goals later in this chapter.)

A former member made a strong case for bringing such questions to legislators or staffers before the lobbyist and the client have decided upon a course of action: "If you think you have a good case, there is no harm in asking us to help you think it through." His larger point is that experienced legislators, if they are sympathetic to the overall objective, may be able to suggest the most suitable course for the lobbyist and his client to pursue. The former member continued: "You don't know. You might hear [from the legislator] 'when you come up with something, let me see it.' . . . He might mean that he will consider taking the lead for you—becoming your horse." [b]

The process he proposed is sometimes referred to as "co-option." Often lobbyists think they must have their ask in hand before they go up to the Hill. Not so. Bringing a legislator into one's confidence, seeking her advice, and incorporating her thinking into a plan can reap two strategic rewards. First, if the lobbyist selects his confidante wisely, he will receive useful insight from an insider. Second, he may have recruited an energetic believer for the cause. One lobbyist, consistent with the view of the member quoted above, offered this advice: "If you can co-opt someone early, that is the best." Asking for advice—especially if you accept it—is an effective way to make the "adviser" feel a part of your team. No one is better positioned than members themselves to be effective lobbyists.

b. The "horse," discussed later in this chapter, is a key congressional ally.

No matter how or by whom a strategy is devised, two things are clear: It must be founded upon a solid understanding of all relevant facts, and it should include a careful design for a practical ask. It must never lead otherwise supportive legislators into a blind alley, and it must ask for sensible relief—not an unequivocal or unlimited exemption.

## Deciding on the Policy Vehicle

The end is the beginning. Think about it. If you are programming a GPS to take you from point A to point B, you must begin by punching point B, your ultimate destination, into your system. The same for lobbying campaigns: You have to know where you want to get to before you can begin to plan how to get there. Although you will alter the initial plan as unforeseen events intervene, the process has to start somewhere, and no better place than to decide upon your final destination. The interviews produced several examples of possible objectives:

- To obtain expedited market access for a product that is tightly regulated by onerous premarket approval requirements.[c]
- To gain a time extension for complying with a federal requirement.
- To establish a grant program for university research.
- To provide tax incentives for companies for job training.

The list of possible objectives is endless. Each opens a set of strategic possibilities and forecloses others. For example, in seeking expedited premarket approval, one may have to advocate for an amendment to regulatory law that will give the regulatory agency authority to grant such access. So doing would necessitate a full-bore legislative lobbying campaign designed to amend current law. At the same time, it would foreclose opportunities to focus solely on the responsible regulatory agency. This is because the by-the-book rule is that executive agencies can do nothing that they are not authorized to do, explicitly or implicitly, by existing law. Before a product can be regulated, there must be an enabling act in effect that either authorizes or directs the executive to establish and promulgate a regulation for that purpose.[d] The rule is important because it weighs heavily on lobbyists' strategic options: "I cannot pursue enactment of a new regulation in the executive branch because executive branch agencies have no

c. Premarket approval is a common regulatory format. The product in question must be approved by a regulatory agency before the manufacturers may sell it to the public.
d. The distinction between authorizing (permitting) and directing is critical. Much legislative blood has been spilt over the choice of words *shall* or *may*.

authority to write such a regulation. Therefore, I have to go the legislative route—that is, I must attempt to have new legislation passed."

## The Strategic Plan

In this discussion of the strategic plan, I begin with the assumption that the vehicle for achieving the final goal is passage of a bill that has been drafted by the lobbyist and, perhaps, a congressional ally. The task of piecing together the initial strategy should rest with a small subset of invested legislative professionals; most likely this will include the lead lobbyist and a few carefully selected associates. But, notwithstanding worries about getting too many cooks in the broth, it should at some future time be subject to an all-hands-on-deck review during which all issues are aired and alternatives thoroughly explored. Even for veteran lobbyists constructive ideas have been known to emanate from the least likely sources, perhaps from a junior person.

There is a second reason for conducting a review, this one defensive. Lobbying in some circumstances is the subject of much hearsay, hyperbole, and ill-informed opinion. In large businesses especially, many executives have had the ubiquitous former roommate who knows someone who lobbies, is related to a lobbyist, or, worse, is a member of Congress. Because there are few rules that define smart lobbying it is almost certain that the roommate's secondhand wisdom will surface before the project is complete; this is particularly true if the venture veers south at some point. The lobbyist should get a buy-in from all possible second guessers before the project is implemented. Getting a buy-in will not necessarily deter second guessers, but it may help to beat them back.

Once the lobbyist and client have settled on their ultimate goal and the vehicle for accomplishing it, they must think about a general plan of attack. Here an important caveat is in order: Lobbying campaigns seldom, probably never, play out as planned. (What campaigns do?) Thus initial strategy sessions should be taken for what they are, at best, first guesses and jump-off points that are subject to constant updates and revision.

So why do these strategy sessions at all? The key is in the phrase "jump-off points." Lobbying is a touchy-feely business. Lobbyists are forever playing off of the vibes they get from other people—most notably, from legislators themselves. The information they gain from reading others—plus the endless numbers of shifting, disappearing, and reappearing variables—keeps strategic operations in a state of flux. Indeed, an important part of the art of lobbying is to make the right reads quickly while maintaining sufficient flexibility to change course if necessary. But none of this can happen if the lobbyist does not begin the process, and it is less likely to begin well if the initial jump-off strategy is not intelligently constructed with careful attention to the variables that might occur as events unfold.

A reasonable beginning point is to identify potential congressional allies.

## Identifying the Horse: The Right Matchup

The matchup is a simple idea that is not always easily applied. It hinges on the ability of a lobbyist to recognize which members of Congress are most compatible with himself (the lobbyist), his clients, their issues, and the congressional exigencies—including committee membership and personalities—that must be successfully managed during the course of the lobbying campaign. The ability to pull these pieces together is what often separates expert lobbyists from also-rans.

The ideal matchup, going by the book, might look something like this: The issue in which you and your client are interested also interests your member of Congress (the member who represents your client's or group's headquarters or major facility). She is a member of your political party and holds the same political, social, and economic views that you hold. She is very bright and energetic with a first-rate staff. She happens to chair the committee with jurisdiction over the issue you are concerned with. She has excellent relations with the White House. And her son wants to attend your alma mater to which you contribute handsomely. Now, that spells the perfect matchup—assuming, of course, that the son is not rejected before your issue is favorably resolved.

In the real world no one can hope for such luck. (Besides, the book might offer prosaic thinking about selecting the horse that is as limiting as it is helpful.) For certain, though, if the chair of the committee that is likely to have jurisdiction over your client's issue has the time and would be enthusiastic as a supporter of the cause, then that person would be among the best possible allies.

But the chair is likely to have many demands on her time, some of which may come directly from her congressional party leadership. Even if she is willing to be supportive, she may not have the time to take on the role of "horse," as one's key congressional ally is sometimes called. These members—the horses—are the most important players on the lobbying team. Unlike lobbyists, they are empowered to offer amendments, contribute language to committee reports, ask questions at hearings, speak in committee or on the floor, and execute many more hands-on legislative activities. It stands to reason, then, that they must be willing to function as something more than supporters; they must be proactive allies who are genuinely interested in seeing the campaign succeed.

This is where some of those touchy-feely instincts, always useful to a lobbyist, become important. The ultimate practical objective is a blending together of those with whom one can work and those who have the interest and clout to get the job done. Lobbyists, in their thinking and planning, should account for all of the factors identified in the ideal match—congresswoman's son excepted. Compatibility of a member (with the lobbyist and the client and other relevant members), energy, intelligence, reputation, commitment, and committee membership are primary desired traits, though they are not always available in a single package. Of course, some prior experience with the subject matter at hand is also a plus.

A former representative with more than thirty years of experience in the House, as senior staff and then as a member, spoke about the dual benefit of working with long-time members of the committee of jurisdiction: "They know the committee [and] how it works. By that, I mean who works well with whom and how the chair likes to work. They also have a good chance of having worked on your issue before, so they will already understand some of the finer points." When pressed, he identified "commitment" as "what I suppose would be the most important thing." Then, after a brief pause: "Well, I suppose being on the committee makes things a lot easier too."

Some of these characteristics are predetermined, and touchy-feely instincts have little or nothing to do with evaluating them. But evaluating matters of compatibility, commitment, and energy are subjective. Remember the former member who said that persistence is the most important trait in determining success in lobbying for an issue? Well, the horse is going to be your internal lobbyist: Is she committed and energetic? Does she get on well enough with you and your client to be motivated to go the extra step in support of your cause?

In some instances a lobbyist has experience in working with a prospective horse and thus can make confident projections in these matters. But, again, ideal circumstances do not always present themselves. Sometimes a lobbyist must rely on gut instincts. As a coach once said to a football team that had just lost for the first time in thirty-four games, "Now we'll find out who you really are."

## Determining the First Foray: House or Senate?

In chapter 2 we saw that the House and Senate, while composing one Congress, are separate institutions with their own styles, rules, and cultures. Certainly, each has its own collective will. Thus what the Senate may decide to move upon quickly, the House may not be so fast to consider. Whether for strategic reasons or in response to member-driven priorities, each body and each committee, absent a leadership directive or an overriding national priority, proceeds at its own pace on its own issues.

Accordingly, the House and Senate do not necessarily work on the same legislation at the same time. Although the Constitution requires each body to pass identical bills before a single piece of legislation is presented to the president for signature, it does not prescribe in detail how this objective is to be accomplished. The only constitutional requirement states that "All bills for raising Revenue shall originate in the House of Representatives; but the Senate may propose or concur with Amendments as on other Bills." [1] The Constitution also says, "Each House may determine the Rules of its Proceedings." [2]

Once again the word *variables* creeps (or, rather, slams) into our discussion. The strategic variables—political and procedural—that govern the decision about which body to approach first are many, each demanding knowledge of the players, the rules, and the overall congressional workload. Here are some of the considerations that the interview subjects noted:

- Where do we have our strongest ally?
- Which body is most likely to act favorably?
- Which body is most likely to give us the best language?
- Which body is about to consider a bill to which we could reasonably attach our amendment? [e]
- Which body will act more quickly?

The corollary questions are even more numerous. Among them: Where is the strongest opposition likely to emerge? What is the chair's interest in this matter? What is the committee's agenda for the next several months? Where do I have my best relationships? Ad infinitum.

Many lobbyists, without paying adequate attention to the consequences, select what appears to be the most immediate course of least resistance. This can be a fatal error when mixed priorities are involved—which is often the case. An example: The common and obvious wisdom is to avoid an early setback where and whenever possible. A former Senate committee staffer remembered: "If the boss saw the House had rejected an amendment, he'd sometimes balk about including it in our bill. He knew that [including the amendment] could be a problem in conference." On the other side of the Hill, a House member saw Senate committee rejection as "a definite red flag."

---

e. Unlike the House, the Senate does not have a germaneness rule requiring that amendments have a reasonable relationship to the main bill. In theory, this makes any amendment ripe to be attached to any bill. But that is theory; it is not always easy to attach an amendment that has little to do with the main body of the bill.

All of that may be true, but actual circumstances may complicate matters and make risk avoidance almost impossible. When the first committee to take up the bill—let's say the Senate committee—has greater interest in and more experience with an issue, its product is likely to have the better chance of surviving conference committee negotiations when differences are ironed out. This situation may present a challenge to the lobbyist and client if they have better prospects of moving their bill through the House. On the one hand, a successfully negotiated provision in the Senate is more likely to survive conference. But, on the other, the chances of seeing a bill through to passage in that body may be much more uncertain. Does one confront the most difficult, yet most important, obstacle first? Or does one attempt to finesse the Senate committee and hope that the House will stand tall in conference?

This is not always a self-evident decision. It is an example of when astute strategic thinking is required to sort out the options and make the best practicable assessment of how the various options will play out.

## Selecting the "Right" Committee

Many of the same points applicable to deciding whether to start with the House or the Senate apply to selecting the right committee. Committee jurisdictions within each body are not always clearly distinguishable, and overlapping responsibilities among committees do exist.[f] Sometimes it is possible to write a House or Senate bill that might ordinarily go to committee X in such a way as to have committee Y granted primary jurisdiction or some form of referral jurisdiction. It is axiomatic that the more committees to which a bill is referred the more time will be taken up by committee deliberations. The result is usually a much-delayed process in getting the bill to the floor.

Because referral is a function of the subject matter contained in the bill, strategic decisions about content must be made during the drafting stage. These decisions are not a job best left to lobbyists or clients before they have consulted with prospective congressional allies. Do their potential allies want the bill? Do they think they can control its fate in their committee? Will the finessed committee take umbrage and demand referral? Can the bill be written in such a way as to ensure that it will be referred to the right committee? A Senate counsel advised: "The sooner we see the drafts the better. We can show them to the parliamentarian and get a sense if they [the drafters] are on the right track."

---

f. House and Senate rules provide for joint (contemporaneous) or sequential referrals to two or more committees when jurisdictional overlaps exist or when a bill contains provisions that clearly fall within the jurisdictions of different committees.

Because referrals usually take extra time, they are sometimes used as a tactic for killing a bill, especially late in a congressional session. Sophisticated lobbyists may attempt to have language inserted in a bill that will act as a poison pill by necessitating referral.

A former House Energy and Commerce Committee member compared the process to "classic forum shopping" in the law: "In my old [law] firm we would sometimes pass on an opportunity to try a case or make an appeal until we found the right judge." The analogy fits nicely; in the final analysis the committee will be the judge and jury for many bills that pass its way; therefore, selecting the right venue—when the option exists—can make the difference between success or failure.

## Setting Interim Objectives

A traveler, setting off on a long trip, might aim for point C as the destination for the first day's drive. In the bigger picture, point C is an intermediate, or interim, destination. A lobbying campaign can be viewed in the same way. If the ultimate objective is to gain expedited access for a product to market, the final legislative goal may be to carve out an exception in existing law that would require (or at least permit) the regulatory agency to make such an exception. In this case interim goals might include getting the *right* legislator (or legislators) to introduce a bill, convincing a bipartisan coalition to signal support by cosponsoring it, inserting language in a committee report, or achieving passage in the first chamber of Congress in which it has been considered. None of these objectives, even when accomplished, produces a change in the law; they are but means to that end. But their importance should not be underestimated. Final victory depends upon achieving them.

## Balancing Outside Support Against Loss of Control

Attracting support from noncongressional sources is often more than desirable; it is frequently a must for lobbyists and legislators attempting to move legislation forward. Without question, a positive word—or better, proactive support from an administration official, a trade association executive, other organizations (usually, the more diverse the better), or even a prominent person held in high esteem by the *right* members of Congress—is a potential boon. A negative opinion or outright opposition may cause a long delay or even spell death.

But the business of attracting allies to even a moderately complex measure is seldom a black-or-white proposition. Few things are done in Washington policymaking circles for reasons of pure generosity or as a consequence of a giving spirit. In the lobbyist's world one must expect that those who are considering signing on to a bill will exact some form of precondition or compensation. The payback may take any of many forms: support for an amendment to the bill; agreement to place slightly more or less emphasis on a particular point; a precondition that Member X be satisfied; or perhaps modification in tactics in order to provide anonymity for an interest group ally. The original authors of a bill may see some of these stipulations as enhancements to their position; they may regard other changes as necessary dilutions that they must accept in order to build a winning coalition.

In the business of legislating—whether being conducted by a lobbyist or a lawmaker—allies can be expensive to attract and to hold. In an environment inhabited by strong-willed people—most with constituents, clients, government officials, or plain old bosses and their own egos to satisfy—it is almost a certainty that control issues will arise among would-be organizers and coalition members. Diana Evans suggests as much: "Potential policy coalition leaders may begin with their own most-preferred policy. However it is very unlikely that major legislation modeled strictly on the views of one leader could gain majority on the merits. Instead the leader most likely must incorporate provisions into the initial version of the bill in response to the demands of desired coalition members." [3]

Further, once the proverbial cat is out of the bag, all legislative hell can break loose. No copyright law protects legislative ideas or language. Once the measure is in the public domain, it is fair game. From the bill sponsor's perspective this can lead to a compromising turn of events: Any legislator is free to offer an amendment. Given the Senate's more lenient conditions for amending legislation on its floor, it is more difficult to protect bills in the Senate than it is in the House. But even in the more restrictive House noncoalition members can and do seek to amend bills in committee and, when permitted, on the floor. Frequently it makes more sense to co-opt a member by accepting her language in whole or in part.

All of this makes timing critical. Here lobbyists are often faced with the classic catch-22. In order to attract congressional allies one may need to demonstrate broad and proactive support from the prototypical coalition. But early formation of the coalition could mean loss of control at the outset. Still, politics is a business of numbers—how many for, how many against. Few members are willing to adopt a cause if they cannot be assured of reasonable prospects for success. An active, supportive coalition provides such a prospect. Control is nice, but the ability to produce allies is usually the more practical path to success.

Perhaps it was for this reason that a northeastern conservative insisted, "I always wanted to be in control. I would decide on *all* strategic matters. That way everyone knew who to look to and we did not have to accept everyone else's brilliant idea." After further questioning, this former member allowed: "Oh sure, you'd have to accept some compromising, but I wanted to be the alpha member, the one with the final say. It was going to be *our* bill." This sort of control is necessary for both credit-claiming purposes and for constructing law that is internally coherent. As the former member said in a somewhat different context in chapter 6, "Someone must be in charge."

For lobbyists, control is not always about strategies, procedures, or policies; reputation can also be a concern. More than one lobbyist has been tarred by association with his allies. In one of the most dramatic and instructive series of interviews conducted for this book, a former House subcommittee chair remembered: "We were livid. We thought we had a deal with [them]. Then they attempted one of those midnight deals over in the Senate. We learned about it just in time and were able to kill it."

A lobbyist who had been part of this coalition was equally upset with his allies: In a subsequent conversation, he had this to say, "Those bastards took off on their own and did not check with anybody. No way we ever would have agreed to that strategy. . . . I went right to the chairman's staff and apologized. . . . I think they believed me, but I also think that we never completely repaired our relationship with them. . . . Those bastards cost us big time!"[g]

Among the most important extracongressional sources of support are the executive branch, trade and public interest groups, and prominent think tanks and universities. Of these, one might think that the president and his minions would be the most important—and sometimes they are. But much scholarship casts some doubt about how consistent and how universal the president's influence is. John Kingdon, for instance, has found that presidents and the cabinet officers are important in influencing congressional agendas.[4]

But Glen S. Krutz argues that in the "winnowing" process, "an important decision process . . . where the biggest cut is made in the population of bills [that will receive committee consideration] . . . presidential bills don't always receive the deference we might expect given the resources available to the executive. Several other factors seem to matter more."[5]

---

g. The instructional value of this incident is underscored by the fact that the maverick ally had retained an independent lobbyist with strong ties to some of the relevant Senate offices. Coming through the revolving door and then building a successful lobbying practice do not guarantee that one will be prudent or engage in ethical tactics.

Other studies have examined for links between the president's influence on congressional activity and his popularity, partisanship, and other factors. The results of these and other studies have produced a mixed bag on the subject of executive influence over congressional decision making.[6]

Executive branch influence in the form of technical advice may be a somewhat different story. There is much anecdotal evidence that career service personnel and congressional staff speak to one another informally on an as-needed basis. Much of this conversation has to do with dotting the i's and crossing the t's in legislation moving through congressional committees. Dotting i's and crossing t's may not sound important, but one person's minute detail is frequently another's mega-issue. For example, the slightest difference in eligibility requirements for participation in a federal program may mean the difference between operating a thriving program and closing its doors.

As we saw in chapter 6, influencing the bureaucracy is not easy for lobbyists to do, especially on matters of legislative (as opposed to regulatory) policy. There is no requirement that career service personnel meet with private-sector representatives. Yet lobbyists are remiss if they do not explore the possibility of such meetings. A well-regarded program expert is likely to carry some weight with information-strapped committee staff. Alert lobbyists, having confirmed support from a career service specialist, will attempt to encourage congressional staff to take advantage of this resource. Other noncongressional sources contribute to legislative policymaking on an issue-by-issue basis. Most members who commented on the matter in the survey found that trade association lobbyists were especially well schooled on both the issues they lobbied and the congressional work environment. As noted by the Blue Dog quoted in chapter 6: "They have lots of resources and know how to put together legislation we can work with."

Marshaling outside resources, whether for political support or subject expertise, often proves to be a valuable strategic move. But, with each expansion of one's resource base, there is also a commensurate risk of loss of control.

Ever try to put the cat back into the bag?

## The Importance of Tactics

The best strategy imaginable will implode if it is not intelligently implemented through the right tactics. The following sections give a brief review—with a few addendums—of the tactical observances that the interview subjects mentioned most frequently.

## Matters of Style

In the fast-paced, never-enough-time, in-the-spotlight world of Capitol Hill, there are parameters for doing business with and among lawmakers. For a lobbyist it is required behavior to recognize and work within these parameters (which are outlined in this section). Long-winded lobbyists who kiss and tell, or who consistently ignore the other basic elements of accepted congressional work style, soon find themselves outside the Capitol looking in. Not a preferred location.

*Be brief.* Members overwhelmingly, but by no means unanimously, said that brevity during office meetings is appreciated. Keeping meetings short necessitates careful planning and full subject knowledge so that questions can be answered succinctly and to the point. Proper use of meetings with staff will enable them to brief their boss prior to a meeting with her, thus conserving time and making it easier to get to the point. The less painful the meeting is for the member, the more likely it is that follow-up meetings will be granted. Getting down to business is almost always the best course, though sometimes the member will say, "Not so fast; let's chat a bit." If that's the case, take full advantage of the opportunity. One lobbyist confided that he once did that and then heard about "every Little League game" the member's grandson ever played.

*Respect the institution and its members.* Institutional pride, a long-recognized congressional norm, is very much alive. Members do not want lobbyists to denigrate their institution by insulting their colleagues. It does not take a psychologist to figure out why: Denigrating a colleague is, after a fashion, denigrating them. Be respectful of the members and the institution. Like it or not, each member is one of 535 representatives of a nation of more than three hundred million people who have been elected to do what may be the most important constitutional charge of all—writing law for the United States.

*Keep allies informed.* Even if not much is happening on your issue, it makes sense to stay in touch with your allies on a regular basis. This does not require long meetings, and, if the office you are updating does not mind, e-mails will suffice. No one is ever hurt by keeping all relevant parties informed of what is, or is not, happening.

*Don't automatically ignore adversaries.* Keeping people informed applies within limits to one's congressional adversaries as well as to one's allies. The cabal-like atmosphere created by huddling in private with allies to defeat the enemy only increases suspicions and exacerbates differences. It is never wise to give the opposition an added incentive to want to defeat you. As one veteran legislator advised, "Don't let [arguments] become ad hominem." Agreeing to disagree is one thing; causing personal enmity is another. Further, talking exclusively to one's allies diminishes opportunities for compromise.

*Remain nonpartisan.* The large independent lobbying firms may be able to afford to hire and maintain a staff of partisans—some with Democratic credentials, others with Republican allegiances. But partisanship is ill advised for most independents and company and association lobbyists. This does not mean that a lobbyist must hide his past political associations; it simply means that he should not trade on those credentials. Rather, he should make clear his present intention to seek close working relationships on both sides of the aisle—a sort of "that was then, this is now" approach. A veteran Republican said with a smile, "Whoever said Democrats have more fun knew what he was talking about. I don't know if I have more than one or two Republican friends in this town, but I have dozens of Democrat friends. Why wouldn't I?"

*Keep confidences.* Lobbyists are sometimes caught between the rock and the hard place. Information gathering and sharing is a big piece of what they do for a living. Certainly, clients expect that their Washington operative is well connected and privy to the behind-the-scenes skinny. Lobbyists, eager to be perceived as earning their keep, delight in sharing this sort of information—the more confidential the better. If clients could be trusted to take any revelations no further, that might be fine. But such assurances are hard to depend on. Clients, like lobbyists, are not immune from the rush that comes with telling industry colleagues what their source in Washington has told them.

Confidences are also tested elsewhere. One would be hard pressed to attend a trade association strategy meeting and not hear lobbyists reporting on the information they had uncovered on the Hill. Sharing these confidences in association settings is one of the things they are paid to do, but there are times when full disclosure is potentially compromising. According to a former Senate chief of staff and revolving-door lobbyist, now retired: "I was very close to some people [in the Senate] and they would speak to me very openly. They wouldn't always say 'Now don't tell anyone this,' but I knew they were speaking in confidence. It could be important information, but I had to be very careful what I said about it. . . . I could usually get my point across by speaking in generalities and by not saying where it came from." One slip of the gabby Washington tongue could turn a friend into a former friend.

Several interview subjects noted their preference for meeting with chief executive officers or other major executives. Sometimes this may have been a form of ego gratification; other times it may have been to ensure that the lobbyist had the full backing of his client. But it may also have been another instance when the 800-pound gorilla was able to creep into the room. Remember the former Republican member who valued a good reputation because it "can get people like CEOs to take note of you, to become allies and to raise money"? CEOs can be wild cards, but if for no other reason than showing the corporate leadership flag, they can serve a useful purpose during meetings with members of Congress.[h]

Trustworthy behavior is more than thou-shalt-not-lie behavior. It encompasses the notion of conduct that is otherwise honorable and dependable and that manifests a person of character. Treating members' staff well, not kissing and telling, and doing what you say you are going to do when you say you are going to do it are all the acts of a person worthy of being trusted. Defensive and busy workhorses in Congress do not have the time or the patience to suffer fools, blabbermouths, or the habitually rude and tardy. There is too much to do and too many other people to do it with to justify tolerance of substandard performers as a daily practice.

The interviews over and again bear out the practical importance of accurate and complete disclosure when lobbying lawmakers. We will address that subject again in the next section.

## Matters of Substance

Throughout this book we have emphasized, iterated, reiterated, implied, and otherwise beaten to death the importance of providing reliable information. But there is good reason to continue to beat it—unlike the dead horse—in part because the message is so powerful and in part because the definition of *trustworthy* is so diverse. The definition goes well beyond the requirement of truth telling to include such matters as timeliness and follow-through.

Truth telling remains at the core of what defines a reliable lobbyist—or any other person for that matter. Michael Watkins, Mickey Edwards, and Usha Thakrar sum it up well: "Shading the truth is the easiest way to lose credibility in the influence game." They quote a former member of Congress: "There is a proper term for a lobbyist who lies or distorts, and that proper term is *former* lobbyist. When you are dealing with each other—member dealing with member and lobbyist dealing with member—the truth is your absolute." [7]

Lobbyists and legislators have strong incentives to hold lobbyists to a high performance standard for credibility. As John Wright observes, "Concerns about interest groups and manipulation of the legislative process are far too important to resolve simply by assuming that groups never

h. The general view is that protocol dictates that CEOs meet only with members, not with staff.

exaggerate, distort or mislead." [8] He later explains how legislators may defend themselves against this possibility: "One very important consideration in the strategic decision to misrepresent the facts is the likelihood of being discovered and punished. . . . Legislators have numerous sources they can turn to for information about legislative or political outlook on any given issue and the possibility that they will turn to these sources provides a strong inducement for lobbyists to report information accurately."[9]

A Texas Democrat, highly respected as a person of character, explained why he favored doing business with well-experienced lobbyists: "Longevity is strong evidence of trustworthiness." Trustworthy behavior works for lobbyists because it is a practical mode of behavior for those doing business with congressional offices: "One of the lobbyist's major tasks, perhaps his most important one, is to ensure favorable reception of his messages by the persons he desires to influence. Easy access and clear communication channels are essential." The Texas Democrat was succinct: "You can get in the door in lots of different ways, but to get something done you must be trustworthy."

Perhaps the surest way the lobbyist can achieve his goals is by developing a trusting relationship with the decision makers he must convince. The lawmakers want this kind of relationship too because they need the information that lobbyists and others outside Congress can provide. When lobbyists provide consistently high information, confidence levels increase and access becomes a matter of mutual benefit for both pleader and member. Again a win-win for both sides.

Serving in Congress is stressful enough without lobbyists unnecessarily adding to the pressure by pushing for unreasonable demands. This means that pleaders should craft what they request of a congressional office to fit what is appropriate and realistic—politically and substantively—for that office. In other words, they should be attentive to the words of the former Democratic congressional leader we quoted in chapter 4: Good lobbying should be about "the art of the possible." Lobbyists should also be prepared to compromise when necessary. Shooting for the moon and digging in one's heels may be effective tactics for labor negotiators, but it is poor practice for those who seek ongoing access to congressional offices.

A corollary is to match one's request with the past positions of the member who is being importuned. This helps to inoculate the member against claims of favoritism or, worse, "selling out," and thus makes it more doable for the member to give a favorable response to the lobbyist's request.

Remember, however, that members will occasionally eschew their preference for consistency, either because of a change of mind, the perceived need to help a friend, or the demands of raw political pressure. The chances of influencing a member who for one reason or another is not deviating from her usual preference are improved when a clever lobbyist is able to design his ask so that the requested act may be performed in an unrecorded venue—for example, in a telephone call to another member or in an intervention with a regulatory official. Of course, the 800-pound gorilla might put in an appearance here as well. Working in the dark provides a setting in which members may feel comfortable doing a favor for a past "supporter."

In ideal circumstance lobbyists should be empowered to make substantive decisions on behalf of their clients. In other words, they should be able to make policy-related commitments. The ability to do so would enhance their credibility and otherwise facilitate their role in policy negotiations. But this sort of autonomy is not often practical. The lobbyist may not know enough about technical ramifications or, if he is an independent lobbyist, he may not feel comfortable with such a broad charge. But none of these factors excuses lobbyists from putting in place the logistical apparatus they will need to seal a deal when the opportunity arises. Sometimes it may be as simple as knowing when matters are coming to a head and making certain that the appropriate executive is available to securing a final resolution. As John Kingdon argues, policy windows open and shut, sometimes rather quickly.[10] Once shut, they may not open again for a long time.

## Conclusion

Lobbying campaigns are like fingerprints: No two are exactly the same. The more complex an issue, the more fitting is the analogy. Various combinations of lobbyists, clients, issues, political circumstances, congressional leadership, oppositional forces, allies, and what-have-you account for the one-of-a-kind nature of the lobbying business and lobbying campaigns.

Notwithstanding the best efforts of seasoned and talented lobbyists, it is impossible to foresee all of the variables that will come into play as a campaign unfolds. But this does not justify throwing up one's hands and leaving matters to fate. Quite the opposite—it means that the right sort of planning is even more important than it would be in managing a highly predictable, patterned undertaking. Early-stage decisions are critical: Who will be your most trusted congressional allies? What organizations will be invited to join in your coalition? Which chamber of Congress and which committee is the best venue in which to launch your effort? Even the most general plan of action helps to establish a loose template against which future deviations may be measured and a corrective course of action adopted.

Selection of the horse (or the horses) who will be your congressional ally is important, but that should not preclude consultations with other members. Many lawmakers take pride in knowing the finer points of doing business within their institution and in giving advice based on that expertise: "I would give advice to anyone who came in to see me. I didn't care what their position was." "Most members try to be even-handed in the people they see and the quality of advice they offer." Some members were especially confident about their ability to evaluate political conditions on the Hill: "I was a better person to sort this out."

These observations should disabuse lobbyists of the notion that all must be in readiness before they take their issue to congressional offices. Far from it: Smart lobbyists will go to the source: the members themselves. Even offices that cannot or will not support their cause may welcome an opportunity to engage in some unrecorded legislative behavior by giving a piece of insider's advice. And, of course, there is always the chance of co-opting a potential ally. Yes, there is the risk of letting the cat out of the bag, and lobbyists will have to evaluate that possibility as information-sharing opportunities and potential alliances arise. But that worry should not automatically preclude expanding one's network of potentially helpful resources.

If insightful planning is the beginning point for a lobbying campaign, then skillful execution is the end point. The substantive and stylistic matters presented in this text (especially in chapter 5), many of them reiterated in this chapter, are the bare bones of expected professional behavior for lobbyists. Failure to gain trust, to act civilly, to be sensitive to the congressional environment, and, perhaps most important, to remember that "it is not about what you want; it is about what the other person needs" will lay waste to even the most skillfully conceived plan of attack.

## Notes

1. U.S. Constitution, Article I, Section 7.

2. Ibid., Article I, Section 5.

3. Diana Evans, *Greasing the Wheels: Using Pork Barrel Projects to Build Majority Coalitions in Congress* (Cambridge: Cambridge University Press, 2004), 38.

4. John W. Kingdon, *Agendas, Alternatives, and Public Policies,* 2d ed. (New York: Longman, 1995), 199.

5. Glen S. Krutz, "Issues and Institutions: 'Winnowing' in the U.S. Congress," *American Journal of Political Science* 49 (April 2005): 324.

6. Among the many studies and tests are Douglas Rivers and Nancy L. Rose, "Passing the President's Program: Public Opinion and Presidential Influence in Congress, *American Journal of Political Science* (May 1985): 183–196 (which looks at the relationship of

presidential popularity and legislative success rates); and George C. Edwards III and B. Dan Wood, "Who Influences Whom? The President, Congress, and the Media," *American Political Science Review* 93 (June 1999): 327–344 (which examines the president's role in agenda setting in relation to other sources of potential agenda influence). For recent overview discussions, see Charles O. Jones, *The Presidency in a Separated System* (Washington, D.C.: Brookings Institution, 1994), chapters 6 and 7; and Matthew Dickinson, "The President and Congress," in *The Presidency and the Political System,* 7th ed., ed. Michael Nelson (Washington, D.C.: CQ Press, 2003), 458.

7. Michael Watkins, Mickey Edwards, and Usha Thakrar, *Winning the Influence Game: What Every Business Leader Should Know About Government* (Wiley: New York, 2001), 173.

8. John R. Wright, *Interest Groups and Congress* (Boston: Allyn and Bacon, 1996), 4.

9. Ibid., 109.

10. Kingdon, *Agendas, Alternatives, and Public Policies,* 168–170.

# 8 Conclusion

At many points I have stressed that my intention in this book is not to put forward or to test hypotheses about what is or is not effective lobbying technique. Rather, my objective here is similar to that of Richard Fenno in *Home Style*. In the appendix to *Home Style,* Fenno asserts that "participant observation," his primary research vehicle, "seems less likely to test an existing hypothesis than to formulate hypotheses for testing by others or to *uncover some relationship that strikes others as worth hypothesizing about and testing.*[1] " (Emphasis added.)

Without presuming to place myself in Fenno's league, I employed a primary research vehicle—open interviews—which, like Fenno's participant observation, was designed to produce the building blocks for future research and analysis when more information about the lobbyist–member exchange has been brought to light and examined.

## Observations About the Study Interviews

I can make quick work of the interview subjects' shared belief that telling the truth and providing good information are at the core of successful lobbying practice. Members of Congress are among the most highly scrutinized individuals working today. National and local media, academics, constituents, interest groups, and potential adversaries all have a stake in watching, listening to (though not always carefully), and evaluating legislators and their work. The decisions made by members of Congress, if not necessarily the right ones, must be defensible. This means that lawmakers are obliged, when challenged, to point to a well-grounded rationale, a solid body of evidence, upon which they have based their decisions. Mistakes may be forgiven; the same is not true for sloppy work that resulted from inadequate deliberation. The legislative lifeblood of these very public players is the right information (right in the sense of "accurate") received at the right time and in the right format. All other needs pale by comparison.

In the next two sections I address those matters on which the interview subjects were not so unified in their views. These issues met one of two criteria, or both: (1) issues most frequently mentioned by interview subjects, and/or (2) issues that generated particularly animated responses. (See Illustration 8.1.) Clearly, the decision to include an observation as one that meets the second criterion is subjective, but I am confident that the correct choices were made.[a]

The following sections, together with chapter 7, provide a rough template for organizing a lobbying campaign and give insight—either directly or through inference—into what one must do or not do in order to comply with members' preferences. I have divided these sections into two categories of responses to the survey questions: (1) those where there was a strong consensus among the interview subjects and (2) those where opinions were mixed.

## Strong Consensus

The points of strong consensus are the matters on which members expressed pronounced, though not unanimous, agreement. Although there may have been occasional variations on themes, and even a few—very few—outright dissents, their comments provide excellent insights into what members look for in professional lobbying practice. Even if one were to disagree, say, about the importance of being as brief as possible when meeting with members or staff, one will never be disparaged for the effort

*Art of the possible.* Few things are more annoying than to be entreated to do something that you simply cannot do. For politicians "doability" is usually measured in political or policy terms, or both. An unreasonable request from a lobbyist is not only irritating, but it also reveals the lobbyist to be an amateur—someone not worth listening to or responding to. (Unless, of course, he is a major constituent: In that case, a politely offered course in Lobbying 101 is in order.)

*Importance of brevity.* Members are hard-pressed to do everything they must do. Lobbyists who have mastered the art of brief, no-nonsense presentations stand a better chance of gaining repeat access to members and staff than do long-winded time sponges.

---

a. For these responses $n = 44$, the number of former members who were interviewed for the study.

## Illustration 8.1 Selected Observations by Interview Subjects

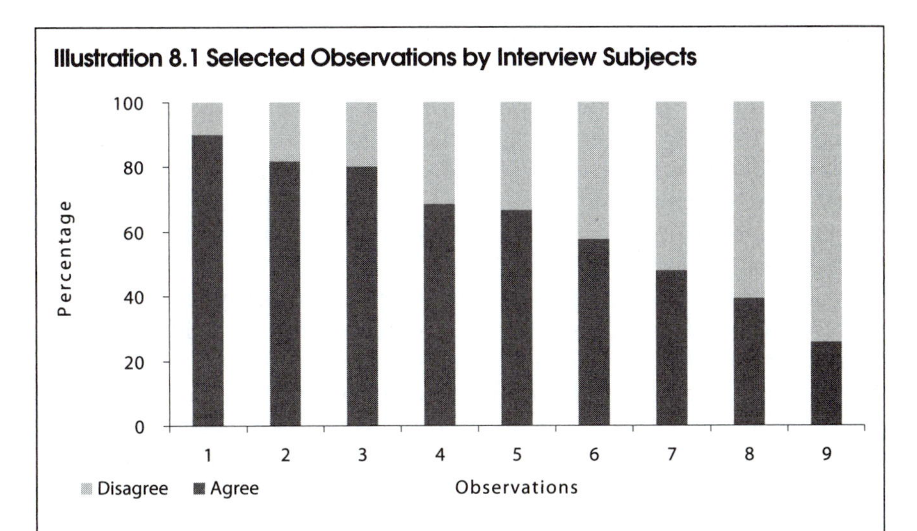


| Observations | No. of interviewees who addressed this matter | No./percentage who agreed |
|---|---|---|
| 1. It was important for lobbyists to understand what a member can do and cannot do—substantively and politically. | 30 | 27/90% |
| 2. Brevity in office visits is appreciated. | 33 | 27/81.8% |
| 3. Courteous behavior matters and is noticed.* | 30 | 24/80% |
| 4. Reasonable amounts of socializing would be a positive for the integrity of the lobbying process. | 35 | 24/68.6% |
| 5. A lobbyist's reputation for excellence was important to me.** | 39 | 26/66% |
| 6. I welcomed legislative drafts, etc., from lobbyists. | 26 | 15/57.7% |
| 7. I had absolute faith in my staff. | 25 | 12/48% |
| 8. I received many ideas for legislation (including amendments) from lobbyists. | 28 | 11/39.3% |
| 9. Most revolving-door lobbyists were quite good.*** | 62 | 16/25.8% |

* Courteous behavior includes behavior directed toward staff. In fact, interviewees most often alluded to staff when discussing this matter. Understandably, few lobbyists would dare to be rude to members, but they might take liberties in working with staff.
** This entry refers to those instances in which legislators knew the reputation of the lobbyist they were scheduled to meet with. The interviews indicate that members often knew very little about these people.
*** In this instance I combined the responses to two separate questions:

- "Most former staff were effective lobbyists." (11 interviewees agreed with this statement, 14 mostly agreed, and 4 mostly disagreed.)
- "Most former members were effective lobbyists." (5 interviewees agreed, 16 mostly agreed, 9 mostly disagreed, and 3 totally disagreed.)

*Behavior norms.* Awareness of and attentiveness to the old congressional norms still seem to matter. Perhaps this explains why many of the interview subjects expressed a preference for veteran lobbyists who have "stood the test of time." It was clear that several interviewees were talking about the idea of respect: In their eyes, respecting congressional norms is another way of expressing esteem for Congress and for the member. Attempting to convince a member to deviate from the norms showed disrespect on both counts.

Good old-fashioned decency and courtesy are other types of behavior that are valued. When lobbyists stray, the penalty can be swift and harsh. Congressional offices will not long tolerate rude or dismissive behavior. Although few lobbyists would even think about offending a member, this is not necessarily the case for their relationships with staff, especially junior staff. Here Mr. Hyde occasionally reveals himself. Former members and senior staff—especially former chiefs of staff—claimed that they were informed of such behavior and often addressed it head on with offending lobbyists. On more than one occasion a lobbyist was declared persona non grata and invited not to return to the office. Put simply, arrogant and rude lobbyists need not apply.

Other forms of rude behavior are noticed and deemed unacceptable as well: Among them are disparaging or badmouthing one's opponents and lobbying a member at what is clearly a social event: "Hi, Representative Jones. That first act was really convincing. Great performance! Now, on this new tax reform bill, my client. . . ." Ouch.

Although the norms may have been identified in the context of relationships within Congress, expectations for certain types of behavior are likely to transcend purely internal application. A case in point is a lobbyist trying to convince a member to blow off a markup. What he is asking the legislator to do is to ignore her professional responsibilities.

*Benefits of socializing.* Modest forms of socializing between members of Congress and lobbyists (for example, lunches and dinners) can be constructive and are valuable in building trust and furthering prospects for the development of good public policies. This argument is based on the belief that "friends don't screw friends." Remember the legislative veteran who was convinced that we have become overly concerned about social interaction between lobbyists and members? The essence of his point was that the friendships that might result from, or be strengthened by, such interaction could serve as a cleansing agent for our politics. A good friend will not encourage a lawmaker to pursue an objective that could someday lead to loss of confidence at home or derision in Congress. It would not make sense to put at risk the trust of a congressional ally. Allies are too hard to come by.

Friendships between lobbyists and members could also lead to higher quality deliberation by facilitating broader, more aggressive discussions on relevant issues. Friends are more likely to float trial balloons and explore out-of-the-box ideas with people with whom they are comfortable than they are with comparative strangers. The tendency in the latter case is to stay on safe ground.

*Reputation.* A lobbyist's professional reputation is a complex matter. First, lobbyists gain reputations in many areas and for many reasons—for example, by proving their reliability, showing their ability to raise money, or demonstrating their knowledge of the ways of Congress and making their asks consistent with congressional norms. The interviews indicate that reputation can be important, for those who have gained sufficient exposure, both in terms of increasing access to members and in improving one's chances for success.[b]

Two of the prime components of reputation are character (providing honest information) and competence (providing good information and wise counsel). Together, these two elements contribute to a lobbyist's reputation for professional behavior. One is not much good without the other.

It was very difficult to pull the two components apart during the interviews because they are so closely linked in the minds of lawmakers. The assumption was almost invariably that good information is by definition honest information. The same can be said of strategic advice. Thus, in terms of the reliability of information and counsel that lobbyists give to congressional offices, the two—honesty and "rightness"—go hand in hand. True, there is such a thing as an honest mistake, but quality professionals are rarely guilty of such lapses.[c]

## Mixed Opinions

Some interview topics elicited responses that I had not expected. What I had thought were sure things did not always turn out that way, not in the minds of the interview subjects. Among these, two topics—legislative subsidies and confidence in staff performance—qualified as "shockers." Ask most lobbyists about these topics, and you will get unqualified answers: "Legislative subsidies are important; they are always valued by members and staff." And "Staff is key. You must get them to buy in." On most occasions those would be accurate statements—nothing here disputes

---

b. Not every lobbyist in Washington is a well-known commodity. In fact, some of the very best try hard not to be well known. If one is not known, then it stands to reason that one cannot have acquired a reputation.

c. I do not attempt here to distinguish between a reputation for honor and a reputation for competence, though further work in this area—pulling issue competence and strategic competence apart—may yield useful observations about how lawmakers view lobbyists and how they decide upon the lobbyists to whom they will provide access.

that—but a surprising number of former legislators did not agree—at least, not whole-heartedly. Their responses are instructive.

*Legislative subsidies.* Most, but by no means all, former lawmakers said they had welcomed legislative subsidies, including drafts of bills, committee report language, floor statements, and suggestions about procedural tactics. But several cautioned that lobbyists, unless they have a long history of working with a member, should seek a go-ahead from staff before offering specific help. Subsidies are likely to be of value to congressional offices only when they are presented in a form that matches the recipient member's work style. Interestingly, and perhaps predictably, staff seemed to value them more than did members.

*Confidence in staff.* One of the most surprising results was the less-than-vigorous endorsement of staff performance by members. Virtually all former members claimed that they preferred lobbyists to begin their work on an issue with their staff people. Yet, paradoxically, a larger than expected number—perhaps 20 percent of the former members—indicated significant doubts about the ability, and most surprisingly, integrity of their staff. They claimed to have worried that some staffers might have "sold earmarks" in consideration for promises of future jobs with lobbying organizations or client businesses.

*Ideas for legislation.* The respondents were even more split on the matter of lobbyist-supplied ideas for legislative proposals. Some interviewees were almost hubristic in their responses. They saw this form of subsidy as coming close to usurping their responsibilities as legislators: You tell me your problem. *I'll* decide what to do about it. Given the possibility of encountering this mind-set, it makes sense for a policy-initiating lobbyist to run his idea by staff first and then, if given the green light, to move forward with a more formal submission to the office.

*The revolving door.* Former members gave the revolving-door phenomenon generally favorable, though somewhat mixed, responses. Their comments focused on two issues: ethical concerns and professional competence. Only two interview subjects (though one of these is a particularly esteemed former member) indicated that they thought longer periods of time between time serving in Congress and practicing as a lobbyist would help in preventing corrupt behavior or blocking other forms of untoward advantage.

Respondents' gave more varied opinions about the competence of revolving-door lobbyists. Many noted that a relatively high percentage of former members attempted to trade on old friendships and past professional associations. They found this approach to be either "pathetic" or a plain nuisance. Some formers, however, did opine that fewer and fewer former members were trying to trade in on past relationships: "They've learned."

Former staff members received uniformly high praise as lobbyists. The message to members of Congress: If one is interested in hiring a revolving-door lobbyist, one might be well advised to think about a former committee counsel.

## A Final Note

Three of the first four items in Illustration 8.1—understanding and asking for the doable, keeping visits brief, and developing and nurturing comfortable professional relationships that help to build trust—along with the requirement for good information, are remarkable for the extent to which they are unremarkable. That may be a letdown for those who suspect, even want to hear, that participating in congressional policymaking is something akin to untying the Gordian knot. It is not.

But this does not suggest that policymaking work is a prosaic affair, quickly learned and easily accomplished. Understanding what is doable in the context of writing the nation's laws often requires extraordinary amounts of substantive knowledge and a deep appreciation for the unique opportunities available to, and the limitations bearing upon, each lawmaker as she engages in each legislative contest. For a lobbyist, functioning efficiently means not only providing lawmakers with reliable information; it also means understanding congressional time—and timing. One must know how and when to seek an audience, make every second of each meeting count, and, then, having made the argument persuasively, take prompt leave. Gaining trust requires that one must do all of these things, and do them all in a way that signals to the lawmaker and her staff an acute awareness of and attention to Congress's unique culture. A combination of long experience on Capitol Hill, native intelligence, and finely honed instinct will increase a lobbyist's chance of success.

A final analogy: Good lobbying is like good cooking. When preparing a meal one finds that few ingredients are, by themselves, out of the ordinary—maybe a rare spice here or a special cut of meat there, but seldom much more than that. What makes the master chef an *artist* is the choice of those ingredients, preparation, blending, timing, pulling together, and presentation of the final product. To say it another way: the master chef pays great attention to the essentials of his art form.

It's no different for the art of lobbying.

## Note

1. Richard F. Fenno Jr., *Home Style: House Members in Their Districts* (Glenview, Ill.: Scott, Foresman, 1978), 249.

# Index

*Note:* Figures and note(s) are indicated by f and n/nn, respectively.

## C

## R

## S